MIDDLE EAST AND NORTH AFRICA:
GOVERNANCE, DEMOCRATIZATION, HUMAN RIGHTS

Contemporary Perspectives on Developing Societies

John Mukum Mbaku, Series General Editor, Weber State University

Mwangi S. Kimenyi, Series Associate Editor, The University of Connecticut

Between 1989 and 1991, there were several changes in the global political economy that have had significant impact on policy reform in developing societies. The most important of these were the collapse of socialism in Eastern Europe, the subsequent disintegration of the Soviet Union, the cessation of superpower rivalry, and the demise of apartheid in South Africa. These events have provided scholars a new and challenging research agenda: To help the peoples of the Third World participate more effectively in the new global economy. Given conditions in these societies, the first line of business for researchers would be to help these countries establish and maintain transparent, accountable and participatory governance structures and, at the same time, provide themselves with more viable economic infrastructure. The *Contemporary Perspectives on Developing Societies* series was founded to serve as an outlet for such policy relevant research. It is expected that books published in this series will provide rigorous analyses of issues relevant to the peoples of the Third World and their efforts to improve their participation in the global economy.

Also in this series

Hope, K. R., Sr. (ed.) (1997), *Structural Adjustment, Reconstruction and Development in Africa.*

John Mukum Mbaku and Julius O. Ihonvbere (eds.) (1998), *Multiparty Democracy and Political Change: Constraints to Democratization in Africa.*

Mwangi S. Kimenyi, Robert C. Wieland and J. D. Von Pischke (eds.), *Strategic Issues in Microfinance.*

Middle East and North Africa: Governance, Democratization, Human Rights

Edited by
PAUL J. MAGNARELLA
University of Florida
Gainesville, Florida, USA

Ashgate

Aldershot • Brookfield USA • Singapore • Sydney

Published by
Ashgate Publishing Ltd
Gower House
Croft Road
Aldershot
Hants GU11 3HR
England

Ashgate Publishing Company
Old Post Road
Brookfield
Vermont 05036
USA

British Library Cataloguing in Publication Data
Middle East and North Africa : governance, democratization,
    human rights. - (Contemporary perspectives on developing
    societies)
    1.Human rights - Middle East 2.Human rights - Africa, North
    3.Democracy - Middle East 4.Democracy - Africa, North
    5.Middle East - Politics and government - 1945- 6.Africa,
    North - Politics and government - 20th century
    I.Magnarella, Paul J.
    323'.0956

Library of Congress Catalog Card Number: 98-073747

ISBN 1 84014 913 2

Printed and bound by Athenaeum Press, Ltd.,
Gateshead, Tyne & Wear.

Contents

Tables   vii
List of Contributors   ix
Acknowledgments   xiii
Map   xiv

1.   Introduction   1
        Paul J. Magnarella

2.   Islam, Governance and Democracy   11
        Manochehr Dorraj

3.   Iraq: Human Rights in the Republic of Fear   37
        Judith S. Yaphe

4.   Syria Resists the End of History   67
        Fred H. Lawson

5.   Jordan   83
        Michael R. Fischbach

6.   Egypt: Human Rights and Governance   103
        Mamoun Fandy and Dana Hearn

7.   Democratization, Liberalization, and Human   125
        Rights: Challenges Facing the Gulf Cooperation
        Council
        Rolin G. Mainuddin

8.   Turkey   143
        Paul J. Magnarella

9.   Human Rights within Israel   173
        Russell A. Stone

10.   Human Rights in the West Bank and the Gaza   191
       Strip: Politics and Law in Transition
       Ilan Peleg

11.   The Rise and Fall of Democratization in   209
       the Maghreb
       Mohammad-Mahmoud Mohamedou

Tables

1.1   General Demographic Information for the
       Middle East, North Africa & United States   4

1.2   Ratifications of Primary International Human
       Rights Instruments   6

3.1   Major Iraqi Dissident Factions   61

List of Contributors

Manochehr Dorraj, (Ph.D. University of Texas), is an Associate Professor of Political Science at Texas Christian University. His publications include: *From Zarathustra to Khomeini: Populism and Dissent in Iran* (1990); *The Changing Political Economy of the Third World*, (ed.), (1995); *Middle East at the Crossrods: The Changing Political Dynamics and the Foreign Policy Challenges,* (co-editor, forthcoming).

Mamoun Fandy, (Ph.D. Political Science, Southern Illinios University), is a Research Professor of Politics at Georgetown University's Center for Contemporary Arab Studies. His research focus is the politics of North Africa and the Arabian Gulf. His articles have appeared in the *Middle East Journal, Comparative Studies in Society and History*, and *Middle East Policy*. He has authored *Saudi Arabia and the Politics of Dissent* (forthcoming).

Michael R. Fischbach, (Ph.D. History. Georgetown University), is an Assistant Professor at Randolph-Macon College, Ashland, Virginia. He is the author of numerous works on Jordanian and Palestinian history, including 'Settling Historical Land Claims in the Wake of Arab-Israeli Peace,' *Journal of Palestine Studies* (1997); 'British Land Policy in Transjordan,' in Rogan and Tell (eds.), *Village, Steppe & State: The Social Origins of Jordan* (1994); and 'The Implications of Jordanian Land Policy for the West Bank,' *Middle East Journal* (1994).

Dana Hearn is a graduate student at the Center for Contemporary Arab Studies, Georgetown University.

Fred H. Lawson, (Ph.D. Political Science, UCLA), is the James Irvine Professor of Government at Mills College. He was a Fulbright Lecturer in International Relations at the University of Aleppo, 1992-93. His major publications include: *Why Syria Goes to War* (1996); *The Social Origins of Egyptian Expansionism during the Muhammad 'Ali Period* (1992); and *Bahrain: The Modernization of Autocracy* (1989).

Rolin G. Mainuddin, (Ph.D. Political Science, University of Kansas) is an Assistant Professor of Political Science at North Carolina Central University. His articles have appeared in the *Indian Journal of Asian Affairs, Journal of Third World Studies, Middle East Policy*, and *Military Review*. In 1995, Dr. Mainuddin was a recipient of the Presidential Award from the Association of Third World Studies.

Paul J. Magnarella, (Ph.D. Anthropology and Middle East Studies, Harvard; J.D. International Law, University of Florida) is Professor of Anthropology and Legal Studies at the University of Florida. He has served as an Expert-on-Mission with the UN War Crimes Tribunal for the Former Yugoslavia and as President of the Association of Third World Studies. He is currently the Association's Special Counsel. His books include: *The Peasant Venture* (1979), *Tradition and Change in a Turkish Town* (1981), *Human Materialism* (1993), and *Anatolia's Loom* (1998).

Mohammad-Mahmoud Mohamedou, (Ph.D. Political Science, City University of New York) held a Post-Doctoral Fellowship at the Center for Middle Eastern Studies, Harvard University and has served as Research Associate at the Ralph Bunche Institute on the United Nations. He is currently Director of Research at the International Council on Human Rights Policy in Geneva. Dr. Mohamedou has authored *Societal Transition to Democracy in Mauritania* (1995) and *Iraq and the Second Gulf War: State-Building and Regime Security* (1998).

Ilan Peleg, (Ph.D. Northwestern University) is the Charles A. Dana Professor of Social Sciences at Lafayette College in Easton, Pa. and the former President of the Association of Israel Studies. Among his books are *Human Rights in the West Bank and Gaza* (1995), which was selected by Choice as an Outstanding Scholarly Book for 1996; *The Middle East Peace Process: Interdisciplinary Perspectives* (1998); *Pattern of Censorship around the World* (ed., 1993); and, *Begin's Foreign Policy 1977-1983* (1987).

Russell A. Stone, (Ph.D., Princeton) is Professor of Sociology at American University, Washington, D.C. He has been visiting professor at the Hebrew University of Jerusalem and Ben Gurion University of the Negev, Beersheba, and a visiting associate at the Guttman Israel Institute of Applied Social Research. Dr. Stone is author of *Social Change in Israel: Attitudes and Events* (1982), co-editor of *Critical Essays on Israeli Social*

Issues and Scholarship (1994) and advisory editor for the SUNY Press book series on Israeli Studies. He has also written on Tunisia, Middle East economic development, and political elites in North Africa.

Judith S. Yaphe, (Ph.D. Middle Eastern History, University of Illinois) is a Senior Fellow at the Institute for National Strategic Studies at National Defense University, specializing in Iraq, Iran, the Arabian Gulf, and political Islam. She has authored papers on radicalized Islam in the Arabian Peninsula, North Africa, and the Eastern Mediterranean region; on the U.S.-Turkish strategic relationship; and, on political stability in the Arabian Peninsula. She is preparing a book on Islamic activism and U.S. strategic interests in the Middle East. Dr. Yaphe has briefed senior U.S. officials and testified before Senate and Congressional committees on regional strategic issues.

Acknowledgments

A collection of this kind involves the efforts of many people, only some of whom I can acknowledge here. I thank John Mukum Mbaku, the general editor of the *Contemporary Perspectives on Developing Societies* series, for commissioning me to put together this work and for advising me in the process. I thank the contributors for their excellent chapters and collegial cooperation. I want to especially acknowledge the fine contributions of two of my graduate students. Mary Sam Allen performed yeoman's service, formatting the text, preparing the map and helping with the editing-proof reading. B.J. Brown expertly prepared the two tables in the introduction. Sharlene Magnarella most graciously proof-read the entire manuscript. Finally, I acknowledge the peoples of the Middle East and North Africa, who long for democracy and respect for human rights in their countries. May they soon achieve their wishes. Collectively, we dedicate this book to them.

The Middle East and North Africa

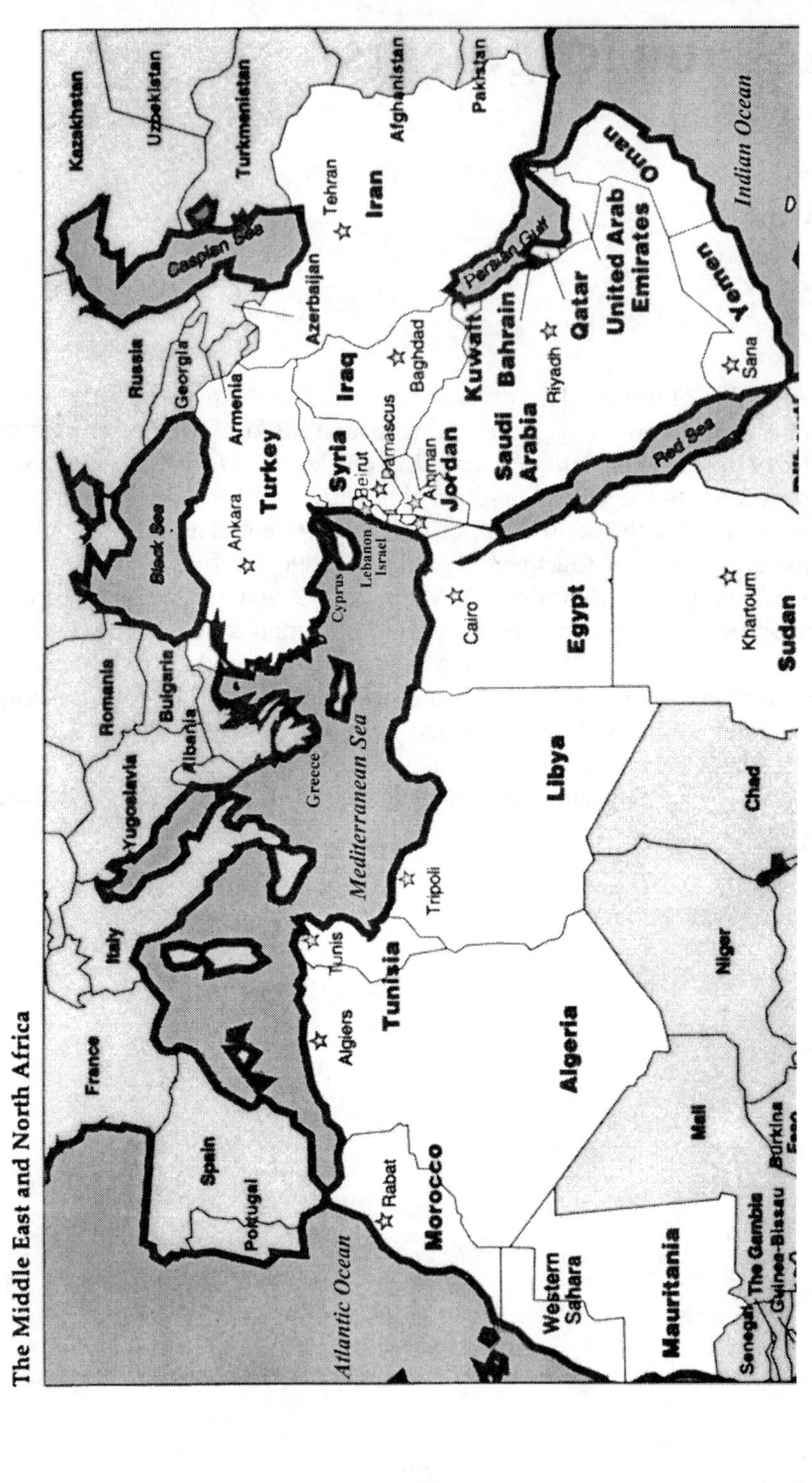

1 Introduction

PAUL J. MAGNARELLA

December 10, 1997 marked the beginning of the 50th anniversary year of the 1948 Universal Declaration of Human Rights. Thus, this is an appropriate time to access the progress that states in the Middle East and North Africa have made towards respecting the human rights of peoples under their jurisdictions. The chapter authors in this volume, each a recognized expert in his/her field, assess the records that countries in these contiguous regions have compiled in the areas of human rights, governance, and democratization.

When the United Nations came into being in 1945, ordinary people enjoyed little protection under international law. The UN Charter affirmed the dignity, worth and equal rights of each person. Article 1 states that the purpose of the UN is to maintain peace and promote respect for human rights and fundamental freedoms. Although the Charter guaranteed human rights, it did not define them. To accomplish this, the UN Commission on Human Rights drafted the Universal Declaration of Human Rights, and the UN General Assembly adopted it on 10 Dec. 1948. At the time, Eleanor Roosevelt, chair of the Human Rights Commission, predicted that the Universal Declaration would become a 'Magna Carta for mankind.'

The Declaration is indeed a bill of rights for the world. The first 21 articles specify certain civil and political rights, including the right to life, liberty, and a fair trial; the right to freedom of conscience, expression and association; the right to leave one's country and return to it; and, freedom from arbitrary arrest, detention and exile. The next nine articles specify social and economic rights, including the right to a decent standard of living, to social security, to work and leisure, to health care, and to education. The Universal Declaration was intended to set an aspirational standard of achievement for all nations. During the following decades, the rights in the Declaration became part of international law through a series of treaties covering civil and political rights, economic and social rights, racial discrimination, religious tolerance, torture, women's and children's rights. Today, there is a full body of treaty law covering the substantive law of international human rights.

The Universal Declaration has certainly created a standard for human rights achievement. In the past two decades the world has witnessed the democratization of Latin America and the fall of repressive communist regimes. Generally, states that observe human rights are democracies that do not initiate wars. These states and their humane legal systems have become the models for peoples everywhere who want to enjoy the rights enumerated in the Universal Declaration. Unfortunately, too many ruling regimes refuse to accept the obligations of the UN human rights conventions and deny their peoples fundamental respect.

The weakness of international human rights law lies in the inadequacy of implementation. Various UN agencies and non-governmental organizations (NGOs) monitor human rights practices in different parts of the world and encourage governments to respect modern human rights standards. NGOs, such as Human Rights Watch, Amnesty International, Minority Rights Group, and the International League for Human Rights send fact-finding missions to repressive countries, provide data to UN bodies and marshal media and public opinion on behalf of victims of human rights abuses. A state mechanism increasingly utilized in the human rights field is linkage. Many repressive states seek trade, technology or security arrangements from Western democracies. In recent decades, some Western democracies have selectively linked trade, technology and military aid with human rights practices and goals. Such linkages should continue, but on a more uniform basis.

This writer assumes that people universally want to be able to make authoritative decisions over their own lives; enjoy some level of economic, physical and health security; have access to educational opportunities; and enjoy the respect of their fellows, the affection of their friends and families, and the spiritual benefits of their chosen religions. He also believes that just systems for distributing and earning these values promote human dignity and a more peaceful world order. Regimes that fail to respect human rights never gain genuine legitimacy, because large segments of the peoples they rule and abuse simply refuse to recognize them as legitimate. Such regimes too frequently resort to military/police force to maintain power by suppressing political opponents and disgruntled civilians. They violate economic, civil, and political rights on the false pretext of 'national security.' Alas, this has too often been the experience in the Middle East and North Africa.

Contrary to the experience in other parts of the world, authoritarian regimes in this region continue to dominate, and the degree of authoritarianism has even intensified over the past several decades. Few human rights NGOs operate freely in Arab countries. Even the Arab Organization for Human Rights (AOHR), which is often called the 'mother of human rights organizations in the Arab World' functions weakly where governments allow it to function at all. Arab human rights advocates avoid openly opposing those political parties that promote a return to the shari'a or Islamic law, even though there are certain incompatibilities between universal human rights conventions and certain interpretations of the shari'a. These incompatibilities include capital punishment for apostasy, gender inequality, physical punishments (including amputations) for crimes, and the unequal status of minorities.

Arab human rights advocates do not regard the Permanent Arab Commission on Human Rights within the Arab League as part of the universalistic human rights movement. This Commission, founded by the Council of the League of Arab States in 1968, has done little to promote human rights in the Arab world. Instead, it has devoted much of its attention to the rights of Palestinian Arabs in the Israeli occupied territories. Significantly, however, it produced an Arab Charter on Human Rights and presented the Charter to the Council of the Arab League States at the 102nd session in 1994 (Resolution 5437). Unfortunately, as of 1 January 1997 not a single Arab state had ratified it. Consequently, unlike Africa, the Americas and Europe, the Arab Middle East- North Africa has no functioning human rights convention-based system. Of the Arab states, Algeria, Egypt, Libya and Tunisia have ratified the African Charter on Human and People's Rights and are therefore subject to the very weak reporting requirements of that regional convention.

Despite their predominantly Arab character, the Middle East and North Africa exhibit a significant degree of ethno-religious diversity (see Table 1.1) and, in the case of some countries (e.g., Iraq and Lebanon), regional factionalism. These characteristics promote particularistic or local identifications and hinder the development of a national identification. They also lead to ethno-religious and/or regional politics involving competition among leaders of different cultural, religious or regional populations for state positions of political and economic power. Sectarian clashes have not been uncommon, as evidenced by the recent history of such countries as Iraq, Lebanon, Palestine, Syria, Israel, Turkey, and Egypt.

A major objective of the UN is: 'To achieve international cooperation in solving international problems of an economic, social, cultural, or humanitarian character, and in promoting and encouraging respect for human rights and for fundamental freedoms for all without distinction as to race, sex, language, or religion; . . .' UN Charter, Art. 1(3). Article 55 of

Table 1.1   General Demographic Information for the
Middle East, North Africa & United States

Country	Population and Ethnic Groups	Major Religions	Life Expectancy	Government
Algeria	29,539,400 99% Arab-Berber <1% European	99% Sunni Muslim; 1% Shi'a Jew & Christian	67.22 years/male 69.46 years/female	Republic; (Now under military junta)
Bahrain	590,100 63% Bahraini; 13% Asian; 10% other Arab; 8% Iranian; 6% others	70 to 75% Shi'a Muslim; 20 to 25% Sunni Muslim	71.78 years/male 76.83 years/female	Traditional monarchy (cabinet-executive system)
Egypt	63,575,107 99% Eastern Hamitic; 1% others	94% Muslim (mostly Sunni); 6% Coptic Christian & others	59.51 years/male 63.46 years/female	Republic
Iran	66,094,264 51%Persian; 24% Azerbaijani; 7% Kurd; 8% Mazandarani; 10% others	95% Shi'a Muslim; 4% Sunni Muslim; 1% Zoroastrian, Christian, Jew & Bahai	66.12 years/male 68.72 years/female	Theocratic Republic
Iraq	21,422,292 75 to 80% Arab; 15 to 20% Kurd; 5% Turk, Assyrian & others	62% Shi'a Muslim; 35% Sunni Muslim; 3% Christian & others	65.92 years/male 68.03 years/female	Officially Republic (In reality a single party dictatorship)
Israel	5,433,200 82% Jewish; 18% mostly Arab	82% Jewish; 14% Muslim; 2% Christian; 2% Druze	76.16 years/male 79.96 years/female	Parliamentary Republic
Jordan	4,212,200 98% Arab; 1% Circassian; 1% Armenian	92% Sunni Muslim; 8% Christian	70.62 years/male 74.45 years/female	Constitutional Monarchy
Kuwait	1,950,100 45% Kuwaiti; 35% other Arab; 9% South Asian; 4% Iranian; 7% others	85% Muslim; 15% Christian, Hindu, Parsi, others	75.92 years/male 78.38 years/female	Nominal Constitutional Monarchy
Lebanon	3,776,982 95% Arab; 4% Armenian; 1% others	70% Muslim; 30% Various Christian sects	67.49 years/male 72.62 years/female	Parliamentary Republic
Libya	5,445,500 97% Berber-Arab; 3% European & Asian	97% Sunni Muslim; 3% other	62.48 years/male 66.97 years/female	Officially Republic (In reality a military dictatorship.)

TABLE 1.1 CONTINUED

Morocco	29,779,156 64% Arab; 35% Berber; 1% other	99% Sunni Muslim; 1% Jewish & other	67.53 years/male 71.61 years/female	Constitutional Monarchy
Oman	2,186,600 99+% Arab; <1% other	75% Ibadi Muslim; remainder mostly other Muslim sects	68.59 years/male 72.57 years/female	Monarchy
Qatar	547,800 40% Arab; 18% Pakistani; 18% Indian; 10% Iranian; 14% other	95% Muslim; 5% other	70 years/male 75 years/female	Traditional Monarchy
Saudi Arabia	19,409,100 90% Arab; 10% Afro-Asian	100% Muslim	67.25 years/male 70.84 years/female	Hereditary Monarchy in Sa'ud family
Syria	15,609,000 90% Arab; 10% Kurd, Armenian, Circassian & Turk	74% Sunni Muslim; 12% Alawite; 6% Druze; 8% Christian & Jewish	65.94 years/male 68.38 years/female	Republic (Currently under left wing military regime.)
Tunisia	9,020,000 98% Arab-Berber; 1% European; 1% other	98% Muslim; 1% Christian; <1% Jewish	71.27 years/male 74.03 years/female	Republic
Turkey	63,700,000 80% Turk; 17% Kurds; 3% other	79% Sunni Muslim; 20% Shi'a Muslim; 1% other	69.53 years/male 74.43 years/female	Republican Parliamentary Democracy
United Arab Emirates	3,057,400 19% Emirian; 23% other Arab; 50% South Asian; 8% East Asian & other	96% Muslim; 4% Hindu, Christian & other	70.64 years/male 74.94 years/female	Federation of Emirates
Yemen	17,300,000 nearly 100% Arab	55% Shi'a Muslim; 45% Sunni Muslim	62.00 years/male 63.00 years/female	Republic
United States	269,000,000	56% Protestant; 28% Catholic; 2% Jewish; 4% other; 10% none	73.0 years/male 79.0 years/female	Federal Republic

Demographic information compiled from the 1998 Wall Street Journal Almanac, New York: Ballantine Books and Global Studies: The Middle East, 7th Ed., 1998, Guilford: Dushkin, McGraw-Hill.

Table 1.1 compiled by B. J. Brown

Table 1.2   **Ratifications of Primary International Human Rights Instruments**

STATE	I	II	III	IV	V	VI	VII
Algeria	Yes	Yes	Yes	Yes	No	Yes	Yes
Bahrain	No	No	Yes	No	No	Yes	Yes
Egypt	Yes	Yes	Yes	Yes	Yes	Yes	Yes
Iran	Yes	Yes	Yes	No	No	Yes	Yes
Iraq	Yes	Yes	Yes	No	No	Yes	Yes
Israel	Yes	Yes	Yes	Yes	Yes	Yes	Yes
Jordan	Yes	Yes	Yes	Yes	Yes	Yes	Yes
Kuwait	Yes	Yes	Yes	Yes	No	Yes	Yes
Lebanon	Yes	Yes	Yes	No	Yes	Yes	Yes
Libya	Yes	Yes	Yes	Yes	Yes	Yes	Yes
Morocco	Yes	Yes	Yes	Yes	Yes	Yes	Yes
Oman	No	No	No	No	No	Yes	No
Qatar	No	No	No	No	No	Yes	Yes
Saudi Arabia	No	No	Yes	No	No	Yes	No
Syria	Yes	Yes	Yes	No	No	Yes	Yes
Tunisia	Yes	Yes	Yes	Yes	Yes	Yes	Yes
U. Arab Emirates	No	No	No	No	No	No	Yes
Yemen	Yes	Yes	Yes	Yes	Yes	Yes	Yes
United States	No	Yes	Yes	Yes	Yes	No	Yes

List of Instruments Corresponding to Numbered Columns

I.   International covenant on economic, social and cultural rights.
II.   International covenant on civil and political rights.
III.   Convention on the prevention and punishment of the crime of genocide.
IV.   Convention against torture and other cruel, inhuman or degrading treatment or punishment.
V.   Convention on the political rights of women.
VI.   Convention on the rights of the child.
VII. International convention on the elimination of all forms of racial discrimination.

Data compiled from *International Instruments Relating to Human Rights: Classification and Status of Ratification as of 1 January 1997* in the Human Rights Law Journal, Vol. 18, No. 1-4 (1997).

Table 1.2 prepared by B. J. Brown

the UN Charter calls for international economic and social cooperation based on 'respect for the principle of equal rights and self-determination of peoples, . . .' The Convention against Genocide defines genocide as, 'acts committed with intent to destroy, in whole or in part, a national, ethnical, racial or religious group, as such: . . .' UNESCO's Declaration of the Principles of International Cultural Cooperation, states that, 'Each culture has a dignity and value which must be respected and preserved,' and, 'Every people has the right and duty to develop its culture.' The principle of non-discrimination against minorities was reaffirmed in the International Convention on the Elimination of All Forms of Racial Discrimination, adopted by the UN General Assembly in 1965. This was followed in 1981 by the UN General Assembly's Declaration on the Elimination of All Forms of Intolerance and Discrimination Based on Religion or Belief. Article 27 of the International Covenant on Civil and Political Rights states: 'In those States in which ethnic, linguistic, or religious minorities exist, persons belonging to such minorities shall not be denied the right, in community with the other members of their group, to enjoy their own culture, to profess and practice their own religion, or to use their own language.' In its *Namibia* (1970) opinion, the International Court of Justice stated that, 'To enforce . . . distinctions, exclusions, restrictions and limitations exclusively based on grounds of race, colour, descent or national origin which constitute a denial of fundamental rights is a flagrant violation of the purposes and principles of the Charter.' The UN General Assembly in its 1960 Declaration on the Granting of Independence to Colonial Countries and Peoples declared that:

1. The subjection of peoples to alien subjugation, domination and exploitation constitutes a denial of fundamental human rights, is contrary to the Charter of the United Nations and is an impediment to the promotion of world peace and co-operation.
2. All peoples have the right to self-determination; by virtue of that right they freely determine their political status and freely pursue their economic, social and cultural development.

The recognition of group rights in international law is closely related to the principles of non-discrimination and equality proclaimed in Article 1 of the Universal Declaration of Human Rights: 'All human beings are born free and equal in dignity and rights. They are endowed with reason and conscience and should act towards one another in a spirit of brotherhood.' The International Covenant on Civil and Political Rights, the European Convention for the Protection of Human Rights and Fundamental Freedoms (Art. 14), the American Declaration of the Rights and Duties of

Man (Preamble, Art. II), the American Convention on Human Rights (Articles 1 & 24), the African Charter on Human and People's Rights (Art. 2, 3, & 19), and the Declaration of the Basic Duties of ASEAN (Indonesia, Malaysia, the Philippines, Singapore, and Thailand) Peoples and Governments (Art. I) contain similar provisions.

Although these international agreements and declarations can be regarded as providing a substantive legal basis for minority cultural rights, international law currently lacks a well-established mechanism for adjudicating violations and enforcing judgments. Representatives of ethnic minorities presently do not have the right to act before international bodies and organizations in representation of their members. Given the fact that a large proportion of states contain one or more significantly sized ethnic or religious minorities, and that in many states (e.g., Turkey and the Kurds, Egypt and the Copts, Saudi Arabia and the Shiites, Iraq and the Kurds, Israel and the Arabs/Palestinians, Muslim countries and non-Muslim peoples, etc.) the denials against and the claims of these minorities have led to internal violence, it is imperative to the cause of intrastate and international peace that the concept of international personality be expanded so that such culturally distinct populations may have recourse to international tribunals to resolve their disputes with state authorities peacefully. Elsewhere I have argued for the necessity of creating partially self-governing culturally autonomous regions and granting such regions standing before the International Court of Justice so that they may resolve disputes with central governments in a more humane and just manner (Magnarella, 1993). As Judith Yaphe points out in her chapter on Iraq, Baghdad promised the Iraqi Kurds a self-governing autonomous region back in 1970, but, unfortunately, Baghdad never delivered. Saddam Husayn's subsequent treatment of the Kurds has been nothing short of genocidal.

As the chapters in this collection so sadly explain, none of the Arab states is a democracy and all have serious human rights problems, despite the fact that most have ratified many of the key UN human rights conventions. In fact, in terms of ratifications alone, some of the Arab countries compare favorably with the United States (see Table 1.2). The main problem has been in implementation. Even the process of liberalization and democratization among these countries has been disappointing for their citizens.

Of all the countries in the Middle East and North Africa, only Turkey and Israel claim to be functioning democracies. Each of these states also has its governance and human rights problems. Israel, at best, can be considered a primitive democracy, because Israel officially classifies its citizens according to ethno-religious criteria and privileges Jews over non-Jews. Lacking a constitution, Israel can offer no constitutionally-based democratic or human rights guarantees to all of its citizens, regardless of their ethno-religious affiliations. Israel has no civil marriage law. Consequently, official marriage is controlled by undemocratic religious organizations that generally prohibit intermarriage between citizens of different ethno-religious affiliations. Such an undemocratic situation reinforces and maintains social barriers between different segments of the population.

In the occupied West Bank and Gaza, Israel follows a colonialist-expansionist policy, incrementally taking lands and livelihoods from their rightful owners in defiance of international law and UN Security Council resolutions. As Ilan Peleg explains in his chapter to this volume, Israel has denied that Geneva Convention (IV), relative to the protection of peoples in occupied territories, applies to its occupation of the West Bank and Gaza, despite the fact that the entire human rights community insists that it does. Consequently, Israel deprives the Palestinians of their most fundamental human rights protection and has abused the Palestinians in its position as a belligerent occupier for decades.

Israel has been able to pursue its colonial, anti-human rights policies for decades because it receives full support from United States. Washington has not only made Israel the biggest recipient of foreign aid in the history of the world, it has repeatedly employed its veto in a manner to cripple the ability of UN Security Council to carry out its Charter duty to deal with the disruptions to international peace that the Israeli-Palestinian problem has caused. The situation in the Occupied Territories is unlikely to improve as long as the US continues to materially support Israeli policies and obstruct the UN Security Council.

Turkey, by contrast, is a constitutional democracy that has moved beyond the primitive stage of ascriptively based distinctions in citizenship. Turkey's official policy has been fully inclusive by defining all citizens, whatever their ethno-religious affiliations, as Turks.[1] Turkey also has a civil marriage law. Consequently, peoples of different ethno-religious background can and do intermarry, thereby reducing sociocultural barriers to integration. Ironically, Turkey's human rights problems stem, in significant part, from its inability to accommodate cultural diversity within its post-WW I concept of Turkish citizenship.

Turkey, by contrast to Israel and its other Middle East neighbors, has submitted itself to the most liberal and rigorous human rights regime in the world today: the European Convention for the Protection of Human Rights and Fundamental Freedoms. Turkey allows its citizens to take their human rights grievances against the state to the European Commission and Court of Human Rights. Turkey has also agreed to honor the judgments of that court. Consequently, Turkey is open to the strict scrutiny and criticism of European human rights advocates. Thus far, Turkey has had difficulty living up to these high standards. It has not, however, responded to criticism by rejecting these standards, nor has it abandoned efforts to meet them. In many respects, Turkey has made the greatest strides towards achieving the promise of the Universal Declaration of Human Rights, although it still has a distance to travel.

Although the current governance and human rights scene in the Middle East-North Africa is rather dismal, most of the contributors to this volume are optimistic about the future. Manochehr Dorraj argues convincingly that Islam, a fundamental cultural feature of this region, is not necessarily an obstacle to either democracy or universal human rights. All the contributors explain that the peoples of every state are thirsty for democratization and respect.

As scholars, with a deep respect and affection for the societies of this region, we, the contributors to this volume, sincerely hope the Middle East and North Africa will soon find political leaders enlightened enough to honor the will of the people and live up to the promise and aspirations of the Universal Declaration of Human Rights.

Note

1. The Lausanne Treaty (1923) minorities are an exception to this generalization. See the chapter on Turkey in this volume.

References

Advisory Opinion (1970) 'Legal Consequences for States of the Continued Presence of South Africa in Namibia (South West Africa) notwithstanding Security Council Resolution 276 (1970),' *International Court of Justice Reports* , 1971.

Magnarella, Paul J. (1993), 'Preventing Interethnic Conflict and Promoting Human Rights through More Effective Legal, Political, and Aid Structures: Focus on Africa,' *Georgia Journal of International and Comparative Law* , vol. 23, no. 2, pp. 327-45.

2 Islam, Governance and Democracy

MANOCHEHR DORRAJ

To declare God's sovereignty means: the comprehensive revolution against human governance in all its perceptions, forms, systems and conditions and the total defiance against every condition on earth in which humans are sovereign . . . in which the source of power is human.

Sayyid Qutb

The state is not something from God but from the people . . . the state has to serve the benefit of the Muslims.

Rashid al- Ghannoushi

The recent intellectual interest in civil society and democratization throughout the Middle East and North Africa has reinvigorated the debate on the compatibility of Islam and democracy. This chapter assays the historical and theological genealogy, the nuances, and the complexities of this debate.

There is no consensus among scholars of Islam as to the relationship between Islam and democracy. While some see Islam as an obstacle to democracy (Tibi, 1990), others perceive of a liberal interpretation of Islamic heritage as the only hope for the success of democracy in the Muslim World (Binder, 1988). Most of the ideological appraisals of Islam that either discard it as 'reactionary' or conservative, or those that dub it as inherently 'revolutionary' or radical overlook the fact that Islam is not a monolithic faith. Throughout its turbulent history, Islam has been interpreted to legitimize the status quo as well as to rebel against it. Therefore, this chapter addresses the following pertinent questions: What are the nuances of Islamic precepts and how do they influence the development of Islamic polity? What is the state of discourse on the compatibility or incompatibility of Islam and democracy? What is the perspective of Islam on human rights? What are the outstanding theoretical issues in these debates among Muslim theologians and Western scholars?

Islam and Democracy: Postulating the Problem Theoretically

The longing for social justice and opposition to autocratic rule has captured the imagination of Muslim intellectuals and progressive theologians throughout recent history. After the western encroachment on Muslim lands and the ensuing ideological challenge, these issues found a new urgency. Facing Western dominance, Muslim scholars and leaders had to grapple with new political and cultural issues. One distinct challenge for Muslim intellectuals was coping with Western dynamism and the vitality of its democratic political institutions. This awareness brought to bear the necessity of reform and renewal of Islam. Hence, Muslim thinkers had to address the question of the compatibility of Islam and democracy.

There are at least two contending concepts of democracy: procedural and substantial. Robert Dahl, for example, defines procedural democracy as 'polyarchy,' a system characterized by free competition among groups and individuals, selection of leaders through popular and competitive elections, and existence of civil and democratic liberties. This concept of democracy is concerned with a series of democratic processes and procedures designed to safeguard a participatory republican system (Dahl, 1971).

The roots of substantial democracy can be attributed to Aristotle, who related the idea of democracy to social and structural issues in society, such as the existence of small territory, self-governing units, and a large middle class. He conceived of self-governance in a Greek city- state as the major cornerstone of democracy. Aristotle defined democracy as the rule of the majority (Aristotle, 1972). The later development of the concept emerged from the social revolutions that swept Europe in the seventeenth and eighteenth centuries. Whereas during the Middle Ages Christianity and Judaism were used to legitimize monarchies and the divine rule of kings, by the seventeenth century, under the influence of the Renaissance, rationalism, and the Reformation, both of these religions were reinterpreted to accommodate nascent democratic ideals. Thus, religious reformation played a significant role in the development of the Western world. Likewise, historically, Islam has been used to legitimize political absolutism and monarchies as well as to mobilize the people against monarchies and arbitrary rule. However, much of the Muslim world never experienced a religious reformation that separated the sacred from the secular. Thus, rationalization of the sacred and its adaptation to the needs of industrial growth and development that were prerequisites to the democratic revolutions of Europe had no corollary in the Muslim world.

The formative origins of democracy are to be found in intellectual and institutional traditions of the Western world and its concern with defining the nature of legitimate government, the limits of its power, and the rights and obligations of its citizens. As such, democracy refers to a system of government with certain legal and institutional structures and processes to define the parameters of social and political life. Democracy is also based on rule by consent of the governed, political accountability, right to dissent, separation of state and 'church,' freedom of conscience and religion, and a legal code based on secular law. Islam, by contrast, is based on immutable principles. As a politicized faith recognizing no separation between state and 'church,' Islam encompasses the personal, the social, as well as the political realms of life. As a 'total religion,' it has specific provisions for social and personal affairs.

There are numerous tensions between Islam and democracy. The word *Islam* means submission to the will of God. Orthodox Muslims believe that God is the only true sovereign on earth. While believers are granted certain political rights, in general, liberties and democratic rights that may challenge 'the rightful' Islamic authority and order, tolerating social permissiveness, are regarded as unnecessary and even dangerous for salvation. Since Islam is the source of individual and collective identity and it permeates both realms of life, the interest of *ummah* (the Muslim community) always takes precedence over that of the individual. Therefore, the very existence of the individual as an autonomous being separate from the community, with certain inalienable rights, is alien to mainstream Islamic orthodoxy. Hence, shari'a (the Islamic holy law) is not born out of communal consensus, open contestation of ideas, or deliberation. It is perceived as the divine law to be interpreted by the highest religious authorities in the community in order to guide the faithful toward the ultimate goal of creating a community of the righteous. Virtuosity is defined in terms of individual conformity to shari'a. There is, however, some room for flexibility, in so far as the decree of one doctor of law or a high ranking cleric can be annulled by another.

The two major sects of Islam have elitist origins. After the death of Muhammad, the Sunnis held that only members of his tribe (Quraysh) were eligible to succeed him. The Shi'ites insisted that only the members of the Prophet's immediate family who had inherited his knowledge and innocence could rule. There is an unresolved tension between the Shi'ites' belief in Imamat (the charismatic rule of the seven or twelve male descendants of the prophet, depending on which sect, Ismai'lis or Ithna'sharis) and the notion of popular sovereignty. In the absence of the twelfth Imam, who is said to be in occultation, the mantle of Imamat is passed down to the Ulama (the learned clergy) as the intermediaries between humans and God. This partially explains why, for example, the leaders of the Iranian revolution of 1979 opted for *Valayat-i Faqih* (the rule of the jurisconsult) and the charismatic leadership of Ayatollah Khomeini. So far as the orthodox Shi'ites are concerned, without the necessary religious leadership and supervision, the community will deviate from the righteous path. It is incumbent on devout Shi'ites to obey the commandments of the leading cleric of the day (the Ayatollah), because he is regarded as 'the source of emulation.' Secular rule, the devout Shi'ites hold, can only usher in moral decay and corruption.

The Sunni doctrine of *khalifah*, in contrast, regards the community as the viceregents of God and allows for limited input by the community in the process of political decision-making. Nevertheless, as the head of a centralized state, the power of the khalif remains supreme with extensive judicial and executive powers and more limited legislative power. These conflicting interpretations of Islamic doctrine have been carried to modern time. Whereas Ayatollah Khomeini, for example, argued for the necessity of the rule by jurisconsult, which would effectively put the clergy in charge of state power, Sayyid Qutb, the leading Egyptian traditionalist (who was executed by Jamal Abdul Nasser in 1966) opposed the need for the stewardship of professional clergy. He argued that,

> the kingdom of God on earth will not be established when religious leaders supervise sovereignty on earth as was the case under the power of the church, nor by men who pontificate in the name of God as was the case under 'theocracy' or divine rule . . . (Tamadonfar,1989, p. 106).

This is only a small indication of the immense diversity in Islam. If democracy is viewed merely in its formal and constitutional dimensions, then it is incompatible with Islam. If the definition is broadened to encompass the broader essence of democracy, then there are possibilities for reconciliation and accommodation despite the profound differences. Democracy, for example, is closely linked with equality. In the Greek concept of equality, individuals were equal only if they owned slaves or property. The Islamic concept of equality, on the other hand, is not contingent upon property or ownership. Theoretically, Islam considers all believers equal members of the community despite their race, origins, or status. The only criterion for superiority is the piety of the believer (Enayat, 1982, pp. 126-128). Despite early Islam's discrimination between believers and non-believers, Arabs and non-Arabs (*Ajams* and *Mawalis*), Muslim men and women and its acceptance of slavery as an institution (Rosenthal, 1960, pp. 29-34), the teachings of early Islam bore a distinct strain of egalitarianism (Marlow, 1997). The roots of this egalitarianism can be detected in the pre-Islamic Arab Bedouin culture. Both the sharing of wealth with kin and the Arab tradition of valuing hospitality and generosity point to a sense of raw equality and the cooperation necessary for survival in the harsh life of the desert (Anderson, Seibert and Wagner, 1990, p. 25). Islam's moral code incorporated these social realities.

Pristine Islam was impacted by two egalitarian elements: monotheism and tribalism. Belief in oneness of God can reinforce a sense of brotherhood of all believers. Tribalism may reinforce a sense of communitarianism. This egalitarian spirit can be found in the Qur'an and the Hadith (alleged utterances and conducts attributed to the prophet Muhammad) as well as the statements of Umar and Ali, the two 'rightly guided' khalifs who succeeded him.

Those who advocate the compatibility of Islam and democracy attempt to demonstrate how the seeds of accountable government were already present in Islamic tradition. They point out that Islam is against arbitrary rule, and they see in the paradigmatic example of the prophet the precedent against tyranny. To strengthen the political solidarity of the community, they assert, the prophet developed a delicate definition of political power: authority of the ruler stems from the ummah, through their *shura* (consultation) and must be accountable to them through *ijma* (consensus) (Esposito and Piscatori, 1991, p. 434). Muhammad also refused to name a successor, thus leaving the decision to the community at large. To prevent a profound rift between the rich and poor in his community, Muhammad encouraged *saddaqah* (contribution to the needy) and *zakat* (legal alms). He also created *bait al mal* (public fund) to finance communal needs (Watt, 1962, pp. 252-253). The electoral process in the Muslim world is traced to the seventh century rule of Ummar, who succeeded the prophet as one of the four rightly guided khalifs. Ummar, it is said, appointed a shura, or electoral committee, to choose his successor, the third khalif (Uthman) (Goldschmidt, 1991).

As the Islamic conquest ushered in new wealth and power and the society became more stratified and hierarchical, a distinct tension developed between the professed egalitarianism of pristine Islamic theology and the existing disparity of wealth and power. This tension remains unresolved and is an animating force in the present Islamic revival and the pervasive populist interpretation of the faith. As the Abassid dynasty incorporated some of the Persian tradition of kingship, administration, and statecraft, the new Arab khalifs became increasingly defensive, attempting to justify the pervading social inequalities in Islamic terms. The egalitarian spirit of early Islam was a major motif in popular rebellion against state power in many parts of the Islamic empire from the eighth to the thirteenth centuries (Marlow, 1997).

This relatively raw egalitarian tradition lacked any trace of individualism, a crucial component of Western democracy. In the hierarchical tribal society of bedouin Arabs, the concept of 'citizens' as autonomous individuals with certain inalienable rights never developed -- as it did not in the West until the emergence of commercial capitalism in the eighteenth century. The harsh life of the desert made individual survival dependent on collective cooperation. The reliance on the tribe for sustenance and security firmly established the primacy of the community over the individual.

Most Muslim khalifs considered the people living in their domain as subjects who owed them 'complete and immediate obedience' (Lewis, 1988, p. 94). In the formative stages of shari'a in the seventh century, slavery was an acceptable institution; women were generally regarded as unequal to men; and religion was the main source of cultural identity. Therefore, the source of discrimination between slaves and free men, men and women, and Muslims and non-Muslims was historically grounded. Close scrutiny of the Qur'an reveals that property and natural and individual rights are subordinate to the collective interest, sanctity and security of the community. The injunction *Al-amri bi ma'ruf Valnahi al-munkar* (rejoicing the good and forbidding the evil) makes it incumbent upon Muslims to watch over public morality.

Preserving the sanctity of the community of the faithful requires leaders with legitimate authority. Muslim traditionalists believed that if the power of the leader were contingent upon a system of checks and balances, the charisma and consequently the authority of the leader would erode. Such was the justification for obeying the authority of charismatic kings and khalifs (Khajeh Nezam al-Mulk, 1960). It is, however, misleading to surmise that Islam supports arbitrary rule. To the contrary, the Qur'an encourages the rule of law (shari'a) and exhorts the faithful to obey legitimate and just Muslim rulers. Enticing 'sedition' (*fitnah*), however, carries a heavy penalty in the Islamic legal code. Since it is not often clear what constitutes 'sedition' and what is rightful criticism, Muslim leaders have much latitude to define fitnah as political expediency would dictate. Muslim lands throughout history have seen their share of autocratic rulers who have charged their opponents with enticing fitnah, thus justifying their annihilation.

In regard to racial and ethnic relationships, however, the Islamic world has fared relatively better throughout modern history than has the Western world. Islam recognizes Jews and Christians as 'the people of the book.' It respects their faith as the two monotheistic religions, and it respects Moses and Jesus as prophets of God. Christianity, by contrast, (perhaps partially because it emerged earlier), does not grant the same recognitions to Islam and Muhammad. Muslim treatment of Jews also demonstrates that the anti-Jewism manifested in Europe never was as extensive in the Muslim world. The mass expulsion and genocide of Jews witnessed in Germany, Poland, Russia and France, for example, has no equivalent in Muslim lands (Enayat, 1982, pp. 129-130). To be sure, the Ottoman government's attacks on Armenians in the early part of the twentieth century, the violation of human rights of Sudanese Christians by the Islamic government of Sudan, and the persecution of the Bahai community in Iran evince that Muslim governments have engaged in abuse and persecution of religious minorities. But this has been done on much smaller scale than the holocaust under Fascism.

To summarize, scholars who argue for the compatibility of Islam and democracy refer to the following five attributes of Islam: (1) The practice of consultation (shura) by the Prophet and the four rightly guided khalifs in pristine Islam. Whereas the traditional notion of shura referred to the ruler asking other members of the court for advice, the modern revisionist concept as formulated by a leading Muslim modernist, Fazlur Rahman, for example, reinterprets shura to mean 'mutual advice through mutual discussions on an equal footing' (Esposito and Voll, 1996, p. 28). (2) Closely related to shura is the concept of ijma (consensus) or the collective judgment of the Ulama that is binding on the Muslim community. Whereas the traditional concept of Ijma referred to the consensus of the leading Ulama regarding the application of Islamic law to social and religious issues, the modern revisionist concept of ijma calls for the popular consensus of the community. (3) Ijtihad (independent judgment) is said to endow the believers with freedom to interpret Islam for themselves, thus challenging the monopoly of the clerics (the doctors of law) on interpretation of holy law. (4) Closely related to the concept of ijtihad is qiyas (analogical reasoning). Muslims can use qiyas to interpret holy law on the basis of rationalism . This potentially renders theirs a reasoned faith that is not based on fear, dogma, or blind obedience. (5) The concept of *bay'ah* is presented as another pillar of democratic governance. Whereas the traditional conservative notion of bay'ah refers to the mandatory allegiance of subjects to the khalifs, the modern reformist interpretation implies the people's approval of a ruler's right to govern and the necessity for free elections. The reformist account also projects bay'ah as a social contract between the ruler and the ruled. If the ruler abuses his or her power, then the community has the right to withdraw its support and oppose him/her. Reformists define bay'ah as the principle of rule by the consent of the governed. (6) The right to criticize the unjust ruler is derived from the duty of the believers 'to rejoice the good and forbid the evil'. This predisposes Muslims to take an active role in the implementation of social Justice in their communities. (7) The respect for the life, private property and equality of all believers is presented as other indications of the compatibility of Islam and democracy. (8) Finally, it is argued that just as democracy emerged from Christian legal canons, so to is it possible for a future democratic legal framework to emerge from reformist interpretations of the shar'ia (Enayat, 1982, Esposito and Piscatori, 1991, Esposito and Voll, 1996).

'Democratic' interpretations of Islamic precepts are more common among Muslim modernists of the late nineteenth and twentieth centuries who favored a representative government and a parliamentary political system. Modernists such as Assad Abadi (Afghani), Abduh, Iqbal, Shariati, Bazargan, Ghannouchi, and Soroosh were inspired by Western rationalism and the dynamism of Western democratic institutions. They abhorred the spirit of fatalism prevalent among many Muslim traditionalists. They used their power of interpretation of the holy law and the Qur'an to reform and revitalize Islam, to encourage participatory politics and to end political absolutism and tyranny. By emphasizing the principle of free will (*ikhtiar*), ijtihad, and qiyas, they argued that Muslims can become masters of their own destiny by educating themselves and becoming engaged in political affairs of their respective communities (Esposito,1984, pp. 44-60). Below I present some of the leading Muslim modernists and traditionalists and briefly explore their divergent ideas on Islam, governance, and democracy.

Muslim Modernists and Muslim Traditionalists

Jamal al-Din al-Afghani (1838-1897), who was born in Iran but lived in various parts of the Muslim world and Europe, aspired to reconcile Islam with the modern world. In contrast to the traditionalists, Afghani called for the revival of Islam based on a new interpretation that would accommodate Western philosophy, science, and rationalism. Afghani's opposition to Western colonialism was complemented by his admiration for Western democracy and its constitutional system. He believed that the archaic members of the Ulama who resisted modernization and social progress were as much responsible for the stagnation of Islam and Muslim societies as were the Western colonialists.
As he put it,

> The Westerners have conquered the world, not because of their
> belief in Jesus or Mary, but because of their capacity to build

railroads; to create the telegram system. We have lost, because we have become the prisoners of our own superstitions and ignorance. (Dorraj,1990, p. 89)

His advocacy of pan-Islamism was based on a dynamic reform and renewal of the faith. Afghani favored the synthesis of religion and science, faith and reason. He promoted enlightened religiosity. He used pedagogical as well as clandestine activities, persuasion of political leaders and called on the masses to revolt in order to instigate social change. He saw tyrants as obstacles to constitutional government and popular sovereignty. Therefore, he urged Muslim leaders to reform their governments and put an end to repression and corruption (Keddie, 1968, pp. 52-62).

Muhammad Abduh (1849-1905), the Egyptian disciple of Afghani, was another influential modernist. He led a reform movement known as *salafiyya* throughout the Arab world. Early in his career he joined Afghani in his anti-colonial struggle against British and French domination of Egypt. This rebellion culminated in Urabi Pasha's unsuccessful nationalist revolt in 1882. After British occupation of Egypt, Abduh was exiled to Paris. Upon his return to Cairo in 1888, he abandoned the path of revolution and opted to transform his country through the reform and renewal of Islam. He advocated the selective adaptation of Western values and institutions and strove to demonstrate the compatibility of Islam and Western rationalism. After he became the head of the shari'a law court system and a member of the legislative council of Egypt in 1899, he initiated a series of reforms in Islamic law, education, and theology. Recognizing the weaknesses of traditional Islamic law regarding equal treatment of women, Abduh opposed polygamy and advocated legal and educational reforms that enhanced the status of women (Esposito, 1984, p. 49, Dorraj, 1992, pp. 96-97). In his ceaseless attempts to find precedents for representative government, he innovatively reinterpreted the Islamic past. Thus *maslah* (public good) was interpreted as utilitarianism, shura became parliamentary democracy, and ijma was presented as the necessity to respect public opinion. His ideal government, however, was a constitutional monarchy (Mortimer, 1982, pp. 175-187).

Muhammad Iqbal (1873-1938) was a prominent modernist whose influence reached as far as India, Pakistan, Egypt and Iran. Like his modernist predecessors, he was also exposed to and influenced by Western civilization and rationalist philosophers. He received his doctorate in philosophy from Heidelberg and Munich. Iqbal considered Islam a complete faith that was superior to both capitalism and communism. An advocate of participatory politics and representative government, he favored modern legislative assemblies over the Ulama. Iqbal presented a critical, rationalist, and democratic reinterpretation of Islam. He admired Western intellectual traditions and democratic institutions as well as some aspects of socialism. He attempted to find precedents for both in Islam (Esposito, 1983, pp. 175-187). Iqbal believed in the absolute inseparability of religion and politics. As he asserted,

> In Islam, God and universe, spirit and matter, Church and state are organically linked to each other. Whatever may emerge, imperialism or democracy, if religion is separated from politics, there remains tyranny, aggression, lawlessness, and exploitation. (Iqbal,1973, pp. 103-104)

Iqbal's ideas on democracy were ambiguous and contradictory. On the one hand, he opposed Western democracy, declaring it to be a cosmetic on the face of imperialism which with 'iron feet... tramples down the weak without remorse.' He also believed that democracy 'lets loose all sorts of aspirations and grievances' which may lead to anarchy. He criticized democracy because it 'counts' rather than 'weighs'. He contended that while in a democracy the individual and individualism are valued, the spiritual well-being of individuals is ignored (Abbott, 1971, pp. 155-175). But Iqbal also regarded democracy as one of the most important aspects of Islam. Individual rights, however, asserted Iqbal, must be subordinated to the welfare of society, and the interests of Islam are more significant than those of the Muslim (Hassan, 1971, p. 157 and Dorraj, 1995, p. 275). Such prevalent ambiguities and contradictions reflect the dual world of Muslim modernists who were caught between their admiration for Western rationalism and democratic institutions, on the one hand, and their abiding loyalty to Islamic authenticity, on the other.

One modernist who was deeply influenced by Iqbal and harbored his ambivalence and ambiguities toward democracy is Ali Shariati (1933-1977). Born in Iran and educated at the Sorbonne, France, where he received a doctorate in sociology, Shariati was influenced by such diverse philosophers and sociologists as Durkheim, Hegel, Marx, and Sartre, and such Third World activists and scholars as Franz Fanon. He applied an innovative approach to Qur'anic exegesis, which enabled him to draw activist conclusions. His politicized interpretation of Shi'ite Islam galvanized and mobilized Muslim youths, many of whom participated in or led the Iranian revolution of 1979. In the eyes of many of his followers he was 'the Luther of Iran' and the leader of Islamic Protestanism (Dorraj, 1990, pp. 140-141). One of Shariati's major contributions was to present a social analysis of Islam and impart social consciousness to his audience. He asserted that, 'It is only through a social struggle that human beings can really grow. In isolation one can become a philosopher, a poet, a virtuous and pious man, but one cannot become a Muslim' (Shariati, 1973, p. 28). Shariati's concept of democracy is linked to his perception of leadership in the Islamic community. He interpreted imamat as the necessity for revolutionary leadership. Imamat should not be confused with a democratic government. As Shariati explains,

> Imamat is not dependent on choice, but recognition. For example, in a democracy the people are the source of power and they are the deciding factor. The government mediates between the leader and the people. In Islam, however, the relation of the people to the Imam is mediated by 'the truth.' People are not the deciding element, they are the recognizing element. (Shariati,1972, p. 127)

Shariati does not say who determines the truth. But he makes it clear that without the leadership of the Imam the individual is lost, like a sheep without a shepherd. As for the duty of community, Shariati clearly states:

> The members of the ummah, despite their race or color, think alike and believe in a single leadership to guide them toward progress and perfection. The goal of society must be progress and not necessarily happiness. It is the duty of the ummah to choose the former over the latter. (Shariati,1972, p. 62)

To dispel possible illusions that any members of the community may have about the nature of the Imam's leadership, Shariati states:

> The Imam need not be democratic in the formal sense of the word. He is not obliged to act according to the wishes of the members of the community. Neither must he consider the well-being and happiness of the masses as his primary goal. The most important duty of Imam is to guide the ummah in the most direct and efficient way toward perfection, even if it would mean great suffering for the community. (Shariati, 1973, p. 63)

Only a Muslim's understanding of this necessity, held Shariati, would set him/her free and prepare him/her for the unity with God. Shariati regarded Western democracy as unsuitable for Muslim societies. Because of the low rate of literacy, asserted Shariati, the majority of the people are not yet in a position to decide what is best for them. He also believed that in so far as democracy is based on maintaining the status quo, it was incompatible with the goal of Islamic societies for revolutionary change (Tamadonfar, 1989,

p. 41). Thus, Shariati's theory of leadership possesses a distinct totalitarian streak that jeopardizes the humanitarian bent of his political ideology and his agenda for social change. Because of his sudden death in 1977, he did not see the Iranian revolution and he did not leave us an evaluation of its leader.

A Muslim modernist and a contemporary of Shariati who participated in the revolution and was, for a brief period, the first prime minister of the Islamic Republic of Iran, was Mehdi Bazargan (1907-1994). His liberal interpretation of Islam quickly put him at odds with the traditionalists who dominated the government. Like Shariati, he was a French-educated Muslim lay intellectual, but with a degree in engineering. Compared to the radical inclinations of Shariati, however, Bazargan was more liberal and moderate in his political temperament. He held that Islam is not based on coercing individuals into compliance with its rule. All individuals, Muslims and infidels alike, must be granted equal protection and equality before the Islamic law (Bazargan, 1982, p. 27). Unlike Shariati, who emphasized the primacy of the community and collective action, Bazargan shifted the emphasis to the inviolability of the individual and individual rights. Since individuals constitute the basis of society, social progress must begin with the transformation of individuals. Thus, individual welfare takes precedence over the collective. Hence, Bazargan regarded Islamic edicts and ordinances as a matter of private values and conscience not to be regulated by the state. No government should legislate morality or persecute people on the basis of their alleged religious deviation (Bazargan, 1982, p. 28). Bazargan opposed a totalitarian interpretation of Islam. He favored popular sovereignty and pluralism, and regarded a synthesis of Islam and democracy as the most desirable form of government. He was also active in the defense of human rights. In 1986, he established the Society for the Defense of Freedom and the Sovereignty of the Iranian People. The society's goals were 'to struggle against despotism, for political and social freedom, and for the equality of all before the law, and to defend Iran's honor in world public opinion' (Chehabi, 1990, p. 302). Toward the end of his life, he opposed theocracy and advocated the separation of religion and politics. He called on the clergy to go back to the mosque and leave politics to the technocrats and politicians. He believed that subjecting a spiritual faith, such as Islam, to mundane politics in a corrupt world, denudes it of its spiritual essence. Ideologization of Islam as an instrument of power politics ultimately diminishes Islam and Muslims (Chehabi, 1990, pp. 278-304).

In the contemporary Muslim World several prominent Muslim leaders have also advocated the compatibility of Islam and democracy. Among them are Sheikh Muhammad al-Ghazali and Sheikh Yusuf al-Qaradawi of

Egypt, Rashid al-Ghannouchi, head of Tunisia's Islamist movement, and Abdol Karim-i Soorosh of Iran. Ghazali perceives democracy as a system that prevents arbitrary rule and protects citizens from the abuse of power by government. Prevention of arbitrary rule and making government accountable, holds Ghazali, is something that Islam and democracy have in common.

Ghannouchi considers the struggle against oppression and for such democratic principles as free elections, majority rule, peaceful transition of power, and the protection of the rights of minorities as universal principles that can and must be respected under an Islamic democracy. According to him, there are no contradictions between the spirit of Islamic precepts and these democratic rights and procedures. He also supports a pluralist electional system in which Muslims are in the minority.

Qaradawi polemicizes against those traditionalists who perceive of democracy as unIslamic and unpious. He considers democracy a system in which people can freely elect their leaders, question them, and depose them if they abuse power. The virtue of democracy, asserts Qaradawi, lies in its opposition to despotism (Ghadbian, 1997, pp. 78-80).

In the same vein, Abdolkarim-i Soroosh, a philosophy professor and one of the leading ideologues of the Islamic Republic in the early years of the revolution, argues for primacy of reason and freedom as the necessary precondition of human development. Having witnessed the suppression of democratic rights and the use of Islam as an instrument of power politics in Iran, he became concerned with the diminishing spiritual essence of Islam and with religious despotism. He has become an advocate of separation of religion and politics. He asserts that religion must not stand as a dominating force above society; it must serve human welfare and well-being. Hence, justice must not be subordinate to the requirements of Islamic doctrine or political expediency. Rather, Islam must meet the standards of social justice and adhere to the universal declaration of human rights. To remain legitimate, religious governments must democratize and respect and protect human rights (Soorosh, 1994, pp. 235-283).

The Muslim traditionalists, on the other hand, such as Sheikh Fadlallah Nuri and Ayatollah Khomeini of Iran and Sayyid Qutb of Egypt opposed democracy and the idea of popular sovereignty and secular law. The attitude of Mawdudi, the leading traditionalist theologian of Pakistan, was too complex and nuanced to fall into this category. Mawdudi was more sympathetic to democratic institutions and ideals than most of the other traditionalists of the twentieth century.

Sheikh Nuri (d.1909) of Iran perceived a constitutional democracy as a threat to the rule of shari'a. He was an ardent opponent of the constitutional revolution of 1906-09 in Iran that sought to end monarchial absolutism. Nuri and his cothinkers opposed the opening of schools for women and the building of factories and 'European' industries. To delegitimize the constitutional movement to adopt a secular constitution modeled after the constitution of Belgium, Nuri emphasized its 'alien' and European origins. Nuri's major objection to constitutionalism and parliamentarism centered around such issues as:

> the inauguration of the customs and practices of the realm of infidelity
> . . . the intention to tamper with the sacred law which is said to belong
> to 1300 years ago and not to be in accordance with the requirements of
> the modern age, the ridiculing of the Muslims and insults directed at
> the Ulama, the equal rights of nationalities and religions, the spread of
> prostitution, and freedom of the press which is contrary to our sacred
> law. (Arjomand, 1983, p. 179)

As the perceived guardians of cultural authenticity and religious sanctity, Nuri and his followers felt threatened by the intelligentsia's adoption of Western secular values. Perceiving the constitutionalists as the agents of Western influence in Iran, they vehemently attacked them.

Another prominent traditionalist who opposed democracy was Ayatolah Khomeini (1902-1989), the leader of the Iranian revolution of 1979. Khomeini was raised in a traditional religious household and received a traditional Shi'ite education in theological seminaries. He came to political prominence by leading the 1963 uprising against the Shah's regime. His subsequent exile put him out of the reach of the monarchy and allowed him to take a more militant political position against the Shah. In order to arouse the masses to political action against monarchy, he developed a populist interpretation of Shi'ism. This increased his popularity and strengthened his stature as a leader. In his treatise on government and Islam, *Valayat-i Faqih* (the rule of the jurisconsult), Khomeini polemicized against both monarchy and Western democracy and called for the creation of an Islamic government. The governments that the Prophet Muhammad and Imam Ali (the first Shi'ite Imam) created were theocracies, argued Khomeini, and it is the duty of Muslims to follow their paradigmatic model. Only such Islamic government and the seizure of power by Ulama can ensure the rule of shari'a and safeguard the sanctity and the salvation of the Muslim community. In an Islamic government a legislative body in the Western sense of the word is not necessary, Khomeini argued; in the Islamic government God alone is the ruler and the legislator. However, a consultative assembly is necessary to conduct consultation among Muslims according to the principle of shura. Thus, he referred to this consultative body (Tamadonfar, 1989, p. 47).

Khomeini explains that the rule of the jurisconsult in Islamic government is not arbitrary. Those who govern are subject to a set of conditions that are specified in the Qur'an and the traditions of the most noble prophet, God's benedictions be upon him' (Khomeini, 1978, pp. 52-53). The rule of the jurisconsult is tantamount to a neo-Platonic idea of the Philosopher King. Since ordinary people lack the wisdom and the necessary religious knowledge to guide the community toward eternal salvation, it is argued, only the jurisconsult can provide a leader who knows what is best for his subjects. The title of *Faqih* (the cleric who is the most knowledgeable of shari'a) bestowed upon him the mantle of the deputy of the Prophet in the absence of the twelfth Imam. This endowed him with great power as the judge, the arbiter and the prosecutor of the holy law. But Khomeini was more than a faqih. He was also a grand Ayatollah (the source of emulation) whose commandments and decrees were binding on his followers, who owed him loyalty and obedience. As such, Khomeini's charisma was rooted both in Shi'ite tradition of folk religion as well as his political legitimacy as the leader of 1979 revolution. This potent combination of religious sanctity and political authority rendered Khomeini's power supreme.

Khomeini regarded Islamic government as the guardian of Islamic ideals and sanctity. Thus, any opposition to the Islamic Republic was tantamount to treason. He exhorted the necessity for the 'unity of words and deeds' among Muslims. He admonished that pluralism and a multiparty system were deadly for the nation. All factions and groups 'should merge into one united Islamic front: the party of God (*Hizballah*') (Tamadonfar, 1989, pp. 46-49). It is not then surprising that both the leftists (the Marxists and the Islamic Mujaheedin) and the rightists (monarchists) opponents of the Islamic Republic were persecuted.

Abul A'la Mawdudi (d. 1979), the founder of *Jama'at-i Islami* (Islamic League) in Pakistan conceived of Islam as a complete system that is the antithesis to Western democracy. He asserted that Islam is opposed to the idea of popular sovereignty; sovereignty belongs to God only. But in so far as humans are regarded as the viceregents of God, some divine power is relegated to them. Mawdudi considered separation of religion and politics as a dangerous phenomenon. When religion is relegated to the personal realm, it gives rise to 'bestial impulses and men perpetrate evil upon one another. In fact, it is precisely because they wish to escape the restraint of morality and the divine guidance that men espouse secularism' (Tamadonfar, 1989, p. 37). Mawdudi also perceived the seizure of state power as an instrumental step in the implementation of shari'a and the creation of the 'kingdom of heaven.' As he puts it,

... the reforms which Islam wants to bring about cannot be carried out merely by sermons. Political power is essential for their achievement ... the struggle for obtaining control over the organs of the state when motivated by the urge to establish the *din* (religion) and the Islamic shari'a and to enforce the Islamic injunctions, is not only permissible but is positively desirable and as such obligatory. (Tamadonfar, 1989, p. 39)

Mawdudi regarded the authority of the Islamic state as all-encompassing, penetrating social and personal realms. This Islamic totalitarianism is, however, perceived to be different from Fascist or Communist totalitarianism, because it rejects dictatorship and grants liberties. In so far as democracy can be reconciled with the rule of Islamic law and subordinated to it, he entertained the possibility of in a new synthesis he termed a totalitarian 'theo-democracy'(Esposito and Piscatori,1991, p. 436; Esposito and Voll, 1996, pp. 23-29). Mawdudi regarded the Islamic polity as the kingdom of God (a theocracy). But Islamic theocracy is different from the theocracies in Europe prior to the Eighteenth century. According to him,

The theocracy built by Islam is not ruled by any particular religious class but by the whole community of Muslims including the rank and file. The entire Muslim population runs the state in accordance with the book of God and the practice of his prophet ... The executive under this system of government is constituted by the general will of the Muslims who have also the right to depose it. (Esposito and Voll, 1996, p. 24)

While every Muslim who is capable is entitled to interpret the shari'a, no one, not even the entire community, has the right to change an explicit command of God (Esposito and Voll, P. 24). Mawdudi's thoughts on Islam and democracy, like those of many other Muslim theologians and theorists of the twentieth century, were full of ambiguities, contradictions, and ambivalence. For Mawdudi, as long as the leader is 'just' and 'right,' his authority remains uncontested and he can disregard the political voice of the legislature. Only Muslims have the right to govern because only they are capable of upholding Islamic law and guiding the Muslim community toward the righteous path (Tamadonfar, 1989, pp. 49-54). Therefore, political contestation and free access to political power despite one's religious convictions or affiliation, which are constituent elements of the democratic process are discarded. Moreover, if the Islamic state is the guardian of the divine truth, as many Muslim traditionalists including

Mawdudi hold, then alternative interpretations of truth and tolerance of diverse ideas become impossible. In Mawdudi's doctrine it is not clear who defines what a 'right' and 'just' leader is, or to whom the community owes allegiance and obedience.

A disciple of Mawdudi who became one of the prominent voices of militant Islamic traditionalism was Sayyid Qutb (d.1966) of Egypt. Unlike Mawdudi's mild political temperament and his desire to reconcile Islam and democracy, Qutb considered all terrestrial powers, secular or religious, as illegitimate. He believed in divine sovereignty and opposed theocracies and rule by professional clergy as the usurpation of power under the name of religion. He also regarded Jamal Abdul Nasser's secular regime as the new *jahalia* (ignorance and barbarism). Since human beings were sinful, argued Qutb, in any government that is based on a group of people legislating for others, equality and absolute dignity cannot be realized (Esposito and Piscatori, 1991, p. 435). Qutb considered both capitalism and socialism as flawed systems that were particularly unsuitable for the Muslim World. He also opposed communism for its preoccupation with materialism and its disegard for human spiritual needs. As Qutb asserted, 'communism in itself is an insignificant idea which deserves no respect from those who think humanely, above the level of food and drink' (Tamadonfar, 1989, p. 42). According to Qutb, Islamic government is a 'system that provides us with the bread that communism provides, and frees us from economic and social disparity, realizing a balanced society while sustaining us spiritually' (Tamadonfar, 1989, p. 42). Qutb's intransigent attitudes brought him early death at the hands of Nasser's regime in 1966. But his impact proved to be resilient especially on the left flank of the Muslim Brotherhood movement in Egypt, inspiring many Muslim militants and their leaders who have opposed Sadat's and Mubarak's governments, often with violence.

Many other contemporary leading traditionalist theologians also oppose democracy. Shiekh Muhammad Mutawwali al-Sha'rawi, a traditionalist religious leader from Egypt, declared in 1982 that shura does not connote simple majority rule, and Islam and democracy are incompatible. Likewise, in Algeria, Ali Benhadj, another traditionalist religious leader, objects to majority rule on the grounds that 'rights and justice cannot be quantified; the greater number of votes does not translate into the greater moral position' (Esposito and Piscatori, 1991, p. 436).

Most Islamic states from Pakistan to the Sudan seem to have opted for a semblance of divine and popular sovereignty. The traditionalists' negation of Western democracy must be perceived in terms of the defensive position of Muslims in the post-colonial era of Western cultural and economic domination. Steeped in tradition and entrenched as the guardians of the Islamic past, they find themselves unable to fully embrace the idea of democracy with its roots in Judeo-Christian tradition. Yet, aware of the appeal of the concept of popular sovereignty to contemporary Muslims, they have opted for a compromise. By reinterpreting the Islamic past to find precedents for participatory politics and a parliamentary political system, they have attempted to respond to the popular sentiment for political participation.

This brief overview of the political thoughts of some leading Muslim modernists and traditionalists is an indication of the complexities involved in analyzing the compatibility and incompatibility between Islam and democracy. This debate is not confined to Muslim theologians. It has been a topic of controversy and polemics among academics as well.

Some academics consider Islam and its patrimonial culture as incompatible with democracy (Huntington, 1991). Others argue that since Islam owes its formative development to a pre-industrial age, it is structurally incapable of coping with the demands of the modern world. One such scholar is Bassam Tibi, who argues that any successful cultural accommodation of social change—including democracy—is dependent upon two central issues. First, there must emerge a democratization of access to science and technology and an elimination of the North-South gap. Second, Islamic monism must be replaced by intellectual pluralism. Muslim societies must desacralize their politics and depoliticize their religion. Only then can they successfully secularize their societies and democratize their political culture (Tibi, 1990, pp. 1-5, 45-55, 179-196). Tibi asserts that Islamic culture is particularly handicapped in the areas of law, language, and education to come to terms with change and accommodate new social realities. Because Qur'anic truth is regarded as eternal and immutable, and the shari'a is all- encompassing, covering the private as well as the social realms of life, its jurisdiction over Muslims' lives is unlimited. A system of law viewed as immutable is extremely hard to change (Tibi, 1990, p. 74). The second element of Islamic culture that Tibi regards as an obstacle to democratic change is the Arabic language. The sources of Islamic law, the Qur'an and Hadith are Arabic proclamations.

Like Islamic law, the Arabic language is not open to change. Arabic is regarded as a sacred language. Thus, it has failed to accommodate new expressions and words. Finally, Islam in its all-encompassing nature also dominates education. Islamic education is not concerned with investigation and inquiry, but with learning in a sacred sense; it is a place for the cultivation of Islamic science and the teaching of the Qur'an and Hadith and branches of knowledge stemming from them. The access to rational science (natural science and philosophy), so critical to the development and growth of democracy in the West, has been obstructed in the Middle East. Thus, the creativity essential to the development of new ideas and the fostering of democratic growth has been limited. Hence, many universities in Muslim states are 'rote-learning' institutions that encourage memorization of material instead of understanding and research (Tibi, 1990, pp. 58, 104-110).

While parts of Tibi's critical assertions bear some merit, other parts can be disputed on several grounds. First, Tibi totally ignores the principle of ijtihad, which allows the Muslim clergy to reinterpret the shari'a and adapt to changing conditions. Indeed ijtihad has made the continuous vitality and relevance of Islam possible over the years. Second, language is the medium of articulation of human perception and the tool of human communication; it evolves with changing human conditions. Therefore, it is both analytically as well as factually wrong to declare Arabic an immutable language. Indeed, both French and English influences in Arabic have abounded since the dawn of the colonial era. Third, Tibi's contention that many universities in the Muslim world are 'rote-learning' institutions is contradicted by his earlier observation in regard to the universalization of science. Hence, his contention that no research takes place in these universities seems an exaggeration. To be sure, research facilities are limited in the Muslim world, but in this age of the transfer of knowledge and technology, no country can close its borders to scientific method and the flow of information. This includes the most conservative of them all, Saudi Arabia.

Other scholars such as Richard Norton are more optimistic about the prospects for civil society and democratization in the Muslim world. He sees the development of an incipient civil society and the strengthening of the middle class as hopeful signs that the chances for democratization in the region are better than generally assumed (Norton, 1995). Yet, others such as Leonard Binder, contend that without a rigorous Islamic liberalism, political liberalism will not succeed in the Middle East, despite the emergence of bourgeois states (Binder, 1988). Unlike some who counterpose the Western intellectual tradition of rationalism to Islamic traditionalism, Binder attempts to find precedence for liberal thought in Islamic intellectual tradition itself. Having witnessed the ideological retreat of secular liberalism in the 1980s, he concludes that the only way liberalism can emerge as a viable ideological alternative is through the rediscovery or reinterpretation of the Islamic sacred past. While Binder's argument for the most part seems compelling, given the preeminent role of Islam in the process of political socialization and cultural life in general, he does not provide a satisfactory response to the assertion made by such scholars as Barrington Moore, who holds that the social conditions that produced Western democracy are not present in the Third World (Moore, 1966).

The fact that some of the alternatives proposed by Muslim liberals seem to be out of touch with the pervading political realities of the Muslim world and, consequently unrealistic, poses an additional problem. For example, the Egyptian liberal Muslim theorist Abd al- Raziq's contention that 'Islam has nothing to do with state' (Binder, 1988, p. 147), a clear attempt to depoliticize Islam, stands little chance of winning wide support among the masses entering the political arena with their traditional Islamic values. Islam not only competes with secular creeds to win the hearts and minds of the people, it also struggles for survival as a vital and relevant cultural medium in the wake of the global hegemony of Western culture. It may well be that liberalization of politics in the Muslim world will not flourish without separating religion from politics and desacralizing the political arena. But for that to happen, fundamental changes in the political landscape must take place to accommodate a vibrant civil society, tolerance, and pluralism. Closely related to the prospect for an Islamic liberalism in the region is the issue of human rights.

Islam and Human Rights

Many educated people throughout the Muslim world are concerned that while the Islamists, as persecuted opposition groups, may appear as advocates of democratic values and human rights, when they seize power they may impose their own variant of totalitarianism under the pretext of protecting Islamic sanctity and truth. There is also concern and trepidation that if an Islamic state is expected to be the guardian of divine truth and sacred principles, then the free competition of ideas which lies at the heart of pluralism becomes impossible. While the spirit of Islamic tenets can be interpreted to conform with many elements of democracy and human rights, there are serious tensions between Islam as a political project and democracy and human rights. Since the present phase of Islamic revivalism is, for the most part, dominated by Muslim traditionalists rather than modernists, anxieties about the protection of human rights by Islamic governments run high particularly among intellectuals and artistic communities.

The skeptics who see Islam and democracy as incompatible emphasize that shari'a is the word of God. It is not a legislated law, but a revealed one. As such, there are serious limitations on its reinterpretation, elasticity, and malleability. In the eyes of orthodox Muslims, shari'a has all the necessary requirements to guide them in this life and prepare them spiritually for the hereafter. Therefore, it has achieved perfection and any fundamental change or reinterpretation will compromise its sanctity and authenticity. It is also argued that human rights are given only by God; they are not inherent to humans. In so far as rights are acknowledged, they are defined as the obligations of the faithful, defined by the dictum, 'rejoicing the good and forbidding the evil.' In this rigid perception of Islam, human logic, rationality, and reason, which are perceived as fallible and ultimately inferior to divine wisdom, take a back seat to the unassailable sanctity of the holy law.

Not surprisingly the Islamic notion of human rights is very different from its Western counterpart. First, rights are defined as religious duties and obligations rather than inalienable rights of the individuals in the Western sense. For example, freedom of expression is tolerated, but only in so far as it does not negate the shari'a or question sacred Islamic principles. Second, the right of the community takes precedence over the right of the individual. Third, Islamists define rights more broadly to encompass social and economic rights.

While medieval Islamic law, like medieval Christian law, had some elements incompatible with human rights, the more modern interpretations of it are not necessarily so. The traditional Islamic penal code as interpreted and executed in Saudi Arabia and Sudan, for example, is clearly incompatible with the universal declaration of human rights. To be sure, many conservative apologists and some Muslim authoritarian regimes have evoked the sanctity of the shari'a to suppress human rights. They may also violate or disregard the principle of Islamic law itself when political expediency or *raison d'etat* (reason of state) requires (Sisk,1992, pp. 26-29).

Certain Muslim scholars, such as Ali abd al-Raziq, Farag Fawdah, and Muhammad Sa'id al-Ashmawi, consider the separation of religion and politics as a necessary prerequisite for democratization and the protection of human rights in Islamic societies. Can an Islamic order tolerate freedom of speech, association, and the contestation of political power by non-Muslims, communists, and liberals who may be regarded as 'apostates,' 'renegades,' 'atheists' and the 'enemies of Islam'? If not can we speak of the compatibility of Islam, human rights and democracy? (Kramer,1995, pp. 117-118). Human rights refer to universal inalienable rights of the people to be free from the coercion of a lawless state. The harsh punishment of political dissidents in Saudi Arabia, the persecution of Bahais in Iran and Christians in Sudan provide a few examples of human rights violations in the Muslim world. In many parts of the Muslim world, the authoritarian state, be it secular or Islamic, regards the people as subjects, whose life, liberty, and property can be trampled on if 'the reason of state' requires it.

Violation of the rights of women and gender inequality also remain rampant in the Muslim world. Patriarchy and a patrimonial political system have proven to be resilient. The rate of political participation of women in the Arab world is among the lowest in the Third World, and female occupations are limited to such traditionally defined roles as nursing and teaching. Women's representation in positions of power also remains meager. In certain countries women are even denied such elementary rights as freedom to travel. In Saudi Arabia, for example, women are barred from traveling alone. Therefore, an essential element of democratization of the political system and expansion of human rights is gender equality and the empowerment of women.

Other scholars while noting the profound tensions between Islam and human rights, seem more optimistic about the possibility of a reconciliation. In her study of Islam and human rights, Ann Mayer (1991) demonstrates how Islamic acceptance of civil and human rights is always circumscribed and confined by the shari'a. Through a textual analysis of the constitutions of the Islamic Republic of Iran, Pakistan, and Sudan (under Numeiri) and an analysis of the writings of Mawdudi and Tabandeh, she discerns a pattern in all three countries:

> they borrow substantive rights from international human rights documents while reducing the protections that they actually afford. This is accomplished by restricting them so that the rights can only be enjoyed within the limits of shari'a, which are unspecified. These emendations leave virtually unlimited discretion to states in deciding what the scope of the affected rights should be. (Mayer, 1991, p. 76)

Mayer is aware of the political, historical and cultural contexts of the Islamic response to human rights, especially in the modern era. By raising such pertinent issues as the impact of colonialism and the concomitant rise of cultural nationalism, she puts the Muslims' reaction and their defensive embrace of shari'a in its proper historical and political context. By doing so, she separates herself from both conservative Muslim apologists, whose retrograde ideas perpetuate autocratic rulers and the patrimonial political culture that nurtures them, and their conservative Western counterparts, who intellectually attack and denigrate anything Islamic. This attribute renders Mayer's analysis more balanced. She concludes that,

> The patterns of diluted rights in Islamic human rights schemes should not be ascribed to peculiar features of Islam or Islamic culture but

should be seen as a part of a broader phenomenon of attempts by beneficiaries of undemocratic and hierarchical systems to legitimize their opposition to human rights by appeals to supposedly distinctive cultural tradition. (Mayer,1991, p. 213)

Mayer sees the solution in a 'synthesis of Islamic and international human rights norms' (Mayer, 1991, p. 207), a synthesis that could be realized if the Muslim world overcomes its present defensive posture. This could happen if the present global power arrangements change in favor of the Muslim world or if the present adversarial relation between some Western nations and parts of the Muslim world are replaced by more accommodating policies.

Conclusion

There is no yes or no, categorical answer to the question of the compatibility of Islam and democracy. To present a balanced response, one must ask which Islam? Who interprets it? And in what historical and social context? The lay and intellectual interpretations of Islam differ profoundly, as do the modernist and traditionalist accounts. The traditionalists have argued that Muslim societies have fallen behind in the race for progress and development because they have deviated from the fundamental teachings of the Prophet and the sanctioned traditions of Islam. Muslims can regain their past glory only if they embrace their tradition and emulate the paradigmatic example of pristine Islam. Imitation of the West can only contaminate the spirit of true Islam and bring moral decay and decline. The modernists, on the other hand, assert that Muslims have fallen behind because they have stagnated, embracing obsolete ideas of the past and refusing to accommodate the realities of the modern world, including rationalism and scientific thought. Only a modernized Islam and a reasoned faith can remain relevant in this rapidly changing world. Such divergent outlooks on how Islam must confront the intellectual and political challenges of the West partially explain the disparate responses of the two schools in regard to democracy and human rights. This also illuminates why the traditionalists, for the most part, harbor a rejectionist attitude toward democracy, while the modernists are, by contrast, more accommodating.

Western democracy evolved out of the Renaissance, the Reformation, rationalism, the industrial revolution and the development of commercial capitalism. These developments decimated the decrepit feudal social structure and the monarchial system associated with it, thus ushering in the democratic revolutions of the eighteen century that swept Western Europe and the United States. Democratic revolutions gave birth to parliamentary republics, put an end to the divine rule of kings, separated state and church and inaugurated open participation of the masses in the political process. It took the Western world two centuries of struggle, trial and error, progress and retrenchment to resolve the conflict between the forces of tradition and modernity, religion and secularism, and competing economic and social interests.

By contrast, the Muslim world has neither had a Renaissance and Reformation nor an industrial or democratic revolution. In many parts of the region feudal structures and norms still persist, as do monarchies, notably among the Persian Gulf Arab states and in Jordan. If posing the question of compatibility of Islam and democracy is intended to ask whether the Western prerequisites of democracy can be replicated in the Muslim world, the answer is emphatically no. 'Islamic democracy' is going to have its own unique attributes and characteristics. Muslim societies have to go through their own process of resolving the contradictions and tensions that emerge on the path to political and economic development, carrying their particular history and cultural baggage. In the process, they will have to define their own variant of 'democracy'.

While democracy is culture bound, human rights are universal. All human life is inviolable and the right to live free from the coercion and abuse of a lawless state is longed for around the globe. Abuse of human rights in the Muslim world may not have as much to do with Islam as it does with social and economic forces that foster authoritarianism. The general conditions of poverty, the high rate of illiteracy, the presence of intrusive militaries, the pervasiveness of military governments, the lack of any longstanding democratic traditions and the weaknesses of civil society are perhaps more significant than Islamic culture in determining the fate of human rights.

As the source of cultural identity, authenticity, and consciousness for a majority of Muslims, Islam plays a preeminent role in social life. Therefore, the following questions raised by Kramer deserve serious thought and debate: Does political democracy presuppose not just economic, but also intellectual, liberalism? Can Islam allow for liberal thought without losing its true essence? (Kramer, 1995, p. 113). Furthermore, can Muslims regard Islam as another ideology, competing in the market place of ideas? Can they concede to intellectual pluralism as liberals do? In the final analysis, given the diversity, contradictions, and nuances inherent in Islam, these fateful questions cannot be answered philosophically, but only practically, in the realm of political life and through the mass action of millions of Muslims inspired by the new dreams through the mass action of millions of Muslims inspired by the new dreams and ideals of their age.

References

Abbott, Freeland (1971), 'View of Democracy and the West' in Malik, Hafeez (ed.), *Iqbal: Poet Philosopher of Pakistan*, Columbia University Press: New York.

Anderson, Roy, Robert Seibert, and Jon Wagnor (1990), *Politics and Change in the Middle East: Sources of Conflict and Accomodation*, Prentice Hall: Englewood Cliff, NJ.

Arjomand, Said Amir 'The Ulama's Traditionalist Opposition to Parliamentarism, 1907-1909', *Middle Eastern Studies*, Vol. 17, pp. 171-86.

Aristotle (1972), *The Politics*, Book 6, Harvard University Press: Cambridge.

Bazargan, Mehdi (1982), *Bazyabi-i Arzeshha (Re-evaluation of Values)*, Vol.3, Liberation Movement of Iran: Tehran.

Binder, Leonard (1988), *Islamic Liberalism: A critique of Development Ideologies*, University of Chicago Press: Chicago.

Chehabi, H.E. (1990), *Iranian Politics and Religious Modernism: The Liberation Movement of Iran Uder the Shah and Khomeini*, Cornell University Press: Ithaca, NY.

Dahl, Robert (1971), *Polyarchy: Participation and Opposition*, Yale University Press: New Haven, CT.

Enayat, Hamid (1982), *Modern Islamic political Thought*, University of Texas Press: Austin, TX.

Dorraj Manochehr (1990), *From Zarathustra to Khomeini: Populism and Dissent in Iran*, Lynne Rienner Publisher: Boulder, CO.

_____ (1992), 'The Politics of Islamic Revival and Counterculture Mobilization in the Middle East: A Comparative Analysis', in Lehman, Cheryl R., and Moore, Russell M., (eds.), *Multinational Culture: Social Impacts of a Global Economy*, Greenwood Press: Westport, CT, pp. 91-105.

_____ (1995), 'The Intellectual Dilemmas of a Muslim Modernist: Politics and Poetics of Iqbal', *The Muslim World*, Vol. 85, No. 3-4, pp. 266-79.

Esposito, John L. (1983), 'Muhammad Iqbal and the Islamic State' in Esposito, John (ed.), *Voices of Resurgent Islam*, Oxford University Press: Oxford.

_____ (1984), *Islam and Politics*, Syracuse University Press: Syracuse.

Esposito, John L. and Piscatori, James P. (1991), 'Democratization and Islam', *Middle East Journal*, Vol. 45, No. 3, pp. 427-40.

Esposito, John L. and Voll, John O. (1996), *Islam and Democracy*, Oxford University Press: Oxford.

Ghadbian, Najib (1997), *Democratization and the Islamist Challenge in the Arab World*, Westview Press: Boulder, CO.

Goldschmidt Jr, Arthur (1991), *A Concise History of Middle East*, Westview Press: Boulder, CO.

Hassan, Riffat (1971) 'The Development of Political philosophy', in Malik, Hafeez, (ed.), *Iqbal: Poet Philosopher of Pakistan*, Columbia University Press: New York, pp. 136-58.

Huntington, Samuel (1991), *The Third Wave: Democratization in Late Twentieth Century*, University of Oklahoma Press: Norman.

Iqbal, Muhammad (1973), 'The Reconstruction of Religious Thought in Islam' in *Kulyah E. Iqbal (The Collected Work of Iqbal)*, Javid Iqbal: Lahor, pp. 95-117.

Keddie, Nikki R. (1960), *An Islamic Response to Imperialism*, University of California Press: Berkeley.

Khomeini, Ruhollah (1978), *Velayat-i Faqih, (The Rule of the Jurisconsult)*, Amirkabir Publisher: Tehran.

Kramer, Gudrun (1995), 'Islam and Pluralism' in Brynen, Rex, Korany Bahgat, and Noble, Paul (eds.), *Political Liberalization and Democratization in the Arab World*, Vol. 1, Lynne Rienner Publisher: Boulder, CO, pp. 113-128.

Lewis, Bernard (1988), *Language of Islam*, University of Chicago Press: Chicago.

Marlow, Louise (1997), *Hierarchy and Egalitarianism in Islamic Thought*, Cambridge University Press: Crambridge.

Mayer, Ann E (1991), *Islam and Human Rights: Tradition and Politics*, Westview Press: Boulder, CO.

Moore, Jr., Barrington (1966), *The Social Origins of Democracy and Dictatorship*, Beacon Press: Boston.

Mortimer, Edward (1982), *Faith and Power: The Politics of Islam*, Vintage Books: New York.

Nizam Al-Mulk, Khajeh (1960), *The Book of Government or Rules for Kings,* Routledge, Kegan Paul: London.

Norton, Augustus R. (1995), *Civil Society in the Middle East*, Vol. 1, E. J. Brill: Leiden.

Rosenthal, Franz (1960), *The Muslim Concept of Freedom*, E. J. Brill: Leiden.

Shariati, Ali (1972), *Qasetin, Mareqin, Nakesin (Oppressors, Deceivers, Betrayers)*, League of Muslim Students in Europe: London.

_____ (1973), *Iqbal: Ma'mar-e Tajdid Bana-ye Tafakor-e Islami (Iqbal: The Architect of the Renewal of Islamic Thought)*, Forugh Publication: Tehran.

_____ (1973), *Ummat Va Immamat (Community and Leadership)*, Association of Muslim Students in the United States and Canada: Houston, TX.

Sisk, Timothy (1992), *Islam and Democracy: Religion, Politics and Power in the Middle East*, United States Institute of Peace Press: Washington, D.C.

Soroosh, Abdolkarim (1994), *Farbeh Tar Az Ideology (More Potent than ideology)*, Sarat Cultural Institute: Tehran.

Tamadonfar, Mehran (1989), *The Islamic Polity and Political Leadership: Fundamentalism, Sectarianism, and Pragmatism*, Westview Press: Boulder, CO.

Tibi, Bassam (1990), *Islam and Cultural Accommodation of Social Change*, Westview Press: Boulder, CO.

Watt, Montgomery W. (1962), *Muhammad at Madina*, Oxford University Press: Oxford.

3 Iraq: Human Rights in the Republic of Fear

JUDITH S. YAPHE[1]

In his disturbing study of Iraq under Ba`thist rule, Kanan Makiyah (1993, p.116) describes what happened to Omar, a young Sunni Arab from Baghdad who was falsely accused of treason by a Kurd and interrogated by a Shiah in an Iraqi prison in the 1980s. Omar's prison, wrote Makiyah, is 'a microcosm of that much bigger prison called Ba`thi Iraq.' Omar had seemingly impeccable credentials. His father was a Sunni Arab nationalist who had served in Iraq's navy and participated in the ill-fated nationalist coup attempt of 1941. Omar himself had served nearly 6 years in the Iraqi army during the war with Iran. Nevertheless, he was arrested and accused of being anti-party and anti-revolution and of calling Saddam names. Omar described his interrogator as a man with immense power who could refer to Saddam as 'Saddam.' 'Never,' said Omar, 'have I been so frightened in my life as I was at that point.' Omar then informed on his informer, who was also said to be 'anti-party' and 'anti-revolution.' The informer and his cousins were executed, their broken bodies sent home in sealed coffins to be buried in secret. After 42 days, Omar was released. There was no hearing, no trial, no judicial proceeding. There was only terror, intimidation, degradation, self-incrimination, and release.

Human Rights in Iraqi History and Tradition

Iraq's People

Iraq has one of the richest mixes of ethnic, tribal, religious, and linguistic populations in the Middle East. The population of approximately 20 million includes Arabs (approximately 65 percent), Kurds (approximately 20 percent), and a smattering of Turkmen, Yazidis, Armenians, Assyrians, and Sabaens. The religious mix is primarily Sunni (approximately 35 percent, mostly Arab, Kurd, and Turkmen), Shiah (55 percent, Arab and a small number of fayli Kurds), and Christian (Chaldean, Armenian, Assyrian, and Jacobite as well as Greek Orthodox, Greek Catholics, and Latin Catholics).

Most of Iraq's Jews had migrated to Israel by the early 1950s and following the hangings in Liberation Square in 1970 of a number of Jews accused of being Zionist spies.

Iraq's rich population mix has been a source of its strength as well as a source of much of its internal conflict. In 1936 the Iraqi Army, led by a Kurdish general, conducted an 'ethnic cleansing' style killing of Assyrian villagers. Revolts by the Kurds in northern Iraq have been endemic since 1919, before the state was established. Periodic overtures to Kurdish leaders to include them in the government in exchange for their loyalty -- Patriotic Union of Kurdistan leader Jalal Talabani twice served as Minister to the North for Reconstruction and Justice in the 1970s under Saddam -- have always failed.

Governance

Political power in Iraq is concentrated in the hands of Saddam Husayn and, to a lesser extent, the Ba`th Party. Saddam is President of the Republic, Prime Minister, Chairman of the Revolutionary Command Council (RCC), and Secretary General of the Regional Command of the Ba`th Party. 'Elected' in October 1995 in a so-called referendum in which he received 99.96 percent of the people's vote, Saddam's is the only voice and vote in Iraq. Saddam appoints the RCC, which exercises executive and legislative authority and heads the government in theory. The size of the RCC varies according to Saddam's whim. Similarly, Iraq has an 'elected' parliament, whose candidates are selected by the Party, and a judiciary that is neither independent nor impartial to presidential directive. There are no secret ballots in the western sense, no independent political parties, and no independent candidates for office. Human rights have long been subsumed under the banner of Arab unity, Iraqi nationalism, and whatever Saddam defined as measures of loyalty to the state and, above all, himself.

Saddam exercises control through multiple and redundant security services headed by his sons and other family and clan members as well as through his hold on the moribund Party apparatus and the military. Militias and security units attached to the President, the Party, the Interior Ministry, and the military watch Iraqis as well as each other for signs of unrest or disloyalty. They are responsible for maintaining the atmosphere of oppression, terror, and systematic intimidation that has been the hallmark of Saddam's regime. These security forces have all committed widespread, serious, and systemic human rights abuses in the nearly 30 years the regime has been in power. This atmosphere of hysteria, fear, and unequal treatment has been exacerbated first by the anti-Iranian paranoia that marked the years of war (1980-1988) and the imposition of economic sanctions following Iraq's occupation of Kuwait in August 1990.

Human rights under the Old Regime, 1920 to 1958

Iraq is an artificial construct, as are many countries in the modern Middle East. It was shaped by the British and French under terms of the 1916 Sykes-Picot and 1920 Versailles Treaties in which France and Britain determined the fate of the Arab East. The treaties united the formerly Turkish-controlled provinces of Mosul, Baghdad, and Basra into the largest and potentially richest of the countries of the Fertile Crescent.

Defined by the British

The British held the mandate for Iraq from 1920 through its declaration of independence in 1932. As state-builders, they created an impressive array of state institutions—a monarchy, a parliament, a Western-style constitution, a civilian bureaucracy, and an army. Historian Phebe Marr (1985, p.29) describes British policy as 'vacillating and indecisive.' She notes that they designed a constitutional structure that was 'less a system of government than a means of control . . . an imposing institutional facade [that] put down few deep roots.'[2] Following the establishment of the mandate and the suppression of a widespread revolt which drew on Sunni and Shiah support, the British in 1920 created a temporary government headed by the aged and venerable Naqib of Baghdad, the head of the Sunni community in Iraq. London also created a cabinet that included representatives of Iraq's disparate religious and ethnic communities, including religious leaders, landowners, tribal shaykhs, Christians, and Jews.

This government was replaced in 1921 when Faysal, son of the Hashimite Amir of Mecca Husayn ibn Ali, was imported to be king. Although an outsider, Faysal was a highly respected leader of the Great Arab Revolt and a descendent of the family of the Prophet. As such, he had impeccable credentials as an Arab nationalist and a Muslim. He soon acquired a reputation for realism and fairness and a vision of Iraq as a state that had to appeal to a wide variety of peoples and groups. Faysal was 'elected' king in a staged plebiscite which indicated he had the support of 96 percent of the population (shades of Saddam's 1995 plebiscite!). A resolution passed by the Iraqi Council of State declared the government of Iraq to be constitutional, representative, democratic, and limited by law. Faysal's rule marked the official introduction of Arab nationalism as political, social, and educational doctrine in Iraq's schools and government institutions. Kurds in the north and Shiah religious leaders who wanted a theocratic government rejected the new government.

Under the constitution passed in 1924, Iraq had an electoral law providing for a two-step indirect election of parliamentary representatives. It also had a monarchy intended to function partly as a symbol of unity but primarily as a means for the British to continue to exercise indirect control over the government. The parliament soon became a stronghold of elements rejected by the British because of their presumed unreliability; these elements included leaders of the tribes of the middle Euphrates, younger members of the Turkish-trained elite, and the growing numbers of Sunnis and Shiah who opposed the British. The British relied mainly, instead, on cabinets dominated by political conservatives or young Iraqis willing to work with the British. Token representatives from the Shiah, Kurdish, Christian, and Jewish communities were carefully included. Despite British mistrust of the parliament, it became representative of the various political, ethnic, tribal, and social groups the British meant to protect in the new Iraqi state.

The other British contribution to modern Iraq was the creation of a modern military institution. The new Iraqi army, intended to be a main pillar of the state, began recruitment in 1921. The lower ranks came from tribal elements, usually Shiah, while the officer corps was drawn from the ranks of former Ottoman officers—all Sunni, many Kurdish in origin. The pattern of Sunni dominance of an officer corps subscribing to Arab nationalist sentiments became the mold for the military that has survived the monarchy and the various republics.

Shaped by the Monarchy

A series of crises in Iraq in the late 1920s—over acceptance of a new treaty with the British and London's decisions to recognize Iraq's independence and support its admission into the League of Nations—enabled King Faysal to introduce more Arab Iraqis into government. These Arab Iraqis, such as Nuri al-Sa`id, subscribed to a different version of civil rights than the generation of the 1920s. A companion of Faysal's during the days of the Great Arab Revolt, Nuri would become a fixture in Iraqi politics until his murder in the 1958 revolution. To deal with the opposition to the British treaty, Nuri used tactics to silence political opponents for which he would become famous—the opposition was silenced, the press muzzled, and parliament prorogued. The first of many rebellions by groups unhappy with the Arab nationalists began—Christians, especially the Assyrians, feared the absence of British protection and the Kurds demanded safeguards from the League of Nations.

The withdrawal of the British and the transition to a throne and government dominated by pro-British army officers and lawyers did not signal protections for Iraq's many groups. Arab nationalists interested primarily in building up Iraq's state institutions and expanding Iraq's influence in the Arab world battled increasingly with social reformers influenced by a variety of left-wing ideologies, including Marxism. Lacking broad-based political institutions through which to express their views, political discourse took place in anti-regime demonstrations, violence, and regime repression. Iraq's first military repression occurred in 1933 with the slaughter of the unpopular Assyrian minority;[3] its first military coup came in 1936 when Arab nationalists in the military were able to defeat moves by Iraqi nationalists intent on internal reform.

Faysal's death in 1933 probably removed the only individual capable of acting as a moderating force among Iraq's diverse ethnic and religious groups. Alone among Iraq's monarchs and republican leaders, Faysal was willing to work with opposition elements to establish government based on the wider spectrum of Iraq's diverse population without resort to violence. There followed a period marked by unstable rule, weak kings and strong regents, and tribal revolts against the authority of central government. The root cause of tribal unrest was the transition from a society based on tribal organization and values to one based on settled agriculture. Part of this transition was the erosion of the power and authority of the tribal shaykh. The shaykh's main function had been to protect the tribe from its neighbors and a predatory central government. Over the years of first British then monarchical rule, this function had been transformed and the shaykh became the agent of the government while the government assumed a much greater role in the internal policing of society. As a result, there were even fewer and weaker voices speaking about civil society and human rights, concepts that were seen as alien to Arab and Islamic society which valued the collective—the community (the 'ummah) and the tribe—over the individual. Iraq's Shiahs remained excluded from the political process. They lacked representation at the local or state level and were denied a fair share of national resources. Shiah tribal and religious leaders opposed central government which they saw as Sunni, secular, foreign-dominated, unlawful, and corrupt. Nor were they won over by the opposition Arab nationalists who saw in their political philosophy a way to overcome Shiah particularism.

The tribal rebellions of the 1930s, like those of the 1970s and 1990s, were put down by the military. Repression was followed by air force bombing of villages, summary executions, and martial law. And thus began another Iraqi 'tradition'—the use of the army as a tool by civilian politicians to intervene and contain civil society. Government became more authoritarian in a system permitting only one political ideology, Arab nationalism, to hold sway. With the exception of the short-lived Baqr Sidqi government of 1936-1937, few Kurds, Shiahs, Christians, Jews or political dissidents played any role in government until the World War II era. Then, many Sunnis with Arab nationalist aspirations were implicated in the 1941 Rashid Ali coup.

After World War II new political parties emerged, permitted and even encouraged by the establishment and representing the new social classes in the cities. The parties represented the educated middle class and an increasingly urbanized working class. Strikes and demonstrations became commonplace, as did the regime's use of violence and the manipulation of elections to restore order and maintain control.

On the eve of the 1958 revolution, political instability reigned in Iraq. The government was dominated by a regent—'Abd al-Illah, who refused to accede power to the young King Faysal II—and a prime minister, Nuri al-Sa'id, who was recycling through his thirteenth cabinet since the late 1930s. Events in 1954 provide an example of the heightened state of repression under the Old Regime. Elections in June 1954, conducted while Nuri was out of the country, were the fairest and freest in Iraq's history. The country's most representative parliament was elected with all licensed parties campaigning and a wide range of delegates from the right and left elected, including a number of leftists and a Communist sympathizer. The stage could have been set for a return of power to the King and the revival of legal political opposition. It never happened. Instead, Nuri threatened to resign rather than work with a parliament that included leftists. The new government, barely three weeks old, fell and new elections were called. As dissatisfaction with the regime grew, Nuri began a systematic suppression of all political activity that surpassed anything yet seen in Iraq. In a series of decrees designed to eliminate the leftists, the Council of Ministers could now strip persons of their citizenship and deport those convicted of belonging to Communist front organizations, anarchists, or working for a foreign government. Professional societies were banned from conducting activities that might disturb public order. Membership in communist or anarchist organizations was already a criminal offense. The new parliament elected that August contained no genuine opposition, and few of the 425 seats in parliament were contested.

For the next four years, there was no significant open political activity in the country. Iraq reverted to a state ruled by Nuri, the police, and the army. The government signed the Baghdad Pact, putting Iraq at odds with the rest of the Arab world, broke relations with the Soviet Union, and rode out the Suez crisis. It also drove the opposition underground, producing the conditions which led ultimately to the 1958 revolution. Other changes were occurring in Iraq by the mid 1950s. Impressive development programs financed by Iraq's oil wealth began to produce results in a new, urbanized, educated middle class that helped erode ethnic and sectarian differences. A small but growing number of Arab Shiah and Kurds moved into the middle class, served in the army, entered the bureaucracy, and joined the clandestine political movements. Kurdish revolts in the north ceased during the Nuri years of 'enforced stability.' And, most significantly, Iraqis were coming into closer contact again with western thought and values. In retrospect, conditions in Iraq, especially regarding political life, civil and human rights, were far better in the 1950s than they were to become when the Ba'thists came to power in 1968.

Reinvented by the Republic

All the revolutions that have occurred since 1958 have shared certain basic characteristics: they were staged by military officers, sometimes in conjunction with civilian plotters; they advocated republican forms of government; and they professed support for democratic institutions and equality in law for all segments of society. And, without exception, all were—and are—authoritarian, dependent on the military and security services for their power. Like the regimes which preceded the revolutions beginning in 1958, respect for the individual civil and human rights were subsumed under security of the state and what was interpreted as the traditional Islamic and ethnic emphasis on the group, the family, the tribe, and the community or 'ummah. Examples from the major political factions seizing power from 1958 through the second—and successful—Ba'thist coup of 30 July 1968 include:

- The leaders of the 1958 coup—'Abd al-Karim Qasim and 'Abd al-Salam 'Arif—called for national freedom, struggle against imperialism, an end to foreign bases and pacts, an end to monarchy and feudalism, democracy, a constitution, social justice, peace, Arab unity, and the return of Palestine to its people. Buried in the middle of their program was a call for complete recognition of the national rights of the Kurds and other minorities 'within the framework of national unity.' Their regime, which lasted until 1963, included a three-man council with representatives from the Kurdish, Shiah, and Arab Sunni communities, a cabinet with a Ba'thist and a Marxist as members, and a constitution. The form of government was a republic in name, with

Iraq declared to be part of the Arab nation and Islam the religion of the state. There was no parliament, and when political parties finally were allowed, army officers, government officials and students were banned from joining them. Real power was wielded by Qasim and the army. Advances were made, however, in personal status law, traditionally governed by Islamic law. Qasim gave more rights to women; he limited polygamy, raised the minimum age for marriage to 18, and, in effect, gave women equal status rights with men in matters of inheritance. Opposed by religious and conservative leaders, the revised code did not survive the Qasim regime. Under Qasim the cult of personality around 'The Sole Leader' flourished, and the courts were used to stage trials to eliminate Qasim's rivals and cow any opposition.

- The Arab nationalists ruled from 1963 through July 1968: first, the Ba`thists briefly in 1963 led by `Ali Salih al-Sa`idi as the real power and Generals `Abd al-Salam `Arif as president and Ahmad Hasan al-Bakr as prime ministers, then a coup and rule by `Arif and his brother `Abd al-Rahman, followed by two other short-lived governments. This first Ba`thist government lasted less than a year but made its mark in eliminating its rivals, especially the Communists. The Ba`thists professed goals were unity, Arabism, and socialism. The reality was elimination of the clause in personal status giving women equality and reintroduction of conservative social policies. The rulers were, without exception, Arab Sunnis from Baghdad and the middle Euphrates; they were conservative Muslims interested in Arab 'unity', an absorption which tended to moderate their revolutionary zeal.

The Kurds under the New Republic

Iraq's Kurds supported the Qasim regime because of the constitutional guaranty that Kurds and Arabs would be partners in the new state. Mullah Mustafa Barzani, the most prominent of the Kurdish leaders to return from exile, wanted to restore the cultural and administrative rights of the Kurdish nation. As would later Iraqis leaders, Qasim saw Barzani's efforts, if successful, as tantamount to the establishment of a separate Kurdish state. Barzani suspected Qasim of paying lip service only to Kurdish demands for autonomy. War began in 1961, wrecking any fiction of Iraqi unity. The Kurds cut a deal with the second `Arif government in 1964 which called for a cease-fire, recognition of Kurdish national rights in the constitution, a general amnesty, and reinstatement of Kurds in the civil service and the military; no mention of autonomy was made. Barzani's acceptance of this agreement led to a split in the ranks of the Kurdish Democratic Party

(KDP) with those advocating a hard line, such as Jalal Talabani, leaving the movement. Barzani emerged as the strongest force in a Kurdish movement divided between intellectuals and tribal loyalists, thereby creating a dissident force that could be used by Baghdad to disrupt Barzani's plans. It also allowed for Iranian meddling in Iraqi Kurdish politics. In October 1964 Barzani issued a set of demands to Baghdad demanding recognition of Kurdish rights on the basis of autonomy and the transformation of his peshmerga force into a regular frontier force. In January 1965 the government rejected all of Barzani's demands, and three months later fighting broke out. A June 1966 accord recognized Kurdish nationality, decentralized administration in the Kurdish areas, recognized the Kurdish language as the official language of the north, guaranteed Kurdish representation in parliament, and reintegrated Kurds into the army and civil service. This settlement was never implemented; it was unpopular with the Arab nationalists and led to further instability in government, especially among Arab military officers.

Human Rights in Ba`thist Iraq

The primary mission of the Ba`thist leaders who participated in the 17 July 1968 coup was consolidation of power under total party control and the elimination of all rivals within the government and party to General Ahmad Hasan al-Bakr and, ultimately, his deputy in the party and government, Saddam Husayn. The first task took two weeks, the latter was completed in stages, culminating in a 1979 internal coup which removed Bakr and placed Saddam firmly and publicly in total control of the party and the state. Saddam ended the years of instability that had plagued Iraq politically, albeit at a terrible cost. Rigidly enforced loyalty to the party, the state, and, most of all, to Saddam himself replaced the traditional ties of clan, tribe, and community that had marked Iraq's Arab and Islamic history since independence.

Some features of Ba`thist politics and Saddam's leadership style were intended to foster creation of the new Iraqi man and woman. The Party in its early days welcomed Arab and Kurd, Sunni and Shiah into its folds. The apparent opportunities to achieve position, status and a secure future on a more equal basis—perhaps even merit, education, and skills—attracted urbanized members of Iraq's minority communities in the early days of the revolution.[4] The constitution defines Iraq as a people's democratic republic aimed at achieving a united Arab state under a socialist system. Article 5 of the Constitution states that 'the Iraqi people consists of two principal ethnic groups, Arabs and Kurds, and recognizes the ethnic rights of the Kurdish people as well as the legitimate rights of all minorities, within the framework of national unity.' Article 19 further states that 'citizens are equal before the law, without distinction on grounds of sex, race, language, social origin or religion.'[5] One provision, aimed at the Kurds, declared that no part of Iraq could be given up. Islam was declared the religion of the state, but freedom of religion and religious practices were guaranteed. In theory, power was given to the Revolutionary Command Council, which had the authority to promulgate laws, determine defense security, declare war, conclude peace, and approve the budget. The president was executive of the RCC, commander-in-chief of the armed forces, and chief executive of the state government. He was given the power to appoint, promote, and dismiss civil, military, and judicial personnel, and prepare and approve the budget. The RCC was to be an arm of the party, its membership controlled by the Regional Command of the Iraqi Bath Party. Reality soon came to mean that decisionmaking was controlled by a small cadre of loyalists, carefully honed over the years, and totally loyal to Saddam.

The Party's appeal was always limited. Shiah were turned away by its emphasis on Arab nationalism, which they interpreted as Sunni Arab nationalist sentiments to join with or compete with Syria, also under Ba`thist rule. Iraq's Kurds to a great extent remained more committed to Kurdish factional interests than integration into a new Ba`thist Iraq. And the government wasted no time in revealing the kind of repressive measures it would use to maintain control and enforce loyalty to the state. Consolidation meant show trials, with accusations including spying for Israel, the United States, and Iran as well as conspiring to overthrow the government; harassment and murder of suspected pro-Western elements; and public hangings of Arabs, Shiahs, and Jews. Iraq under Saddam began its long-standing 'custom' of being an equal opportunity killing field. Arab nationalists, Christians, and Kurds were as likely to be attacked for not being sufficiently loyal to the state and its leader than purely for their religious, tribal, or ethnic backgrounds. Disloyalty to Saddam rather than ethnicity or religion per se became the chief criterion for social safety. Government under Saddam persecuted the Kurds in the horrific retribution known as the anfal (see below), drove out of Iraq hundreds of thousands of Shiah of Iranian origin, many of whom had lived in the holy cities of Najaf and Karbala for generations, and publicly hanged Jews whose families had lived in Iraq since the days of the Babylonian exile. But, over the years, Saddam also persecuted Arab Sunnis from the 'center', from Tikrit and from important tribal confederations that had long supported him and the revolution.

Saddam's First Kurdish Solution: Contained Autonomy

When the Ba`thists came to power in 1968 they faced the still unresolved issue of Kurdish demands for autonomy. Mullah Mustafa Barzani was receiving military aid and political support from the Shah of Iran and had begun a long relationship with Israel. The government soon sided with Barzani's chief rival for leadership of the Kurds, Jalal Talabani, and in the winter of 1968 clashes between the Iraqi army and the Kurdish militias were increasing. The Iraqis used their air force to bomb Kurdish villages suspected of harboring Kurdish dissidents, and the Kurds in December attacked government-owned oil installations in the north. The military situation was at a stalemate. In March 1970 Saddam orchestrated a settlement with the Kurds. Its terms included:

- Recognition of Kurdish autonomy and guaranteed proportional representation for Kurds in a national legislative assembly;
- Appointment of a Kurdish vice-president to the national government (Taha Muhyi al-Din Ma'ruf remains as Kurdish vice president today) with Kurds or Kurdish speakers to be civil servants in administrative units inhabited by a Kurdish majority;
- Commitment to spend a proportion of Iraq's oil revenues in the autonomous region;
- Recognition of Kurdish and Arabic as the official languages in Kurdish Iraq;
- Promise to carry out a census to determine areas where Kurds formed the majority of the population.[6]

Barzani, in turn, agreed to turn in his heavy weapons and integrate his peshmerga (the term means those who face death) fighters into the Iraqi army. Implementation of the agreement was to be delayed four years. With its signing, the government withdrew support for the Kurdish opponents of Barzani and five Barzani loyalists were put on the Council of Ministers (Gunther, 1992, pp. 14-16).

The peace negotiated in 1970 was short-lived. The Iraqis recognized the governates of Irbil, Sulaymaniyah, and Dohuk as comprising the Autonomous Region; the Kurds claimed much more, including the oil-rich region of Kirkuk, which was not a predominantly Kurdish city. Amid accusations of bad faith, assassination attempts against Barzani and his sons, and government attempts to move Arabs into predominantly Kurdish areas to change the population's balance, fighting once again broke out.[7] In mid 1972, the Kurds began receiving aid from the Shah and the CIA, authorized by President Nixon.[8] In October 1973 the KDP demanded inclusion of the city of Kirkuk in their area of control. Baghdad refused, demanding instead that the Kurds accept the government's autonomy plan. The Kurds refused, Baghdad announced its plan would be implemented, the Kurdish ministers withdrew from the government, and war resumed in April 1974. The Shah and Saddam both decided on peace one year later for reasons that go beyond the scope of this chapter. It was to their mutual advantage to resolve their long-standing border dispute, end Iranian assistance to the Kurds and Iraqi interest in trying to subvert Iran through its dissident, Kurdish, and Arab populations, and institute strict border regulations. Baghdad insists that its 1970 agreement with the Kurds is still in effect, including the puppet parliament for the so-called autonomous region.

Containing Shiah Aspirations

Saddam's priorities of personal and national security created the most egregious of human rights violations in the 1980s. The decade began with deep mistrust of Iraq's Shiah clerics, suspicions of the intentions of the new Islamic Republic in Iran, and Saddam's assumption that the opportunity existed to take advantage of the clerical regime before Tehran could reassert territorial claims or export its Islamic revolution to Iraq and the Arab states of the Persian Gulf. The violations included mass deportations of thousands of innocent civilians suspect only because of their Iranian origins and mass murder by chemical attack of hundreds of Kurds suspected of harboring dissidents in their villages. It ended with the invasion and occupation of Kuwait, an event marked by brutality and destruction of the people as well as the fragile environment of the small Gulf state.

Saddam moved methodically to curb Shiah dissidence. Anti-regime and anti-Saddam protests had grown in the Shiah holy cities of Najaf and Karbala in the years following the 1968 revolution. In 1974 more than two dozen Shiah clerics were secretly tried and five of them executed. In 1977, riots broke out in Najaf and Karbala, sparked by Shiah opposition to the regime and government claims that a Syrian agent had been discovered carrying explosives into the shrine in Karbala (Marr, 1985, pp.236-37). The town was closed to pilgrimage traffic, and riots erupted again, to be quelled by military troops. The government banned demonstrations during the Shiah observance of `Ashura, when Shiah Muslims commemorate the martyrdom of Husayn, grandson of Muhammad, with passion plays and self-flagellation. The deportations of Iranians and Iraqis of Iranian origin at the end of the decade was not a new tactic for Baghdad. They had been done before Saddam but not on the scale—perhaps as many as 800,000 ordered to march to the border—nor speed.[9] It marked the culmination of a decade of persecution of Iraq's Shiah community that also saw the arrests and murders of Shiah clerics, members of their families and students.

Saddam's most prominent victims included Ayatollah Muhammad Baqr al-Sadr, an Iraqi Arab cleric and the founder of the opposition al-Hizb al-Da'wa al-Islamiyyah (the Islamic Call Party) in the 1960s, and his sister. Muhammad Baqr al-Sadr, described as having a 'charismatic aura', was the most prominent and intellectual of the radical Shiah clerics gaining in popularity after the 1958 revolution. He preached against the Sunnization of the government and called for a return to Islamic precepts in government and social justice. His movement appealed to religious Shiah who lived in Najaf and Karbala as well as those who lived in the poor suburbs of Baghdad. By the early 1970s its appeal had spread in particular to those in search of Islamic answers in place of rejected ideologies of Arab nationalism, Ba'thism, or communism. At some point it became dedicated to the overthrow of the Ba'thist regime and encouraged by Iranian radical Islamists (see Mahallot, 1988). It is not clear that a majority of Iraq's Shiah subscribed to Khomeini's precise vision of the vilayat-i faqih, but by the mid 1970s radical Iraqi Shiah scholars had begun to call for religious leadership to guide the nation. In 1979, riots broke out again in the holy cities.[10] The government denied Baqr al-Sadr permission to demonstrate, the army suppressed the riots, the clandestine Da'wa organization was uncovered, and Baqr al-Sadr was arrested and executed.

Over the next decade many Iraqi Shiah clerics, members of their families and students would also be executed or escape into exile in Iran to join the Da'wa Party and the Iranian-backed umbrella group the Supreme Assembly for the Islamic Revolution in Iraq (SAIRI). Other prominent clerics, such as the aged and venerated Grand Ayatollah Kho'i, the leading mujtahid of an apolitical, quietist Shiah community, would be kept under virtual house arrest and denied medical treatment or visitors. Kho'i's alleged support of the Shiah rebels in the February 1991 uprising—he did not encourage rebellion but did issue a decree (fatwa) calling for civil order to allow the dead to be buried—only confirmed to Saddam the ailing cleric's 'guilt.' Iraq's Shiah, for the most part, supported the Iraqi state in the long war with Iran and, according to many accounts of the Shiah rebellion in February 1991, were appalled by the activities of the Iranian-backed SAIRI militia (the Badr brigade) when it entered Iraq garlanded with headbands and banners bearing Khomeini's picture. Most Iraqi Shiah, like their Gulf counterparts, admired the ability of Iran's radical Islamists to replace the Shah's oppressive regime with rule by Islamic law under the clerics but did not appear to want a complete replication of the revolution and clerical rule in their own country.

Saddam's Second Kurdish Solution: Anfal

Throughout the 1970s and early 1980s, Baghdad continued its policy of Arabizing traditional Kurdish lands. Arabs were moved into Kirkuk and other cities and a Kurd-free buffer zone was created along Iraq's northeastern border with Iran. Some sources claim more than 3,000 villages were destroyed and 500,000 Kurds forcibly moved to the plains of southern Kurdistan or to desert regions in southern Iraq. Besides eliminating Kurdish territorial claims, the buffer zone was meant to cut the Iraqi Kurds off from their kinsmen and potential allies in Turkey, Iran, and Syria, and prevent their joining with Iran in fighting Iraq in the war (Gunther, 1992, p. 35). The policy attracted very little outside attention until Baghdad's defeat in the Gulf War, when Western humanitarian organizations documented abandoned Kurdish villages in the south and destroyed villages in the north.[11] During the war with Iran, Iraq's Kurdish Democratic Party, led by the Barzanis, supported Iran. The KDP saw further advantage following Iran's victory at Haj Omran in July 1983; it joined with other anti-Baghdad dissidents, including the Tehran-based Shiah Da`wa Party and Iraqi exiles based in Damascus, to fight Saddam. In retaliation, Baghdad rounded up nearly 8,000 Barzani Kurdish loyalists between the ages of 12 and 80 who were being held in camps near Irbil. Saddam accused them of loyalty to the KDP and assisting the Iranians at the Haj Omran offensive. They were taken to Baghdad and never heard from again. They were almost certainly murdered. Until 1984 Talabani's PUK backed Baghdad, as did Iran's Kurdish factions. Talabani believed advantage could be gained by dealing with a weakened Saddam. In fact, Baghdad paid little attention to the Kurdish region and allowed many Kurds who had been deported south to return to the north. Saddam offered amnesty to Kurds accused of anti-government activities, including Kurdish deserters from the army, and allowed elections (rigged of course) to be held for the Legislative Council of the Kurdish autonomous region.

The calm in Kurdistan was short-lived. Iraqi-PUK negotiations soon failed, and by 1986 Talabani was looking to oppose Baghdad. In 1988 the KDP and the PUK, along with several small Kurdish factions, joined together to form the Iraqi Kurdistan Front. Its goals were to overthrow Saddam Husayn's regime, establish democratic government in Iraq, and develop a federal status for Kurds in Iraq. Barzani and Talabani were co-presidents. The combined strength of the Kurdish forces has been estimated at about 60,000 peshmerga plus an unknown number of anti-Turkish Kurdish dissidents, all armed with anti-aircraft missiles and other weapons looted from the Iraqis or obtained from Iran. Fighting in the north escalated in 1987 and early 1988. It was a commonplace observation that the Iraqis controlled the roads by day, but the night belonged to the Kurds. In January the PUK captured one of Saddam's palaces (Gunther, 1992, pp. 33-35).

Baghdad's response was anfal. The word, meaning the 'spoils,' is the name of the eighth sura of the Quran and the official military codename used publicly by the Iraqi government to refer to its actions against the Kurds. Beginning in April 1987 and continuing through 1988, Iraq conducted a systematic campaign attacking villages in Iraqi Kurdistan suspected of harboring Kurdish dissidents. In June 1987 Baghdad declared all Kurds living in the prohibited rural areas of northern Iraq to be coterminous with the peshmerga insurgents; a shoot-to-kill policy would be applied. A second order also issued in June modified and expanded these orders to allow army commanders 'to carry out random bombardments, using artillery, helicopters and aircraft, at all times of the day or night, in order to kill the largest number of persons present in these prohibited zones.' All persons captured were to be detained and interrogated by the security services and those between the ages of 15 and 70 'shall be executed after any useful information has been obtained from them, of which we shall be duly notified.'[12] The October 1987 census was the final step in identifying the target group. The census gave those registering two options: to declare their nationality as Arab or Kurd; and for those living in the proscribed area, a choice of returning 'to the national ranks,' i.e. abandon their homes and accept resettlement in camps elsewhere or lose their Iraqi citizenship. Those who rejected resettlement would be regarded as military deserters. The second option was equal to a death sentence, since the census decree also made those who refused to be counted subject to an RCC decree imposing the death penalty on deserters. When the census was completed, those living in the region identified as Kurds—women, children, and the elderly for the most part—were forcibly transferred to the rural areas to join those accused of being peshmerga. Similar standards and consequences would later be applied to many Assyrian and Chaldean Christians and Turkmen who, when they refused to choose Arab or Kurd as their ethnic designation, were labeled Kurd and treated in the same brutal fashion (M.E. Watch, 1993, p.15).

The actual anfal began four months after the census, in February 1988. On 16 March 1988 the Iraqi military attacked Halabjah, a Kurdish city of 70,000 located approximately 15 miles from the border with Iran; the city had recently been captured by peshmerga aided by Iranian Revolutionary Guard forces. In what was part counter-insurgency operation and mostly retaliation for its capture, more than 5,000 civilians were killed in operations using chemical weapons—mustard, nerve, and cyanide gas. Chemical attacks against civilian targets recurred through the summer. More than 60,000 Kurdish refugees, declared terrorists and criminals by Saddam, fled across the Turkish border. Baghdad also began forced resettlement of Kurdish villagers to camps in southern Iraq. Middle East Watch quotes Kurdish sources who claim that 4,000 villages were destroyed and that an estimated 182,000 persons disappeared during 1988 alone (M. E. Watch, 1993, p.xii). The Middle East Watch estimates that at least 50,000 and possibly as many as 100,000 persons—many of them women and children—were killed between February and September. The killings were not the result of battle nor were they conducted by rogue commanders acting out of anger; rather, the Watch states, they were part of a systematic plan by the central government to kill as many Kurds as possible and destroy their villages. In language similar to the 'special actions' and 'resettlement in the east' used by the Nazis, Iraqi records of the anfal describe 'collective measures,' 'return to nationalist ranks,' and 'resettlement in the south.' The intent, as the Middle East Watch methodically documents, was genocide, 'to destroy, in whole or in part, a national, ethnic, racial or religious group.'[13]

The anfal campaign was headed by Saddam's cousin `Ali Hassan al-Majid. Known in Iraq as 'Chemical `Ali,' `Ali Hassan was then Interior Minister and secretary-general of the Bath Party's Northern Bureau. He would later serve as Defense Minister and be in charge of the brutal occupation of Kuwait. In 1988, he commanded two corps of the Iraqi Army, the General Security Directorate (Mudiriyat al-Amn al-Am) and Military Intelligence (al-Istikhabarat al-Askariyyah). In a meeting with Kurdish representatives demanding to know the fate of the disappeared, a number they estimated to be 182,000, `Ali Hassan replied that it 'could not have been more than 100,000' (M. E. Watch, 1993, p. xviii). Special security units carried out the killings. On the eve of Operation Desert Storm, Jalal Talabani claimed that 'more than 5,000 Kurdish villages [had been] razed by the Iraqi Army' and 'two million Kurds moved to concentration camps at the edges of major cities in Kurdistan.'(Gunther, 1992, p.47). The State Department reported that 'an estimated 250,000 to 300,000 Kurdish villagers were forcibly relocated in 1988; since . . . 1987, an estimated 500,000 people have been uprooted.' (Ibid).

Occupying Kuwait

Any one following the course of Ba`thist rule in Iraq could not have been shocked by the brutality of Iraq's occupation of Kuwait. Saddam—and his surrogate in Kuwait, `Ali Hassan al-Majid—applied the methods used against political opponents, suspected Shiah dissidents, and rebellious Kurds to cajole and control the so-called 19th province after 1 August 1990. The story of the occupation has been told in the press, Congress, and by those who lived in occupied Kuwait.[14] Kuwaitis suspected of aiding the resistance were killed in front of their families, while others were marched away to imprisonment, torture, and execution. Many disappeared, including several thousand civilians reportedly taken indiscriminately from their homes, mosques, and other public places on the retreat from Kuwait.[15] Following Kuwait's liberation on 27 February, the Government of Kuwait requested that the UN send a mission to Kuwait to assess the practices of the Iraqi occupation force against the civilian population and the damages to the country's economic infrastructure. In addition to detailing the wanton destruction of Kuwait's economy, culture, and environment, witnesses told the UN commission of the violations of the Fourth Geneva Convention. These included ill treatment of detainees, arbitrary arrest and/or detention, deportation, collective punishment, and random killings. As of 1997, Kuwait claimed more than 600 of its nationals were still missing in Iraq.

The UN took several actions to condemn Iraq's abuse of human rights during and after the war for Kuwait. In December 1990 the General Assembly condemned Baghdad and the occupying forces for 'their serious violations of human rights against the Kuwaiti people and third-State nationals.'[16] Three months later, in March 1991, the Commission on Human Rights appointed two special rapporteurs to study the human rights situation in Kuwait and Iraq.[17] The situation in Iraq at this time was especially critical. Saddam's military forces and intelligence forces were busily suppressing a chaotic rebellion by Shiah in the shrine cities and villages of southern Iraq which resulted in the near destruction of Karbala and Najaf. Many Shiah fled to the marshes only to watch the Iraqis begin a systematic destruction of the marshes to ease their access and ferret out dissidents. At the same time the Kurds were in open rebellion in the north. The situation in the north, where the Kurds had risen in revolt one month after the Shiah, was just as grim. By early April 1991 a humanitarian catastrophe clearly was underway. More than 1.5 million refugees fled to the mountains to escape a vengeful Iraqi military. On 5 April the UN Security Council passed Resolution 688, which 'condemned the repression of Iraq's civilian population in many parts of Iraq, including most recently the Kurdish-populated areas' and called on Baghdad to 'allow immediate access by international humanitarian organizations to all those in need of assistance.'[18] Unlike UN Security Council Resolution 687, which included punishments for Baghdad if it did not adhere to the resolution, Resolution 688 provided for no punishment if/when Saddam violated human rights or failed to adhere to the resolution.[19]   The Resolution was used by the Coalition, however, to establish two no-fly zones—one created in June 1991 covering the territory above the 36th parallel, the other established in June 1992 extending the flight ban below the 32nd parallel.

Iraq's Human Rights Record Since Operation Desert Storm

Kanan Makiyah writes in his book Republic of Fear that 'The measure of a regime of terror is the victims of its peace, not the casualties of its wars.' (Makyah, 1989, p.24). That Saddam Husayn remains in power today, after two major wars which devastated his country, numerous coup attempts, and the impoverishment of his country under UN-imposed sanctions, is a testament to the effectiveness of his arbitrary style of rule, the fear engendered by his retributive justice, and the inability of Iraqis to control their political lives. Concern for human rights in a country which has seen its expectations and standards of living rise dramatically since the 1958 revolution and fall precipitously since 1991 is probably lower on most Iraqis list of daily priorities than is the struggle for survival, a decent wage, and freedom from the watchful eyes of the mukhabbarat (secret police). Tribalism, with its stress on family and clan origins, and a careful resurgence of Islam, with its emphasis on the community of believers, place the interests of the group over those of the individual. Both are being manipulated by Saddam's regime to maintain control over a troubled society. Both lack the leaders and organization necessary to challenge the government within Iraq, essential ingredients if there is to be any change in how or who rules Iraq.[20]

Government Policy

Iraqis lack virtually all the basic rights guaranteed by their constitution. They have no right to change their government. Referendums, such as the October 1995 one which saw Saddam 'win' 99.96 percent of the vote, are a mockery, according to UN Special Rapporteur Max van der Stoel. Van der Stoel described voters at the polling stations as presenting their ballot cards and official papers to referendum administrators in the presence of Iraqi security forces and Ba'th Party officials. They deposited the second part of a two-part ballot in an opaque sealed box. The question on the ballot was, 'Are you in favour of Saddam Hussein assuming the post of President of the Republic of Iraq?' Van der Stoel observed that 'virtually no one voted against Saddam' in the southern governates, including Karbala and Najaf, that had been the scene of bloody uprisings in April 1991. The population, he stated, 'has now been totally subdued, made to

conform, become economically exhausted and totally dependent.'
Widescale military movements were carried out in the south before the
election to intimidate the population, and security forces dispatched to the
marshes warned people that their ration cards would be confiscated if they
did not vote for Saddam. Van der Stoel concluded that

> . . . the conditions necessary to ensure that the free will of the Iraqi
> people is the basis of the authority of the government do not exist in
> the present legal and political order of Iraq . . . . the almost total control
> of information coupled with an all-pervasive and generalized fear
> among the population of severe sanctions for non-support of the
> prevailing order, maintained through abuses of power and facilitated
> by the absence of the rule of law in the country, combine totally to
> undermine and distort apparent expressions of the 'will of the
> people.'[21]

The government forcibly transfers government employees and military
personnel constantly to prevent any government or party bureaucrat or
military officer from acquiring a popular base of institutional support. The
government conducts arbitrary arrests, searches and seizures of property,
and executes citizens with or without a 'trial.' The judiciary is an adjunct
of the regime. Saddam can override any court decision and certainly
dictates those in trials of accused coup plotters, assuming they live to trial.
Citizens are denied their right to due process and privacy. As detailed by
the UN Special Rapporteur for Iraq in his biannual reports, Iraqis are
denied freedom of the press, assembly, speech, and association, except in
areas of the north not under Saddam's direct control. Freedom of religion
is severely limited—but then it is in many Muslim Arab countries. Iraq's
'minorities'—the Kurds in the north and Arab Shiah in the south— remain
targets of repression, denied access to whatever humanitarian resources are
available to Iraqis in the Arab Sunni center. Yet, the Arab Sunni center is
not as protected as it once was. Abortive revolts have been attempted by
members of tribes and families known for their loyalty to the regime; for
example, members of the Jaburi, a large tribal group that has been overly
represented in the military and security services, have been implicated in
several coup attempts over the last several years, with several prominent
members executed by the regime. Many Iraqis and observers of Iraq
believe Saddam ordered the return and execution of his sons-in-law,
Hussein and Saddam Kamil, who defected in 1995 only to be wooed back
and murdered the following year ostensibly in a clan reprisal.

The record as defined by the UN and the U.S. State Department's
annual report on human rights practices is dismal. The reports all note that

Iraq is 'run through extrajudicial measures.'[22] This includes those parts of Iraq under Saddam's direct control and those parts of the north where Kurdish factions led by Mas'ud Barzani and Jalal Talabani continue to fight each other, in league with Baghdad, Tehran, and/or Ankara. The Kurds pay lip service to ideals of civil liberties and human rights but apply their own brand of judicial revenge in the areas under their control. Amnesty International noted in a report released in February 1995 that the clashes between Kurdish parties that had occurred over the previous two years 'signified . . . an abandonment of fundamental human rights principles to which the Kurdish leadership had publicly committed itself.'[23] The report blamed the abuses by the Kurdish parties—the KDP, the PUK, and the Islamic Movement of Independent Kurdistan—on two factors: the impunity enjoyed by their 'military' forces, and their active undermining of the judiciary and lack of respect for its *independence*.

Government Practice: The Role of the Courts

Iraq does not have an independent judiciary. There is no system of checks and balances to protect the courts from the President's power to override or dictate their decisions. Iraq has two parallel judicial systems: the regular courts that try common criminal offenses; and the special security courts that generally try national security cases. There is a Court of Appeal and a Court of Cassation, which is the highest court.

The theory of trial in Iraq includes procedures for protections, at least in the regular courts. Trials in the regular courts are public, and defendants are entitled to counsel, at government expense in the case of indigents. Defense lawyers have the right to review the charges and evidence brought against their clients. There is no jury system. Panels of three judges try cases, with defendants having the right to appeal to the Courts of Appeal and Cassation.

The reality of the judicial system is quite different. The state can assign a trial to whatever court it chooses, often assigning cases to the security courts that would appear to belong in the civil court. Favored groups—such as members of Saddam's family—are shielded from prosecution for their alleged crimes. A 1992 decree grants immunity from prosecution to Ba'th Party members and to members of the security forces who kill anyone while in pursuit of army deserters.[24] Most political prisoners are tried by special courts in camera with no right of appeal. The special security courts have jurisdiction in all cases involving espionage and treason, peaceful political dissent, smuggling, currency exchange violations, and drug trafficking. Lawyers are government-appointed and access to them severely restricted. The detainee probably does not meet with his/her lawyer until the day or hour of the 'trial.' According to the Special Rapporteur and the U.S. Department of State, military officers or civil servants with no legal training head these tribunals, hearing cases in secret. Defendants are held incommunicado, and confessions extracted under torture are frequently used as the basis of conviction. Defendants, including those on trial for their lives (virtually all of them) are not usually allowed to call witnesses or submit evidence in their defense. Amnesty International reports that some convicts sentenced to imprisonment have been executed regardless of sentence.[25]

Ba'thist Iraq has no shariah courts for personal status law. Regular courts are empowered to administer Islamic law in cases involving personal status matters, such as divorce or inheritance. After the Kuwait war, in order to win over support of the tribal confederations that he had virtually ignored for twenty years, Saddam granted them power under tribal law. In 1997 a government decree reminded Iraqis that state law took precedence over tribal or any other law.

The Role of the Military and the Security Services

The Iraqi army has intervened in the nation's political and social life since independence in 1932. It led coups in 1936 and 1941, and military officers played major roles in each of the coups since 1958. With the exception of the 8-year war with Iran, Iraq's military forces have been engaged primarily in internal policing, suppressing rebellions, and fighting a near continuous civil war with Iraq's fractious Kurds. The security services include the Special Security Force (Jihaz al-Amn al-Khas), the General Security Directorate (Mudiriyyat al-Amn al-Amm), Military Intelligence (al-Istikhabbarat al-Askariyyah), the paramilitary force of the People's Army (Ba'th Party militia), and the secret police (mukhabarrat). When popular resentment against the government spilled over in one of Baghdad's poorest slums in March 1991, a crowd of mostly unarmed demonstrators estimated by one witness to number 5,000 gathered in a market area of al-Thawra district, a predominantly Shiah quarter of the city. Forewarned, security forces and party loyalists from the Popular Army shot into the crowd, killing approximately 600 people. The district was surrounded for one week while security forces arrested thousands of people in security sweeps (M. E. Watch, 1993, p.3).

Respect for the Integrity of the Person

Political and extrajudicial killing is commonplace. It is impossible to estimate the number of killings, although both the UN and the State Department assume that the numbers have increased since the end of the war in 1991. Again, Hussein and Saddam Kamil and more than 40 of their relatives were killed despite receiving an amnesty and without due process. Following the Iraqi attack on Irbil in late August 1996, numerous eyewitnesses claimed that nearly one hundred army officers and soldiers who had deserted the army and fled north were executed in the town center while other dissidents were hunted down and murdered for their alleged opposition to the regime. In October 1996, representatives of the UN's Human Rights Commission (UNHCHR) interviewed refugees from the north and recorded what happened after the army and special security services, assisted by the KDP, entered the territory. These witnesses described a campaign intended to eliminate the opposition. All non-Kurds living in the area were presumed to be members of the opposition; several were arrested and taken to Mosul, Kirkuk, or Baghdad. Hundreds were said to have been subjected to extrajudicial executions, the use of excessive force, confiscation and destruction of personal property, arbitrary arrest and detention, and forced relocation. According to witnesses, members of the Iraqi National Congress (INC), the Iraqi National Turkmen Party (INTP), the PUK, students, and doctors known for their support for human rights were especially targeted. Non-Arabs were ordered to sell their property only to Arabs.[26]

In the south, suspicions linger over the true cause of the automobile accident which took the life in 1994 of Taki al-Kho`i, a prominent Shiah opposition figure who was the son of the late Grand Ayatollah Kho`i. Other members of the Grand Ayatollah's family who were arrested in 1991 have still not been accounted for, and the regime refuses to respond to queries about their status.

It is equally impossible to place an accurate estimate on the number of 'disappeareds' in Iraq. The UN has documented more than 16,000 cases of missing persons, most of them from the anfal of 1988. Human Rights Watch and Amnesty International place the total of missing at a much higher number. Those detained by the security service are routinely tortured, psychologically and physically, even though the Constitution prohibits torture. Former detainees have described to the Special Rapporteur, Amnesty International, and other non-governmental organizations branding, the use of electric shocks on the genitals, beatings, burning, suspension from ceiling fans, rape, the breaking of limbs, denial of food and water, and the imprisonment and threats to harm innocent family members. In 1994, the RCC enacted criminal penalties involving physical mutilation, including the amputation of hands, feet, ears, and the branding of marks on the forehead. The decrees included:

- Decree No. 59 of 4 June 1994 providing for the amputation of the right hand for theft, including bakers for contravening regulations concerning the production of bread;
- Decree No. 92 of 21 July 1994 prescribing life imprisonment or amputation of the right hand for falsifying an official document for illicit benefits or depriving another person of rights;
- Decree No. 115 of 25 August 1994 mandating the amputation of an ear and branding on the forehead for any person evading military service, deserters, and those sheltering evaders or deserters.

According to the Special Rapporteur, these punishments have been applied to several thousand prisoners. Other information indicates doctors have been forced to carry out amputations or branding without anesthesia. Doctors refusing to carry out mandated procedures were executed. The Special Rapporteur also received reports of executions of members of the political opposition; their bodies were returned to their families with signs of torture. The Special Rapporteur noted extenuating circumstances for applying punishments in Iraq under sanctions, saying that Iraq's international isolation and the effects of embargo have increased crime and the need for severe social penalties as a deterrent. Amputation is permissible under Islamic shariah law.[27] Other decrees grant immunity to men who kill their mothers, daughters, or other female members of their family who have committed 'immoral deeds', such as adultery, or who have been raped. This practice was—and still is—acceptable in societies governed by traditional standards of tribal law or custom.

Respect for Civil Liberties

There is no freedom of the press, assembly, or free speech in Iraq. Political dissent is not tolerated, even in humor. Under a 1986 decree, anyone insulting the President or other high government officials can be sentenced to death. Section 214 of the Penal Code prohibits singing a song likely to cause civil strife, and the Press Act of 1968 prohibits the writing of articles on specific subjects, including those detrimental to the President. The government, the Party, the military, and Saddam's son Uday own all print and broadcast media, operating them as propaganda outlets. Journalists are expected to join the Ba`th Party and laud Saddam. The Ministry of Culture and Information defines the parameters of press freedom. Books can only be published with Ministry authorization. Uday has extensive control over press publication and censorship in Iraq; he uses his newspaper Babil to criticize government ministers and threaten members of tribes, clans, or other organizations in Iraq's meager civil society believed to be insufficiently supportive of the regime. Allegations printed in Babil apparently have reflected discord within the family; Hussein Kamil may have fled Iraq because of attacks in Babil against him in early 1995. In areas of Iraq not under government control, political factions such as the KDP and the PUK control the media and do not allow dissent.

Other freedoms assumed in the West are denied in Iraq. Only political parties approved by the state are allowed; membership in some—the Communist Party or the clandestine Da`wa Party, for example—is punishable by death. The Provisional Constitution of 1968 declares Islam to be the religion of the state, just as do the constitutions of other Arab Muslims countries, but religion has always played a special role in the lives of many Iraqis. Iraq is home to two of the great shrine cities of Shiah Islam —Najaf and Karbala—centers of religious education, law schools, and burial societies; Ayatollah Khomeini spent 15 years in exile here. Like other Arab Muslim countries, Iraq severely limits the practice of religions other than Islam. The Ministry of Endowments and Religious Affairs monitors places of worship, appoints the clergy, and approves the publication of religious literature. The suppression of religion has been particularly harsh on Iraq's Shiah. Clerics, students, and their families have routinely been arrested over the years and subject to deportation on allegations they were Iranian in origin, sympathetic to the Iranian Islamic revolution, or had given assistance to individuals suspected of belonging to banned political movements. Actions by Baghdad against the Shiah include:

- Desecration of mosques and shrines during the 1991 rebellion. The Iraqi military bombed major shrines and mosques in Najaf and Karbala, creating a swath of destruction around the major shrines in the center of the cities to create free-fire zones. The shrine of the Imam `Ali in Najaf was used as an interrogation center, Najaf's chief theological school is used as a public market. Saddam's refurbishment of the major shrines several years ago did little to allay the impact of his retribution for rebellion.

- Ban on the Muslim call to prayer in certain cities, the broadcast of Shiah religious programs on radio or television, the publication of Shiah books, including prayer books, funeral processions, and processions such as the passion play (taziyah) which commemorates the death of the Imam Husayn in the seventh century.

- Accusations of collaborating with the enemy (dissident Kurds) leveled against Iraq's 350,000 Assyrians, most of whom live in northern Iraq. Many Assyrians have been subject to torture and execution, along with confiscation of property and forced relocations.

What Does the Future Hold: Scenarios for a More Civil Society?

Iraq's future behavior as a denier of human rights and abuser of human freedoms seems easy to predict. While Saddam rules, power will continue to be concentrated in the hands of a few and loyalty to the state linked to personal loyalty to the leader. There can be no other standard in a state that perceives itself to be under siege. If Saddam has shown himself unwilling to alleviate the suffering of the Iraqi people by complying with UN-imposed sanctions, why should he suddenly display an uncharacteristic—and unhistoric—concern for human rights or the protection of civil society? Again, if history is a reliable guide, then Saddam is likely to continue to manipulate the mechanisms he uses to control government and society. The same could happen under a successor regime.

Table 3.1   Major Iraqi Dissident Factions

Faction	Type	Leader	Objective
Iraqi National Congress (INC)	Umbrella group of Sunni, Shiah, KDP, PUK	Ahmad Chalabi	OverthrowSaddam; secular government; U.S., Western, Arab backing
Iraqi National Accord (INA)		Iyad al-Allawi	Overthrow Saddam
al-Da`wa al-Islamiyya	Shiah		Democratic rule under Islamic law; Iranian-backed
Supreme Assembly for the Islamic Revolution in Iraq (SAIRI)	Shiah umbrella organization	Muhammad Baqr al-Hakim	Democratic rule; Iran-backed
Kurdish Democratic Party (KDP)	Kurdish	Mas`ud Barzani	Self-rule; was member INC; links to Turkey, Iran; allowed Baghdad to occupy Irbil
Patriotic Unition of Kurdistan (PUK)	Kurdish	Jalal Talabani	Overthrow Saddam; self-rule; occasion Iranian, Turkish aid was member INC

Two scenarios for Iraq's future are worth considering. In the first and more likely scenario, Saddam remains in power. To maintain control, he is likely to manipulate the several basic components which have long dominated Iraqi politics, including resurrected Tikriti family or clan members, a reconstituted Ba`th Party, and reinvigorated tribal structures.

At the end of the Gulf War Saddam appointed as Prime Minister Sa`dun Hammadi, a Shiah party loyalist who had been educated in the United States and would presumably woo favorable attention and quick relief from sanctions from the West. He lasted less than three months. Over succeeding years Saddam kept power in the hands of his close family members, reining in the current generation of son Uday, cousin `Ali Hassan al-Majid, and son-in-law Hussein Kamil only when their excesses threatened his hold on power. Appointments to government positions in 1997 suggest that Uday, seriously wounded in a December 1996 assassination attempt, is being rehabilitated by reappointment to his party and extra-governmental posts, and that Saddam is probably grooming a new generation of extended family members to assume key posts. Saddam's second son Qusayy remains supervisor of the Republican Guard. At the same time, Saddam has given preference in admission to Iraq's military academies and universities to loyal tribe and clan members, thereby assuring him of their continued loyalty. He held elections for Ba`th Party leadership positions in October 1997, bringing in new men loyal to him and stripping power from those he holds responsible for the Party's collapse after the Gulf war.

None of these developments suggests Saddam's vision of Iraq and the proper place for its diverse people will change. Nor is it likely he will perceive a need to shore up popular support by releasing political prisoners or easing the security restrictions that dominate the lives of most Iraqis. Under this scenario, Saddam will continue to apply the same tests for loyalty he has used since the 1968 revolution. In a speech marking the 29th anniversary of the 17 July 1968 revolution, Saddam warned Iraq's Kurds that 'nobody has the right to interfere in or speak about' Iraqi Kurds' trust in—or lack thereof—in Baghdad:

> . . . we give dialogue and agreement on disputed issues precedence over the use of force with respect to the Kurdish issue. Dialogue might take a long or short time before it reaches its goals. This is an Iraqi affair. . . . Nobody may claim he has the right to interfere in this issue, peg his failure on it, or conceal its intentions toward it . . . . Our Kurdish people know very well that their national Iraqi higher leadership will not abandon them in any circumstances or case, regardless of how hard the road or the sacrifices may be.[28]

On a similar note, Saddam accused Iran of wanting to save Iraq's Shiah from his leadership, 'as if the Iraqi Shiites had no nationality or national and pan-Arab roots and as if the Shiites needed foreigners to care for them and establish a foreign canopy for them in their own country.'[29]

In the second scenario, Saddam is gone, removed by assassination or natural causes. However he goes, it is unlikely a member of his immediate family will succeed him. It is also unlikely to be a democratically minded regime, although a successor might be willing to include a wider spectrum of political representation in a coalition government in order to win foreign, especially western, approval. The immediate successor will most likely be a member of Saddam's extended clan, a Tikriti, probably a military officer. An Iraq without Saddam would seem to offer an opportunity for an Iraq with some allowance for civil liberties and human rights. This will depend, however, on how the succession occurs and the amount of scrutiny brought to bear by Europe and the United States. A new Iraqi regime dependent on Western recognition for survival and acceptability in diplomatic and investment circles would probably pay some attention to human rights, but there is no reason to assume this would be a significant relaxation of the repressive standards which have marked all Iraqi regimes until now. Many successors would probably equate implementation of human rights policies—to include civil and political rights—as encouraging opposition from fractious Kurds, disgruntled Shiah, and overly ambitious Arab Sunnis in the so-called center. It does not seem likely that opposition elements based outside Iraq who advocate democratic rule have much of a chance of coming to power in Iraq.

Opponents of the Iraqi regime will continue to seek international backing in their efforts to restrain Saddam. In early September 1997 a group representing Iraq's Kurds called on the U.S. administration to demand an end to Saddam's 'ethnic cleansing' of Kirkuk. They accused Baghdad of violating UNSC resolution 688 by forcing mass deportations of Kurdish nationals, destroying hundreds of villages, and resettling Arabs in traditionally Kurdish and Turkman areas around Kirkuk.[30] In November the U.S. House passed a resolution reflecting the sense of Congress in condemning Saddam Husayn and senior Iraqi officials for committing crimes against humanity. Critics in Iran draw attention to Baghdad's continued repression of Shiah Muslims in southern Iraq. Ayatollah Muhammad Baqr al-Hakim, the Iraqi cleric who heads the Supreme Assembly for the Islamic Revolution in Iraq claimed that Iraqi troops had killed more than 200 Shiah pilgrims commemorating `Ashura in the major shrine in Karbala in July 1997.[31]

One final alternative remains, that of Iraq in chaos. At least one casual observer of recent history in Iraq has suggested that an Iraq divided among the three primary interest groups—Arabs, Shiahs, and Kurds—would do more to ensure that a strong Iraq headed by an authoritarian leader would not emerge than does the possibility of the same if Iraq remains united (Byman, 1996, pp.48-60). Is it in the interest of Iraqis and their neighbors that Iraq remain united? The argument is a false one, since there is no natural division of Iraq except that sought by some Kurdish factions, and there is no way a weak and divided series of statelets would pose any less a threat to themselves or their neighbors. It would not serve as seedbed of democracy, a development better sought through manipulation of a successor regime.

Notes

1. The views expressed in this article are those of the author and do not reflect the position of the National Defense University, the Department of Defense, or the US Government.

2. See also Hanna Batatu's classic study, *The Old Social Classes and the Revolutionary Movements of Iraq*, (Princeton: Princeton University Press, 1978), for the most comprehensive examination of Iraq's political and social development from 1920 through the early days of the Ba'thist regime.

3. The Assyrians had been forcibly resettled in northern Iraq after World War I and recruited into paramilitary, pro-British levies feared by the fledgling Iraqi army. Their claims to autonomy without the ability to sustain those claims came at a time of rising Arab nationalism. Following a skirmish with Iraqi troops in July 1932, 100 unarmed villagers were killed in Dahuk and Zakhu; several days later another massacre occurred among civilians clustered at a police station for protection. To many outsiders, the massacre of the Assyrians signified Iraq's inability to deal fairly and firmly with a dissident minority. To Iraqis, however, the Assyrians represented a threat to national unity. See Marr, *The Modern History of Iraq*, pp. 57-59.

4. In the formative years of the Bath Party—the late 1950s and early 1960s—Arab Shiah dominated the party leadership, holding 53 percent of all leadership positions. Substantial numbers of Shiahs also belonged to the Communist Party. See Marr, p. 283.

5. Report submitted by the Government of Iraq to the UN Committee on the Elimination of All Forms of Racial Discrimination, CERD/C/240/Add.3, 14 June 1996.

6. Under subsequent legislation, Iraq's Turkmen and Assyrian communities were accorded similar 'rights,' that their language would be the language of instruction in the primary schools, that cultural rights for writers and intellectuals would be preserved, and that special studies programs would be established in schools of higher education. See RCC Decree No. 288 of 11 March 1970; Act No. 33, The Iraqi Kurdistan Regional Autonomy Act of 11 March 1974; RCC Decree No. 89 of 24 November 1970 for the cultural rights of Iraq's Turkmen community; and Decree No. 251 of 20 February 1972 for the cultural rights of Iraq's Syriac-speaking citizens.

7. Baghdad expelled approximately 40,000 Shiah (*fayli*) Kurds who had lived for generations in Baghdad and near Khanaqin on the grounds that they were Iranian nationals. Gunther, p. 17.

8. For information on the CIA role, see the portions of the Pike Report that appeared in the *Village Voice* (New York), 16 February 1976, pp. 72-92.

9. Forced deportations of Iranians to the borders first occurred in 1969 when tensions heated up between Baghdad and the Shah over control of the Shatt al-Arab and Iranian claims to islands in the Persian Gulf also claimed by the Sharjah and Ras al-Khaymah. An unknown number of people from the holy cities of Karbala and Najaf were bundled

into trucks and driven to the border with Iran.

10. Marr claims that the 1979 riots were sparked by Baqr Sadr's efforts to lead a procession to Iran to congratulate Ayatollah Khomeini. Ibid. Yitzhaq Nakash is less certain; in his view the Shiah masses lacked the 'genuine revolutionary frame of mind' and the socioeconomic infrastructure necessary for carrying out an Islamic revolution. See Nakash, *The Shi'is of Iraq*, p. 137.

11. Kurds returning from exile first found mass graves around Irbil and Sulaymaniyah. See the reports issued by Middle East Watch, a division of Human Rights. Their reports include *Genocide in Iraq: the Anfal Campaign Against the Kurds* (NY: 1993), *Unquiet Graves: The Search for the Disappeared in Iraqi Kurdistan*, (NY: 1992), and *Endless Torment: The 1991 Uprising in Iraq and Its Aftermath*.

12. Orders issued to Ali Hassan al-Majid, Secretary-general of the Bath Party's Northern Bureau from records obtained by the Middle East Watch; see *Genocide in Iraq*, pp. 8-9. *Genocide in Iraq* documents the steps of the *anfal* from conception to completion based on documents uncovered by the Kurds in 1991, interviews with survivors of the *anfal*, and forensic research on remains found in the mass graves.

13. The definition is that of the Convention on the Prevention and Punishment of the Crime of Genocide, 78 UNTS 277, approved by GA Res. 2670 on December 9, 1948; cited in Genocide in Iraq, p. 5.

14. See for example, John and Roberta Hogan, *Trapped in Kuwait: Countdown to Armageddon*, Lynnwood, Washington: The Charles Franklin Press, 1991. The Hogans were Americans caught in Kuwait when the Iraqis invaded; this is their account of life in hiding from the Iraqis.

15. *The United Nations and the Iraq-Kuwait Conflict, 1990-1996*, (NY: UN Information Office, 1996), p. 39; for the text of the interim report assessing loss of life in Kuwait under the occupation and Iraqi practices against the civilian population of Kuwait, see S/22536, 29 April 1991, in *The United Nations and the Iraq-Kuqait Conflict, 1990-1996*, pp. 229-234.

16. A/RES/45/170, 18 December 1990, cited in *The United Nations and the Iraq-Kuwait Conflict*, pp. 178-179.

17. The Special Rapporteur for Iraq submits reports twice yearly to the Security Council. See, for example, the UNHCHR, *Situation of Human Rights in Iraq*, Report A/51/496 of 15 October 1996 and UNHCHR, *Situation of Human Rights in Iraq*, Report A/51/496 of 8 November 1996.

18. S/RES/688 (1991), 5 April 1991, cited in *The United Nations and the Iraq-Kuwait Conflict, 1990-1996*, p. 199.

19. *The United Nations and the Iraq-Kuwait Conflict, 1990-1996*, pp. 40-41. See also Laith Kubba, 'Human Rights, Sanctions and Soverignty,' *Iraq Since the Gulf War*, (London: Committee Against Repression and for Democratic Rights in Iraq, 1994), pp. 147-152.

20. On tribalism in Iraq, see Amatzia Baram, 'Neo-Tribalism in Iraq: Saddam Hussein's Tribal Policies, 1991-96,' *International Journal of Middle East Studies*, vol. 29, no. 1 (February, 1997), pp. 1-31.

21. *Report on the Human Rights Situation in Iraq* of 4 March, E/CN.4/1996/61, pp. 12-13.

22. Special Rapporteur on Iraq Max van der Stoel in his November 1996 report to the UN Human Rights Commission; U.S. Department of State, *Iraq Report on Human Rights Practices for 1996*, (Bureau of Democracy, Human Rights, and Labor: January 30, 1997).

23. Cited by the Lawyers Committee for Human Rights in *Critique: Review of the U.S. Department of State's Country Reports on Human Rights Practices for 1995*, July 1996.

24. According to the U.S. Department of State, this decree may have been used to protect

Saddam's son Uday from prosecution in 1996. See *Iraq Report on Human Rights Practices for 1996*, p. 8.
25. Amnesty International Newsletter, vol. XIX, no. 5, May 1989; see also Amnesty International yearly reports for Iraq.
26. UNHCHR, *Situation of Human Rights in Iraq, Report* A/51/496, 8 November 1996.
27. See UN High Commissioner for Human Rights, *Report of the Special Rapporteur on Torture*, UNESCO: 16 January 1996, pp. 74-77; and UNHCHR, *Situation of Human Rights in Iraq*, 15 October 1996.
28. Speech by President Saddam Husayn marking the 29th anniversary of the 17-30 July Revolution, 22 July 1997.
29. Ibid.
30. Press release from the Washington Kurdish Institute, September 4, 1997.
31. See Hasan Salehi, 'Is the Prophet Happy,' *Tehran Keyhan International*, 22 July 1997, p. 2; 'SAIRI Chief Says Saddam Troops Kill Over 200 in Kerbala,' *Voice of Rebellious Iraq*, 13 July 1997.

References

Amnesty International, *Annual Reports for 1981-1985, 1993, and 1994*.
Baram, Amatzia (1997), 'Neo-Tribalism in Iraq: Saddam Hussein's Tribal Policies, 1991-96,' *International Journal of Middle East Studies*, vol. 29, no. 1, February.
Batatu, Hanna (1978), *The Old Social Classes and the Revolutionary Movements of Iraq*, Princeton University Press: Princeton.
Byman, Daniel (1996), 'Let Iraq Collapse,' *The National Interest*, Fall.
Gunther, Michael M. (1992), *The Kurds of Iraq: Tragedy and Hope*, St. Martin's Press: New York.
Hazelton, Fran (ed.), (1994), *Iraq Since the Gulf War: Prospects for Democracy*, The Committee Against Repression and for Democratic Rights in Iraq: London.
Mahallat, Chibli (1988), 'Religious Militancy in Contemporary Iraq,' *Third World Quarterly*, vol. 10, no. 2, April.
Makiyah, Kanan [Samir al-Khalil] (1993), *Cruelty and Silence: War, Tyranny, Uprising, and the Arab World*, W.W. Norton: New York.
Makiyah, Kanan [Samir al-Khalil] (1989), *Republic of Fear: The Politics of Modern Iraq*, University of California Press: Berkeley.
Marr, Phebe (1985), *The Modern History of Iraq*, Westview Press: Boulder.
Middle East Watch (1993), *Genocide in Iraq: The Anfal Campaign Against the Kurds*, Human Rights Watch: New York.
Nakash, Yitzhak (1994), *The Shi`is of Iraq*, Princeton University Press: Princeton.
The United Nations and the Iraq-Kuwait Conflict, 1990-1996 (1996), The United Nations Blue Books Series, Vol. IX, UN Department of Public Information: New York.
United Nations High Commissioner for Human Rights (4 March 1996), *Report on the Situation of Human Rights in Iraq*, Report E/CN.4/1996/61.
UNHCHR (16 January 1996), *Report of the Special Rapporteur on Torture*.
UNHCHR (15 October 1996), *Situation of Human Rights in Iraq*, Report A/51/496.
UNHCHR (8 November 1996), *Situation of Human Rights in Iraq*, Report A/51/496.
UNHCHR (21 February 1997), *Report on the Situation of Human Rights in Iraq*, E/CN.4/1997/57.
U.S. Department of State (30 January 1997), *Iraq Report on Human Rights Practices for 1996*.

4 Syria Resists the End of History

FRED H. LAWSON

Syria's formal governmental structure provides for a highly centralized, strictly hierarchical political system that concentrates power in the presidency of the republic and the top leadership of the Ba'th Party. This system emerged after military supporters of the Ba'th seized power in March 1963, and it remains in place as the 1990s draw to a close. In the years since November 1970, the presidency has been held by Major General Hafiz al-Asad, who also serves as commander-in-chief of the armed forces, secretary-general of the Regional (Syrian) Command of the Ba'th and head of the National Progressive Front, the ruling alliance in the national assembly. Furthermore, since the 1963 revolution, the country has been under a continuous state of emergency, in which the minister of the interior is empowered to enforce statutes that tightly regulate public gatherings, the press and the disposition of property. Persons charged with offenses under the state of emergency regulations are almost always remanded to state security courts, where deliberations are carried out *in camera*. Proceedings in the state security courts have most often resulted in summary verdicts and in the immediate sentencing of those convicted of political crimes.

Major Political Organizations

Syria's most important political organization, the Arab Ba'th Socialist Party (*Hizb al-Ba'th al-'Arabi al-Ishtiraki*), was founded in the early 1940s by a trio of ardent Arab nationalists: Michel 'Aflaq, Salah al-Din Bitar and Zaki Arsuzi. The party grew out of an earlier grouping, called the Arab Resurrection (*al-Ba'th al-'Arabi*), that had been formed by Arsuzi in Damascus in 1940. Angered by 'Aflaq and Bitar's appropriation of the earlier organization's name, Arsuzi disbanded the Arab Resurrection in 1944. Meanwhile, the newer party led by 'Aflaq and Bitar began to pick up steam, attracting two of Arsuzi's most prominent disciples, Sami al-Jundi and 'Abd al-Halim Qaddur, as well as winning the support of younger reformers such as Akram al-Hawrani and Jamal al-Atasi.

By the time Syria gained its independence in May 1946, the Ba'th had set up local branches throughout the country. 'Aflaq and Bitar traveled to Latakia at the beginning of 1947 in an attempt to persuade Arsuzi to join them in forming a unified national organization. These discussions led directly to the convening of an inaugural congress of the Ba'th Party in Damascus that April. The congress elected 'Aflaq as head of the party and selected Bitar, Jalal al-Sayyid (from the northeastern province of Dayr al-Zur), and one of Arsuzi's colleagues, Wahib al-Ghanim, to serve as a governing council. These four leaders supervised the publication of a party newspaper, *al-Ba'th*, and authorized the establishment of official district branches in Syria's larger cities and towns.

Government efforts to restrict the activities of radical organizations prevented the Ba'th from winning any seats in Syria's first National Assembly elections in July 1947. But as mainstream parties fragmented along regional lines over the next two years, Ba'thi activists stepped up their criticism of the 'feudalists, reactionaries and exploiters' who dominated the post-independence political order. Such attacks prompted President Shukri al-Quwwatli to close down many of the party's offices and order the arrest of 'Aflaq in the fall of 1948. Nevertheless, the Ba'th Party leadership's consistent demands for comprehensive political-economic reform continued to attract new members from all sectors of Syrian society. This theme even played a role in motivating Colonel Husni al-Za'im to overthrow the country's elected government in March 1949.

During the weeks following the 1949 coup, the Ba'th Party joined the peasants' movement led by Akram al-Hawrani in expressing guarded approval for the economic and social reform policies adopted by the al-Za'im regime, on the grounds that such measures would prepare Syrian society for the long-awaited revolution. It was not long, however, until the party's demands for greater freedom of expression began to grate on the new president, and in mid-June al-Za'im ordered the arrest of the Ba'thi leadership. After al-Za'im was overthrown in August 1949, the Ba'th initiated talks with the liberal People's Party to put together a combined list of candidates for the revived parliament. When the discussions collapsed, Ba'thi leaders made overtures to al-Hawrani's newly-established Arab Socialist Party. These negotiations bore fruit, and in February 1953 the two parties formally merged to form the Arab Ba'th Socialist Party.

Reinvigorated by an influx of supporters from the Arab Socialist Party, and gaining popular support for its unwavering commitment to a nonaligned foreign policy, the Ba'th became more and more influential in Syrian politics as the 1950s passed. Paradoxically, the party exerted considerably less influence over the comparatively radical governments of 1956-57, which drew their strength from the Ba'th's primary leftist rivals, the Syrian Communist Party and the independent socialist Khalid al-'Azm. Confronted with the rising power of these competitors, the Ba'thi leadership took the initiative in persuading Syrian and Egyptian officials to create the United Arab Republic in February 1958.

Egypt's President Gamal 'Abd al-Nasir proved to be no more palatable a partner than had Syria's indigenous radicals, so the Ba'th Party reversed course and joined the forces that orchestrated the dissolution of the United Arab Republic in September 1961. Military officers sympathetic to the party seized control of the central administration following a coup d'état in March 1963; the next year, militant Ba'thi cadres in the north-central cities began sequestering private enterprises and turning them over to workers. These actions set the stage for a series of nationalizations over the course of 1965-66, which culminated in a February 1966 coup that brought a radical Ba'thi leadership to power in Damascus. The new leadership steadily increased state control over the local economy, while forging closer ties to both the Syrian Communist Party and the Soviet Union. The 1966-70 period also saw the consolidation of party control over the country's trade unions, student and youth organizations, farm laborers' union and women's federation, each of which became a virtual subsidiary of the Ba'th. Intramural struggles that pitted the radical wing of the party against a relatively pragmatic faction led by Minister of Defense Hafiz al-Asad ended with the latter's taking power in November 1970.

Ba'thi doctrine has been most authoritatively codified in the party's major theoretical statement (*Ba'd al-Muntalaqat al-Nadriyyah*), which was drafted by Michel 'Aflaq for the Sixth National (Pan-Arab) Congress held in Damascus in October 1963. This statement introduced the party's longstanding slogan: 'Unity, Freedom and Socialism' (*Wahdah, Hurriyyah wa Ishtirakiyyah*). Steps to promote effective unity among the existing Arab states were thus accorded highest priority among the Ba'th's stated objectives. The party's concept of freedom appears to be largely derived from the political philosophy of Jean-Jacques Rousseau: it bears little resemblance to liberal-democratic precepts, evidencing little tolerance either for individual liberties or for representative governance. The third objective, socialism, has proven to be the most elastic of all. During 1963-66, it signalled the party's commitment to a mixed economic program that included not only measures designed to redistribute property and income but also state support for 'non-exploitative' private enterprise; from 1966 to 1970, a more radical notion of socialism that entailed public ownership and comprehensive state planning predominated. With the advent of the al-Asad regime in 1970, economic doctrine shifted once again to promote the reintroduction of private ownership. The very flexibility of Ba'thi ideology thus provided a touchstone for the disparate leaders that have governed Syria in the party's name in the years since 1963.

Dissident offshoots of the Ba'th Party have been subjected to systematic harassment and repression by the state security services. Among these is the Democratic Socialist Arab Ba'th Party (*Hizb al-Ba'th al-Dimuqrati al-Ishtiraki al-'Arabi*), whose membership consists primarily of former Ba'this loyal to Salah Jadid, the leader of the radical regime that ran the country from 1966 to 1970 (Lobmeyer, 1994, p. 85). Located equally beyond the pale are the Revolutionary Workers' Party, a grouping of ex-Ba'th Party radicals founded by the former Ba'thi ideologue Yasin al-Hafiz, and a dissident faction of the Arab Socialist Union led by one of the Ba'th Party's early supporters, Jamal al-Atasi (Lobmeyer, 1994, p. 164).

Standing opposed to the Ba'th has been a heterogeneous collection of Islamist organizations. Most of these groups are offshoots of the Egypt-based Society of the Muslim Brethren, which gradually took root in Syria when religious scholars and students returned from Egypt during the late 1930s and 1940s and set up local benevolent societies (*jama'iyyat*) to carry out the Muslim Brethren's program of social and moral improvement. The jama'iyyat put pressure on the authorities in Damascus to provide assistance to Palestinian Arabs during the 1936 rebellion, and then orchestrated a series of mass demonstrations against French-sponsored reforms in Syria's educational system during the Second World War. As the war drew to a close, the jama'iyyat banded together to form a national organization, and in the summer of 1946 nominated Mustafa al-Siba'i of Homs to be general director (*al-Muraqib al-'Amm*) of a Syrian branch of the Muslim Brethren (*Ikhwan al-Muslimin*). The association set up headquarters in Damascus and established a close working relationship with the Egyptian Muslim Brethren, led by Hasan al-Banna.

Syria's Muslim Brethren played an active part in local-level politics throughout the late 1940s and early 1950s, when it vied with the Ba'th Party and the Syrian Communist Party for popular support. General Director al-Siba'i consistently refused to characterize the organization as a political party, referring to it instead as a 'spirit that permeates the very being of the community.' In accordance with this conception, the leadership declined to sponsor candidates in successive parliamentary election campaigns. Nevertheless, the Muslim Brethren did form a short-lived Islamic Socialist Front at the end of 1949 to block an attempt by the People's Party to federate Syria and Iraq. Eight years later, the organization vehemently but unsuccessfully opposed Syria's union with Egypt, whose government had crushed the Egyptian Muslim Brethren in 1953-54. The Syrian Muslim Brethren's inability to prevent the creation of the United Arab Republic convinced the organization's leadership to take a more active part in political affairs, and it authorized a series of popular demonstrations against the regime during 1963-64. In the wake of these protests, al-Siba'i's successor as general director, 'Isam al-'Attar, was deported to Germany.

As the 1960s went by, the Muslim Brethren gradually split into a quietist wing clustered around the senior leadership in Damascus and a more militant wing based in Syria's north-central cities. Northern activists, led by Marwan Hadid of Hamah province, organized themselves into clandestine cells (*usrahs*) consisting of a dozen or so activists. These cells orchestrated a succession of anti-Ba'th Party uprisings in Aleppo, Hamah, Homs and Idlib in 1968-69. Sometime in the early 1970s, they coalesced to form an association called the Fighting Vanguard (*al-Tali'ah al-Muqatilah*), and gained the endorsement of one of Syria's most prominent Islamist ideologues, Sa'id Hawwa. The campaign of armed struggle against the Ba'thi regime precipitated a leadership crisis inside the Muslim Brethren, which eventuated in the division of the organization into two distinct entities. The northern branch escalated its campaign of assassination and sabotage against the government throughout the 1970s, culminating in a virtual civil war that rocked the north-central cities in the spring of 1980. Following the forcible suppression of the rebellion by the armed forces and security services, several surviving fragments of the Muslim Brethren formed an Islamic Front in Syria (*al-Jabhah al-Islamiyyah fi Suriyyah*). In October 1980, the front elected Shaikh Muhammad Abu al-Nasr al-Bayanuni of Aleppo to be its secretary-general (*al-Amin al-'Amm*). That November, it published a comprehensive manifesto that called for the overthrow of the Ba'thi regime and its replacement with a liberal-democratic political system, which would be firmly rooted in the principles of Islam.

Continuing operations against the Islamic Front by the security forces in 1981-82 heightened the level of anti-regime sentiment in the cities and towns of the north-central provinces. The front's leadership repeatedly advised the inhabitants of these districts not to resist the security services, lest such resistance provide the authorities with a pretext for obliterating the Muslim Brethren and its sympathizers. When a large-scale rebellion nevertheless erupted in Hamah in February 1982, Islamic Front militants took an active part in the fighting. Armed Islamist fighters fought off the Syrian army's efforts to dislodge them from the city for almost three weeks, but eventually succombed to indiscriminate artillery and air bombardment that reduced whole neighborhoods to rubble. Meanwhile, appeals by al-Bayanuni and Hawwa for a general uprising against the al-Asad regime went largely unheeded by the Muslim Brethren's supporters in Damascus and Aleppo.

After the Hamah rebellion was quashed, the Islamic Front's leadership-in-exile joined forces with liberal and socialist opponents of the Ba'th Party to set up a National Alliance for the Liberation of Syria (*al-Tahaluf al-Watani li-Tahrir Suriya*). This step was strongly condemned by militants led by 'Adnan 'Uqlah of the Fighting Vanguard, who vowed to carry on the armed struggle against the Ba'th inside Syria itself. In response, the leaders of the Islamic Front expelled 'Uqlah from the organization and appointed Hawwa as commander of the front's paramilitary units. In January 1985, 'Uqlah finally surrendered to the authorities under the terms of a general amnesty, bringing to an end overt political activity on the part of Syria's Muslim Brethren.

More ambiguous has been the relationship between the Ba'th and the Syrian Communist Party (*Hizb al-Shuyu'i al-Suri*). The party was founded in Beirut in 1924 and came under Syrian control eight years later following the election of Khalid Bakhdash to the post of first secretary. It was recognized as a legal entity and authorized to carry out activities inside Syria and Lebanon when the Popular Front came to power in France in 1936. Syrians on the party's central committee finally split with their Lebanese counterparts in July 1944 and set up a separate Syrian Communist Party. The party planned to take part in the parliamentary elections of July 1947, but was prevented from doing so when President Shukri al-Quwwatli banned all radical organizations. Popular support for the party was further undermined by Bakhdash's persistent ties to the French Communist Party, as well as by the Soviet Union's decision to support the creation of a Jewish state in Palestine in November 1947. These developments convinced the central committee to formally disband the party in January 1948.

Communist activists re-emerged during 1953-54 as part of the opposition to the military regime of Colonel Adib Shishakli. Following Shishakli's ouster, Bakhdash attempted to build alliances with both the Ba'th Party and the independent socialist Khalid al-'Azm, but failed to overcome the deep-seated anti-communist predispositions shared by these two actors. Party members campaigned in the parliamentary elections of September 1954, but were forced to run as independents, since the newly-installed civilian government maintained the ban on the organization that had been imposed during the era of military rule. In the end, the party succeeded in winning only a single seat in the National Assembly, which was occupied by Bakhdash.

Beginning in early 1955, the Syrian Communist Party started to gain influence once again. In fact, the steady rise in popular support for the party throughout the decade contributed significantly to the Ba'th Party's decision to pursue union with Egypt in 1958. Bakhdash himself decamped to eastern Europe as soon as the United Arab Republic was formed. Those party cadres who remained in Syria soon found themselves imprisoned, and kept in custody until well after the dissolution of the union in September 1961. The party started to revive when Prime Minister al-'Azm at last revoked the legal prohibition against autonomous political parties in the fall of 1962, but quickly fell out with the military leadership that seized control of the country in March 1963.

Party officials openly applauded the nationalization program that was implemented by the Ba'thi regime in January 1965. Communist sympathizers emerged victorious from the comparatively free trade union elections that were held later that same year. As a result, prominent members and allies of the Syrian Communist Party were offered key cabinet posts in the wake of the February 1966 coup d'état that put the radical wing of the Ba'th Party in control of Syria's central administration. The central committee of the party launched a concerted campaign to augment the size and influence of the Syrian Communist Party in February 1968. But at the Regional (Syrian) Congress of the Ba'th convened in Damascus that October, simmering discontent over the rising level of communist involvement at all levels of the government came to a boil in the form of a lengthy diatribe directed against Prime Minister Yusuf Zu'ayyin by the minister of defense, Major General Hafiz al-Asad. The cabinet reshuffle that took place at the end of the congress substituted comparatively compliant apparatchiks for the outspoken ministers who had played such an important role in previous governments.

When the radical wing of the Ba'th Party was overthrown in November 1970, the al-Asad regime invited the Syrian Communist Party to join the Ba'th-dominated National Progressive Front (*al-Jabhah al-Wataniyyah al-Taqaddumiyyah*). Participation in the front was enthusiastically encouraged by officials in Moscow, who saw collaboration with the new regime as a step toward consolidating socialism in Syria. Under the auspices of the National Progressive Front, the party fielded candidates for successive elections to the People's Assembly, winning six seats in the elections of 1977 and eight in 1986.

Factions opposed to Khalid Bakhdash's leadership regularly split off from the Syrian Communist Party during the 1970s and 1980s. Bakhdash's longtime rival Riyad al-Turk headed one of these breakaway groups, which adopted the name Syrian Communist Party Political Bureau (*al-Hizb al-Shuyu'i al-Suri al-Maktab al-Siyassi*); after al-Turk was imprisoned in 1980, this party issued a series of strongly-worded manifestos but engaged in virtually no political activity. In 1980 the maverick communist Yusuf Faisal declared himself head of another breakaway organization, originally known as the Base Organization (*Munazzamah al-Tasis*). Throughout the

1990s, international human rights monitors protested the drastic measures taken by the security forces to root out such clandestine splinter groups as the Union for Communist Struggle (*Ittihad al-Nidal al-Shuyu'i*) and the Party for Communist Action (*Hizb al-'Amal al-Shuyu'i*), which drew its early cadres from Syria's minority 'Alawi and Isma'ili communities.

Following the 1991 Gulf war, marginal communist organizations associated with an umbrella National Democratic Gathering (*al-Tajammu' al-Watani al-Dimuqrati*) began to issue communiques calling for the establishment of a liberal-democratic political order in Syria (Lobmeyer 1994, p. 88). This fundamental ideological shift provided a basis for co-operation with dissident Ba'thi and Islamist groups, resulting in an unprecedented degree of unity among anti-regime activists. Opposition pronouncements have generally emphasized the injustices that have resulted from the perpetual state of emergency and the excesses practiced by the state security services (Lobmeyer, 1994, p. 93). But they have also tended to be, in the words of Hans Gunter Lobmeyer (1994, 95), 'highly abstract and sometimes even purely theoretical.' Consequently, even though such communiques 'deal with problems that may stimulate the interest of academics, and the slogans may sound revolutionary, ...none of this affects the ordinary Syrian who tries hard to surmount the difficulties of everyday life and who is tired of political slogans.'

Somewhat less abstruse were the activities of an indigenous human rights organization founded in early December 1989. This organization, known as the Committees for the Defense of Democratic Freedoms and Human Rights in Syria (*Lijan al-Difa' 'an al-Hurriyyat al-Dimuqratiyyah wa Huquq al-Insan fi Suriya*), drew most of its initial adherents from the ranks of the state-affiliated lawyers' syndicate, whose members have a history of questioning the legality of government policy in general and the state of emergency in particular (Picard, 1994). On 8 March 1990, the organization issued a manifesto demanding an end to the 27-year-old state of emergency. In addition, several members signed one of two open letters that circulated in the country toward the end of 1990, 'sharply criticizing the allied attack on Iraq and thus indirectly accusing the Syrian regime of participating in what one communique considered a 'criminal war'' (Lobmeyer, 1994, 95). The authorities immediately detained a number of those individuals who had signed the letters, as well as virtually the entire leadership of the human rights organization. The latter remained imprisoned seven years after the war.

The People's Assembly

Shortly after coming to power, the al-Asad regime convened an appointed parliamentary body, the People's Assembly, and charged it with drafting a permanent constitution to supersede the provisional ones that had been promulgated by previous Ba'thi leaders in 1964 and 1969. Delegates to the assembly were selected by the president and his closest advisers to represent the Ba'th and the four parties whose programs most closely mirrored its own: the Arab Socialist Union (*Hizb al-Ittihad al-Ishtiraki al-'Arabi*), the Socialist Unionists' Movement (*Harakah al-Wahdawiyyin al-Ishtirakiyyin*), the Arab Socialists' Movement (*Harakah al-Ishtirakiyyin al-'Arab*) and the Syrian Communist Party. A small number of independents was also included among the assembly, along with representatives of the country's trade union federation and other popular front organizations. In March 1973 the assembly submitted a draft constitution for presidential approval, and it was subsequently ratified by plebiscite.

The 1973 constitution vests primary authority in the president, who enjoys a seven-year term of office. The president must be nominated by the Ba'th Party leadership, approved by the People's Assembly and confirmed by an absolute majority of eligible voters in a national referendum. After being confirmed in office, the president is empowered to appoint one or more vice presidents, as well as a prime minister and other members of a council of ministers that enjoys the right to promulgate laws. The president is also authorized to dissolve the People's Assembly and assume its legislative functions until it is reconvened, to call for national plebiscites to approve measures not ratified by the assembly, to nominate judges for the high courts and to appoint provincial governors. The People's Assembly is granted the right to veto or amend presidential decrees by a two-thirds vote, but this provision has remained dormant in practice. In fact, for the first two decades of its existence, the People's Assembly served at best as a sounding board for policies being considered by the council of ministers, and at worst as a rubber stamp for initiatives put forward by the president and council of ministers.

Parliamentary elections in May 1990 signalled a subtle shift in the role of the People's Assembly in Syrian politics. Ba'th Party candidates still won some 137 of the 250 seats contested, while other parties in the Ba'th-dominated Progressive National Front captured another 31. But the number of independent representatives who won seats in the assembly rose to 82 from a previous total of 35 (out of of 195) (Perthes, 1992, p. 16). Among the independents were a prominent Islamic television commentator from Damascus, four other religious notables from Aleppo and Idlib, several tribal leaders—including the son of the leader of the 1925 rebellion in Jabal Druze—and an influential but heterogeneous collection of wealthy merchants and successful entrepreneurs (Perthes, 1992, p. 17). Besides allocating patronage among their supporters, the new delegates set out to 'use parliament as a forum to call for economic reform and liberalization, presenting themselves as the people who know how to run economic affairs, and probably—in the long run at least—claiming that private sector representatives should also share political responsibility' (Perthes, 1992, p. 18).

During its four-year term, the assembly that was elected in 1990 debated a variety of pressing economic and social issues. In April 1992, for instance, leftist Ba'thi and communist delegates expressed their displeasure over the government's draft annual budget. At the same time, representatives of the Ba'th Party-affiliated workers' and farm laborers' federations criticized planned reductions in social spending and the generally low tax rates levied on private enterprise (*Middle East Economic Digest* [*MEED*], 8 May 1992). Eberhard Kienle (1997, p. 199) notes that 'on several occasions during its four-year term the Assembly even used its right to pass a vote of no confidence in individual ministers leading to their resignation.' The unprecedented activism of the 1990-94 assembly prompted the local press to dub it 'the session of opening' (*ahd al-infitah*) (Zisser, 1997, 18).

By the time of the August 1994 elections, the number of candidates for positions in the People's Assembly had dropped from around 9000 to just over 7400. Nevertheless, competition for many seats increased sharply, a trend that was particularly evident in electoral districts surrounding Aleppo, where some 1200 candidates contested 52 openings (Zisser, 1997, p. 11). Campaigning among rival lists of independents often proved heated, even though independent candidates were not permitted to run directly against those representing parties inside the Progressive National Front. In the end, 83 independents emerged victorious from the balloting, virtually the same proportion of total assembly delegates as four years before. As Kienle (1997, p. 200) has observed, 'While the arrangements governing the 1994 elections failed to extend participation beyond the limits set in 1990, they nonetheless confirmed and consolidated the policy of restricted liberalisation; more would have been surprising at a moment when the regime had to make critical decisions concerning its negotiations with Israel.'

Trends Toward Popular Initiative in Politics

Evidence of heightened popular political initiative in Syrian politics appeared in three different arenas as the 1990s opened. First, elections to the governing councils of the country's semi-autonomous chambers of commerce became increasingly contested. Campaigning for the December 1992 elections to the Damascus council got underway some two months before the vote was to be taken, and the local media devoted considerable attention to the platforms and statements of the various candidates involved. Three years later, the campaign in the capital proved even more animated (Kienle, 1997, p. 200). One prominent venture capitalist published an open letter to the chamber's members detailing a platform that called for the immediate creation of a stock exchange, the implementation of a unified exchange rate and substantial reductions in taxes levied on private enterprise, as well as for the abrogation of the laws that prohibited the operations of private and foreign banks inside the country (*MEED*, 22 November 1996). This candidate somewhat surprisingly won a seat on the council.

Second, Syria's workers' and farm laborers' federations expressed growing discontent over the regime's efforts to encourage private enterprise and implement market-based economic reforms. Grumbling among the rank-and-file of the farm laborers' federation heightened in August 1992, after Prime Minister Mahmud al-Zu'bi announced that the government planned to increase support for export-oriented projects in the private agricultural sector (Lawson, 1996, p. 148). More important, the General Federation of Workers' Unions compiled a lengthy list of grievances concerning the adverse impact of economic liberalization in preparation for its December 1992 congress. An influential faction within the federation even proposed to sever the organization's longstanding connections to the Ba'th, so that workers' demands could be presented to the authorities outside existing channels. This proposal was in the end not introduced for discussion on the floor of the congress, but was subsequently taken up by the People's Assembly (Kienle, 1997, p. 202).

Third, nonviolent political demonstrations occurred sporadically. A small group of women gathered in front of the presidential palace in December 1989 to demand an accounting of the country's political prisoners. The following February a somewhat larger crowd, made up of 'as many as 100 women, from several Syrian cities and various political orientations, assembled in front of the Presidential Palace and asked to see Asad.' According to Middle East Watch, 'When officials denied their request, the women refused to disperse and some cried out in protest. Police then violently broke up the demonstration, and three women had to be taken to the hospital with injuries' (Human Rights Watch, 1991, pp. 505-506). Two years later, during the course of the 1990-91 Gulf crisis, there were persistent reports of a series of popular demonstrations in support of Iraq in the eastern town of Al Bu Kamal. Such demonstrations were quelled after the Syrian government opted to co-operate with Egypt and Saudi Arabia in pushing the Iraqi armed forces out of Kuwait.

Prospects for Liberal Democracy

Most observers of contemporary Syria presume that the prospects for the emergence of a liberal-democratic political order brightened during the 1990s, partly as a result of the unexpected collapse of the al-Asad regime's primary external patron, the Soviet Union, and partly due to the government's continuing commitment to economic liberalization. The most nuanced statement of this position is offered by Eberhard Kienle (1997, p. 209), who argues that the conjunction of these two factors prompted the leadership in Damascus to loosen its grip on the People's Assembly, the chambers of commerce and other avenues of popular participation 'in order to reward, please, and even functionally associate [itself with] the private sector which played such an important role in and after the economic crisis of the mid-1980s.' The regime's decision to expand political participation, he emphasizes, represents a deliberate exercise in 'coalition-building from above, not one of pluralistic politics of pressure groups from below' (Kienle, 1997, p. 211). At the same time, it is only the most privileged and best-connected of Syria's private capitalists and entrepreneurs who are likely to enjoy the fruits of 'enhanced political participation and a greater respect for civil and human rights.' Those who find themselves in a position to take advantage of any further steps toward political liberalization can be expected to 'have little interest in sharing their benefits with society at large. Even if they overcome their present divisions and fears and develop into something like a bourgeoisie,' Kienle (1997, p. 212) concludes, 'they will hardly become the defenders of liberal political values as such.'

In a similar vein, Raymond Hinnebusch claims that the policies implemented during the Ba'thi era have worked to offset the historic imbalance between state and society that pervaded Syrian politics before 1963. Thanks to the economic and social reforms adopted by successive Ba'thi regimes, literacy rates have jumped, the distribution of wealth has become substantially less skewed in favor of the rich and contact between the countryside and urban centers has increased. At the same time, membership in professional associations and in informal housing and transportation co-operatives has soared, increasing the weight of these 'ostensible networks of civil society' (Hinnebusch, 1995, p. 229). More recently, the country's revitalized bourgeoisie has started to chip away at the underpinnings of the military elite that has controlled the party-state apparatus: 'The bourgeoisie is now ...accorded growing access to decision makers. Asad has explicitly approved greater political 'pluralism' (*ta'addudiyyah*) in which the regime will take account of the views and interests of the bourgeois elements in the more complex social coalition it is putting together. Thus, the populist dominated corporatist system has been opened to the bourgeoisie' (Hinnebusch, 1995, pp. 233-234). So far, Hinnebusch (1995, p. 235) asserts, powerful private interests remain deferential to the authorities, but if further economic deregulation were to push workers and farm laborers out of their longstanding alliance with the state, then it is quite possible that they would join forces with 'the bourgeoisie in a cross-class liberalizing alliance with the potential to advance pluralization.'

Others are less optimistic that economic liberalization will provide a basis for political liberalization. Elizabeth Picard (1994, p. 223) notes that the spectacular prosperity that Syria's commercial elite enjoyed during the early 1990s came about not so much as a result of the workings of the market as it did from monopolies granted to their companies by state officials. Meanwhile, high rates of population growth and stagnant employment opportunities threaten to generate a 'social crisis,' which might prompt representatives of the workers' and farm laborers' federations to exercise their leverage inside the People's Assembly to launch a democratic counterattack against further deregulation of the economy, but is more likely to precipitate a fundamentally anti-democratic outcome. Persistent communal tensions, the marginalization of important sectors of the local population and the state's overriding interest in preserving the public sector combine to militate against the emergence of a liberal-democratic order any time soon (Picard, 1994, p. 225). Moreover, the wave of political violence that swept across the country during the early 1980s convinced most Syrians that they are better off avoiding politics altogether and going about their daily lives in peace (Picard, 1994, p. 230).

In fact, the prospects for liberal democracy in Syria may be even dimmer than Picard allows. To borrow terminology proposed by Valerie Bunce, Syrian politics continue to be characterized by uncertain procedures combined with certain results. The great majority of candidates for the People's Assembly is still nominated through a process that can best be called 'informal, irregular and secret' (Bunce, 1991, p. 149). At the same time, the outcomes of parliamentary elections are clear even before voting occurs: not only are specific numbers of seats reserved for the Ba'th, for the other parties that make up the National Progressive Front and for independents, but the composition of the independent component of the assembly appears to be meticulously worked out in advance (Picard, 1994, p. 149). Liberal-democratic governance is predicated upon precisely the opposite conditions: certainty regarding procedures and uncertainty about outcomes. Establishing a liberal-democratic order in Syria would require not simply incremental reforms, but a complete transformation of the status quo.

Even steps that might be interpreted as conducive to political liberalization remain plagued by uncertainty regarding the procedures whereby they have been adopted. In November 1995, for instance, President al-Asad marked the silver anniversary of his taking power by issuing Decree Number 18, which granted an amnesty to individuals imprisoned for engaging in nonviolent opposition to the regime (Amnesty International, 1996, pp. 288-9). The decree was immediately ratified by the People's Assembly, and led to the release of some 1500 prisoners by the end of the year. A second wave of detainees was freed in March 1996. The majority of those released consisted of members and supporters of the Muslim Brethren; others were dissident members of the lawyers', physicians' and engineers' syndicates who had taken part in a one-day general strike in 1980 (Amnesty International, 1996, p. 289). Although the amnesty was undoubtedly beneficial to those released, it did little to alter the fundamental character of Syrian politics. The fact that the presidential decree was promulgated by fiat underscores the power of the regime, reinforcing what Bunce (1991, p. 149) aptly calls 'the Party's security and the insecurity of others.'

To make matters even more complicated, the al-Asad regime finds itself squarely in the middle of what Perthes (1994) has termed Syria's second *infitah*. By encouraging the expansion of private enterprise and the development of an unregulated market, state officials have heightened the degree of uncertainty concerning economic outcomes, but without institutionalizing regular procedures to govern the operation of the domestic economy. On the contrary, further liberalization threatens to fragment the national market by facilitating the emergence of discrete local economies scattered throughout the country (Lawson, 1997, p. 12). The regime has attempted to stabilize the increasingly anarchic domestic marketplace by maintaining strict control over the financial sector. Under these circumstances, there is little incentive for government to risk throwing Syrian society into total chaos by opening up the political arena as well.

Conclusion

Despite Syria's lengthy history of competition among organized political parties, as well as its abbreviated experience with parliamentary politics during the 1940s and 1950s, individual liberties and liberal-democratic procedures have virtually no place in the either the principles or the practices that structure the country's political order as the 1990s draw to a close. This is partly due to the Ba'th Party's longstanding conception of democracy as a transformative, collectivist enterprise, rather than a system of governance designed to guarantee the rights of individuals. It is also one of the legacies of two decades of armed struggle between the Ba'th and the Islamist movement, which culminated in a virtual civil war at the beginning of the 1980s. In addition, deep-seated suspicion of, and intolerance for, liberal-democratic institutions reflects the historic symbiosis between the party and a secretive group of military commanders that laid the foundation for the succession of Ba'thi regimes that have governed the country in the years since 1963 (Rabinovich, 1972).

What happens when President al-Asad at last exits the scene is anyone's guess. However, perhaps in an attempt to prevent a recurrence of the overt jockeying that erupted among Syria's most powerful military commanders when the president fell ill in 1984 (Drysdale, 1985), several key officers have been relieved of their posts and replaced by individuals with experience administering civilian agencies (*MEED*, 26 August and 4 November 1994). More important, the president has consistently refused to designate a successor. When he was asked in a November 1992 television interview how Syria's next leader would be determined, al-Asad replied that the country had a constitution which set down a clear procedure for nominating and confirming the president. Neither of these straws in the wind signals the imminent approach of a liberal-democratic order, but the steadily increasing role accorded to regular administrative procedures at least opens the possibility that Syria will be able to avoid having to choose between dictatorship and chaos in the post-Asad era.

References

Amnesty International (1996) *The 1996 Report on Human Rights Around the World.* New York.
Bunce, Valerie (1991) Democracy, Stalinism and the Management of Uncertainty. In Gyorgy Szoboszlai (ed.) *Democracy and Political Transformation.* Budapest: Hungarian Political Science Association.
Drysdale, Alasdair (1985) 'The Succession Question in Syria,' *The Middle East Journal* 39 (Spring): 246-257.

Heydemann, Steven (1991) 'Can We Get There From Here? Lessons from the Syrian Case.' *American-Arab Affairs* no. 36 (Spring): 27-30.

Hinnebusch, Raymond A. (1995) State, Civil Society and Political Change in Syria. In Augustus Richard Norton (ed.) *Civil Society in the Middle East*. Leiden: Brill.

Human Rights Watch (1991) *World Report 1990*. New York: Human Rights Watch.

Kienle, Eberhard (ed.), (1997) Authoritarianism Liberalised: Syria and the Arab East after the Cold War. In William Hale and Eberhard Kienle (eds.), *After the Cold War*. London: I. B. Tauris.

Kienle, Eberhard (1994) *Contemporary Syria: Liberalization Between Cold War and Cold Peace*. London: British Academic Press.

Lawson, Fred H. (1997) 'Private Capital and the State in Contemporary Syria,' *Middle East Report* no. 203 (Spring): 8-13.

Lawson, Fred H. (1996) *Why Syria Goes to War*. Ithaca, N. Y.: Cornell University Press.

Lawson, Fred H. (1994) Syria. In Frank Tachau, ed. *Political Parties of the Middle East and North Africa*. Westport, Conn.: Greenwood.

Lobmeyer, Hans Gunter (1994) *Al-dimuqratiyya hiyya al-hall?* The Syrian Opposition at the End of the Asad Era. In Kinele, Eberhard (ed.), (1994) *Contemporary Syria: Liberalization Between Cold War and Cold Peace*. London: British Academic Press.

Middle East Economic Digest. Various issues.

Perthes, Volker (1994) Stages of Economic and Political Liberalization. In Kienle, Eberhard (ed.), (1994) *Contemporary Syria: Liberalization Between Cold War and Cold Peace*. London: British Academic Press.

Perthes, Volker (1992) 'Syria's Parliamentary Elections,' *Middle East Report* no. 174 (January-Feruary): 15-18.

Picard, Elizabeth (1994) 'Infitah Economique et Transition Democratique en Syrie.' In Riccardo Bocco and Mohammed-Rez Djalili (eds.), *Moyen-Orient: Migrations, Democratisation, Mediations*. Geneva: Graduate Institute for International Studies.

Rabinovich, Itamar (1972) *Syria under the Ba'th, 1963-66*. New York: Halsted Press.

Zisser, Eyal (1997) 'Syria--Exercising Democracy?: Elections to the People's Assembly, August 1994.' Paper presented at the annual meeting of the Middle East Studies Association, San Francisco, California.

5 Jordan

MICHAEL R. FISCHBACH

Introduction

Jordan's recent experiment in democratization and respect for human rights is often cited as one of the most unique in the Arab Middle East. Indeed, the return of political parties and a more open political climate in the early 1990s has changed the face of Jordanian politics considerably. Yet this has not merely come about as a result of a change of heart on the part of Jordan's long-ruling monarch, King Husayn bin Talal. Jordan's internal political scene has long reflected both a domestic 'opposition' pushing for greater rights and the relentless pressure of external events that have buffeted the country and affected its politics.

The path of democracy in Jordan during the past decade started out with great fanfare and excitement. More recently, popular enthusiasm has waned as the limits of the regime's commitment to the process have been made apparent. As in the past, the future success or failure of Jordanian democracy will depend both upon the resilience of domestic forces committed to expanding democratization and to the ability of the country to maintain a democratic trend in the face of exogenous constraints. Yet the final arbiter will be democracy's ability to serve the populace's interests.

Historical Background to Democratization and Human Rights in Jordan

The Hashemite Kingdom of Jordan is characterized by a long tradition of powerful monarchical authority punctuated by periods of relatively liberal political freedoms judging by Middle Eastern standards. While retaining a high degree of power in the hands of the monarch, the Jordanian system has been at the forefront of democratization and political liberalization in the Arab world since the late 1980s. The roots of Jordan's current experiment in liberalization and democratization can be traced to two main historical factors: the long-standing presence of an indigenous 'opposition' struggling against an authoritarian regime and Jordan's intimate connection with the Palestinian problem.

Both of these factors were the result of the creation of Jordan by Britain following the First World War. British authorities constituted the Emirate (Amirate) of Transjordan in April 1921 as part of Britain's 'mandate' for Palestine, thus tying the new entity not only to Britain but to the growing conflict between Zionist Jews and Palestinian Arabs in neighboring Palestine as well. Rather than governing Transjordan directly, the British established Amir (Prince) `Abdullah bin Husayn of the Hashemite family of Mecca as ruler and granted him considerable domestic power while retaining overall control of the country's financial and security matters.

Democracy served the interests neither of `Abdullah nor the British. A formal arrangement delineating governmental structure in Transjordan emerged in 1928, when `Abdullah and the British reached agreement on a Basic Law that granted the Amir and his executive council (cabinet) both executive and legislative authority. It also created a weak legislative council that could not propose legislation, but could be summarily dismissed by the Amir. The first legislative council elections were held in February 1929.

The institutional curbs on democratic government agreed upon by both `Abdullah and the British spawned the growth of an opposition within and outside the legislative council that called for greater democratization and reduced British interference in Transjordan. Yet `Abdullah maintained his power throughout the period of the mandate (1921-46) and beyond. Following independence in 1946, whereupon the country changed its name to the Hashemite Kingdom of Jordan and `Abdullah his title to King, politics continued in the same vein until the tumultuous events of 1948.

Both the monarchy and the opposition were irrevocably affected by the first Arab-Israeli war of 1948 and the Palestinian problem that ensued. During the fighting, Jordan ended up controlling that portion of Palestine later known as the West Bank and formally annexed it in 1950. The state of war with Israel that continued after 1948, the wider anti-Israeli and anti-Western feelings that developed in the Arab world in the 1950s, and the presence of large numbers of new Palestinian citizens both in Jordan proper (the East Bank) and in the West Bank, subjected Jordanian politics to new forces and constraints illustrated by `Abdullah's assassination at the hands of a Palestinian in July 1951. Native East Bank proponents of greater democratization were emboldened in their oppositional stance by Palestinians angered by `Abdullah's moderate stance toward Israel, while the wider anti-Western, Arab nationalist attitudes that emerged in the 1950s, affected the opposition by aligning it with the pan-Arab and anti-Western Egyptian leader Jamal `Abd al-Nasir.

The twin forces of an opposition calling for increased democracy and the passions unleashed by Arab-Israeli conflict, and the growing polarization of the Arab world into pro and anti-Western nations led to a tumultuous period of politics in the 1950s, the echoes of which still reverberate in Jordan today. The opposition benefitted from constitutional changes in 1952 and 1954 approved by `Abdullah's successor and his son Talal. These changes made the cabinet responsible to parliament for the first time. King Talal's teenage son Husayn assumed the throne in 1953, following his father's deposition for health reasons, only to be confronted by a vibrant opposition that openly supported Nasir and other regime rivals. The opposition succeeded in forming a government under Prime Minister Sulayman al-Nabulsi in 1956 during an era of relatively free elections based on the 1952 constitution. Bolstered by Anglo-American support and loyal units in his military, Husayn moved against the opposition by foiling an attempted coup d'état in April 1957, dismissing Nabulsi's government, banning political parties, and declaring martial law. Aspects of this repression remained in place until the early 1990s.

The Palestinian problem, the Arab-Israeli conflict and the regime's hostility to a return of the democratic era of the 1950s continued to affect politics in Jordan well into the 1990s. Parliamentary elections were held in 1962, but parties were still illegal. Following Israel's occupation of the West Bank in 1967, Jordan's parliament did not meet until 1984 since half its deputies represented the West Bank and were under Israeli occupation. As Palestinian nationalism began to grow in the 1960s, and the Jordanian army fought a bitter domestic war with Palestinian guerrillas in 1970 and 1971, the question of how integrated were the Palestinians into Jordan's political system became a significant issue. The mid-1980s saw Jordan make major concessions to the claims of the Palestine Liberation Organization (PLO) to represent West Bank Palestinians, Jordan also decided to forge a joint negotiating team with the PLO in the event of Arab-Israeli peace talks.

By 1988, King Husayn decided to concede PLO preeminence in any future diplomatic moves aimed at an Israeli withdrawal from the West Bank. This decision was the beginning of Jordan's march toward democratization. In July 1988, Jordan announced it was severing administrative ties to the West Bank. Since one half of the Jordanian parliament represented the West Bank, parliament was dissolved and plans made to hold new elections for an all-East Bank body. Although parties were still banned, those elections marked the beginning of a sea change in Jordanian politics.

Democratization in the 1990s

King Husayn initiated a wide series of political reforms in response to the disengagement from the West Bank and to the serious disturbances in April 1989 among the regime's traditional East Bank supporters in central and southern Jordan. Riots broke out following the government's decision to abide by an International Monetary Fund austerity program. Significantly, the demonstrators not only called for the resignation of the government of Prime Minister Zayd al-Rifa`i, but also for expansion of democratic freedoms in Jordan. Rifa`i was replaced and the stage set for reform.

The three most important changes initiated by the regime in 1989 bode well for democratic reform in Jordan. They included the return of legal political parties vying for votes in parliamentary elections, the lifting of aspects of emergency rule and martial law left over from earlier periods, and the creation of a more open political atmosphere. The return to party politics actually began after the groundbreaking parliamentary elections of November 1989. Those elections, the first complete parliamentary elections since 1962, took place in an atmosphere of great expectation. Scheduled after the king dissolved parliament following the severing of administrative ties with the West Bank in July 1988, and prior to the April 1989 disturbances, the elections were seen as one of the first major tests of the king's new political changes. While regarded as free elections, the polling for the parliament's 80-member chamber of representatives was conducted among individual candidates, since parties were still illegal. Election in Jordan is by universal adult (19 years of age) suffrage.

The stunning victory of candidates associated with the Society of the Muslim Brotherhood, which as a legally-chartered 'society' and not a party could campaign openly, offered the regime the first of many challenges it would face on the road to democratization. The Brotherhood captured 22 of the 80 seats in the lower house of parliament, the House of Representatives. Eight seats were won by independent Islamist candidates. The 40 members of the House of Notables were appointed by the king as stipulated in the constitution. The Brotherhood, and no longer the leftist, pan-Arab, or Palestinian organizations of the 1950s-1970s, would thereafter constitute the core of a new anti- regime opposition. The regime's response to this opposition would later constitute a significant roadblock on the road to full democratization.

The legalization of parties began following the signing of the National Charter in 1991. The Charter represented the king's attempt to establish a broad framework for political life outside of the constitution, and was drafted by a 60-person royal commission appointed by the king in April 1990 and representing various political persuasions. Upon issuance of the

Charter in June 1991, King Husayn emphasized that while political parties could henceforth be established, they must be uniquely Jordanian parties and must function responsibly within a democratic atmosphere. Parties began forming thereafter according to the 1992 Law on Political Parties and fielded candidates for the November 1993 parliamentary elections. According to law, parties were required to obtain a license from the ministry of the interior and to meet a number of criteria that promoted the regime's policy against 'foreign-oriented' parties. These included having a minimum of 50 founding members possessing Jordanian citizenship for at least ten years, agreeing to uphold the constitution and Jordan's independence, and having no organizational or financial links outside Jordan. These requirements were clearly designed to prevent the establishment of parties tied to Palestinian or other foreign Arab organizations, leftist parties advocating an internationalist position, and pan-Arab or pan-Islamist parties articulating merging Jordan within some wider Arab or Islamic order. The memory of an opposition aided and abetted by foreign Arab powers in the 1950s was clearly still on the king's mind. Thus the restrictions were designed to guarantee the formation only of 'Jordanian' parties willing to work within a purely Jordanian context.

Between 1993-1996, 26 parties, representing a number of different political views, were licensed. The most significant party to emerge was the Islamic Action Front Party (IAFP), technically an independent front, but in fact a party associated with the Muslim Brotherhood. Three different parties advocating the principles of the pan-Arab Ba`th (Renaissance) Party emerged, as did parties from underground groups formerly associated with such Palestinian resistance groups as the Popular Front for the Liberation of Palestine and the Democratic Front for the Liberation of Palestine. Leftist parties, like the Jordanian Communist Party, non-ideological parties that represented narrow interests, and pro-regime parties, such as the National Constitutional Party, also emerged.

An early test of just how far the regime was willing to move toward democratization came in late 1992 when the ministry of interior rejected the licensing applications of the Jordanian Communist Party (JCP), the Jordanian Democratic People's Party (known by the Arabic acronym HASHD), and the Jordanian Arab Socialist Ba`th Party (JASBP). The JCP had been the leading leftist underground party since the 1950s; HASHD emerged from an underground group associated with the Democratic Front for the Liberation of Palestine; while JASBP extended allegiance to the Iraqi wing of the Ba`th Party. The government initially claimed the three parties' ideologies violated the stipulations set forth in the political parties law. The government later reversed itself and granted them licenses. The episode revealed the ongoing hostility of the regime toward certain political trends.

While parties continued to form in the mid-1990s, the king and the government soon expressed dissatisfaction with certain aspects of party politics. The regime complained about the plethora of parties on the Jordanian political scene, noting that many expressed the same viewpoints. This coincided with a wave of party consolidations that began around 1995 much to the regime's satisfaction. Eight parties coalesced into the pro-regime National Constitutional Party in 1997 and two new, consolidated leftist parties—the Jordanian Nationalist Democratic Front and the Jordanian Unionist Democratic Party—created in 1997 and 1995, respectively.

More serious was the regime's fear of the growing power of the Islamist movement and of the Islamic Action Front Party in particular. The Jordanian electoral system contained provisions that had long worked to the advantage of pro-regime constituencies as well as against the regime. For example, special seats in parliament are allocated to religious and ethnic minorities: Christians and the Circassian and Chechen communities (descendants of Ottoman-era immigrants from the Caucasus mountains). These groups traditionally support the regime. Additionally, electoral districts for parliamentary elections were drawn so as to give a disproportionally high number of seats to poor, rural regions outside the capital Amman where the regime traditionally found some of its most loyal East Bank supporters. By contrast, the poor districts of East Amman, heavily populated by Palestinians, and the upper-middle class districts of West Amman that were home to many liberals in the opposition, received fewer electoral seats than some of the aforementioned rural districts despite their considerably greater population. On the other hand, the regime was hurt in 1989 by the fact that voters could cast as many ballots as there were representatives from their district; a person voting in a district where there were four seats, for example, could cast four ballots. This worked to the advantage of the Muslim Brotherhood in 1989, because voters could 'vote their conscience' and still have votes left over for others (such as a candidate fielded by their tribe, a Christian ally of the Muslim Brotherhood, etc.) (Amawi, 1994, p. 17).

In a move that clearly indicated the regime's concern over a repeat of the Brotherhood's 1989 victory, King Husayn changed the election law in August 1993 in advance of the November parliamentary elections. First the king dissolved parliament, then he decreed amendments to the election law. The new amendments created a system of 'one person, one vote'. The government anticipated that with their votes now limited to one, citizens would most likely vote in a 'tribal' way for someone representing their family rather than 'vote their conscience' in an ideological way. The move worked: the Islamic Action Front Party garnered only 16 seats in the elections, compared with 22 captured by the Muslim Brotherhood in 1989. The 'one person, one vote' formula would later feature large in the Islamist candidates' grievances that provoked their decision to boycott the 1997 elections (see below).

The 1993 changes in the election law demonstrated that the regime maintains significant control over the political process in Jordan. The prime minister and the cabinet are appointed by the king, who is not obliged to select ministers from parliament. To be sure, the cabinet and its overall political program technically must be ratified by the House of Representatives within one month of the cabinet's formation. And legislative authority remains constitutionally shared both by king and parliament, which has the ability to override a royal veto of legislation. Yet the king remains the leading arbiter of Jordanian politics.

A second major feature of the regime's move toward democratization was ending martial law and emergency rule. These laws had coexisted alongside regular civil law for decades, and had granted the authorities considerable latitude in curbing political freedoms and due process. Martial law, which was declared in June 1967 and which created the special military Martial Law Court, was suspended in December 1989 at the outset of the new reforms. It was finally repealed in April 1992. That same month the regime lifted the state of emergency technically still in place since the onset of the Second World War in 1939. Declaration of a state of emergency was based upon the 1935 Defense Law.

While martial law and the state of emergency were lifted, their reimposition is still allowed under the Jordanian constitution, and a new type of military court was in fact established during the period of liberalization. The 1935 Defense Law was replaced by a new Defense Law in March 1992. This law grants the king the power to declare a state of emergency if national security or public safety are threatened. Such a state of emergency can last indefinitely. The law grants the government the power to place persons in administrative detention and restrict movement and assembly. Similarly, article 125 of the constitution still allows the cabinet and the king the power to declare martial law if emergency law is deemed 'insufficient for the defense of the kingdom'. Lastly, a new military State Security Court was created in 1991 to take the place of the old Martial Law Court. This new court came into existence on the basis of the 1959 Law on the State Security Court. Like that of its predecessor, verdicts of the State Security Court were initially not subject to appeal. The king vetoed a 1991 attempt to amend the 1959 law to allow for such appeals.

However, he eventually approved such an amendment in 1993. Consequently, the court's decisions can now be appealed.

The State Security Court began considering cases almost immediately. One of the first noteworthy cases involved eight men whom the government alleged belonged to the underground Liberation Party and plotted to assassinate King Husayn during his visit to al-Mu'ta University. The State Security Court and not civilian courts still regularly hears political cases dealing with 'security' in the broadest internal and external sense. It is an extraordinary court created by the prime minister. Its procedures were liberalized somewhat in 1993, when death sentences and lengthy sentences were referred automatically to the Court of Cassation.

The specter of special states of emergency, emergency laws, and martial law continues to haunt Jordan's future. The National Charter recommended making future cabinet decisions regarding the reimposition of either martial law or a state of emergency subject to parliamentary approval, but this has still not occurred. The Charter also called for unifying overlapping measures relating to these types of extraordinary rule.

The third aspect of democratization in Jordan since the 1980s has been a more relaxed political atmosphere. Beginning in 1989, the regime carried out a number of changes which have revitalized free speech, association, movement, and debate. Political exiles were allowed to return, passports confiscated from those accused of political opposition to the regime were returned, and a number of political prisoners released. Additionally, the 1953 Law on Resistance to Communism was repealed in February 1992.

One of the most visible and widely-debated aspects of this new atmosphere has been the emergence of a free press. While there is no official state newspaper in Jordan, the government influences the press through its partial control of major publishing companies. The government controls 47 per cent of the company that publishes one of the two leading Arabic-language daily newspapers, al-Ra'i, and 32 per cent of the firm that publishes the other, al-Dustur. Beyond this, journalists and editors have traditionally exercised a considerable degree of self-censorship to avoid problems with the authorities. Jordan's television and radio stations are government stations, and their importance in the regime's eyes is indicated by the fact that the broadcasting station in Amman is guarded not by the police, but by the Royal Guards unit of the army.

The era of greater political freedom has seen the establishment of numerous private publications and greater media debate, although the regime has made clear its impatience with the free-wheeling pace of press freedoms. Among the publications that have emerged in the 1990s are papers associated with political parties or trends and weekly tabloids which were quite open in their attacks on corruption among public officials.

Several tabloids contained stories on social scandals and carried biting cartoon commentaries as well. In May 1993, parliament passed a new Law on Press and Publications to regulate the Jordanian press. Human rights activists decried the Law's provisions, which included requiring journalists to join the Jordanian Press Association and newspapers to obtain an official publishing license. Other provisions limit the content of what can be published and offer vague guidelines for free speech. Such provisions include a prohibition on publishing anything 'offensive' about the king or the royal family (also a crime under other statutes), anything that might endanger 'national unity', or 'personal insult(s)' directed at heads of states on friendly terms with the government. Moreover, the Law prohibits articles that offend 'public morals', that show contempt for any religion recognized by the constitution, that provide information on the military, or injure an individual's reputation. Violators faced prison sentences if convicted.

Official frustration with the stories that began appearing in the Jordanian press as journalists began reaching beyond the traditional standards of self-censorship was almost immediately made manifest. Several journalists were prosecuted under the Law on Press and Publications and other laws such as the Penal Code. Charges included defamation of parliament and the State Security Court. Journalists face prosecution not only in civil courts, but in the new State Security Court as well. In 1997, two were tried by the State Security Court for violating press restrictions. Between 1993 and 1997, the government brought some 60 cases of alleged violation of various press laws to court. The vast majority of these were against weekly publications, including the tabloids that so irked the regime and many ordinary citizens as well with their sensational stories about society and politics. Most cases resulted in acquittals.

The degree to which the regime's frustration with the press continued to grow became apparent in 1997 as parliamentary elections approached and as popular disenchantment with the government's generally warm embrace of Israel mounted. As the regime changed the election law in advance of the 1993 parliamentary elections, so too did it act to change the Law on Press and Publications prior to the 1997 elections. The king issued a royal decree in May 1997 that amended the 1993 Law on Press and Publications in several significant ways. While abolishing prison terms for violations, the amendments raised the fines for those convicted of breaking the press law from a maximum of 6,000 Jordanian dinars (JD) to a maximum of JD25,000 (and a minimum of JD15,000). Beyond that, the amendments increased the amount of capital a publication must possess in order to be licensed drastically. The capital requirements for daily newspapers rose from JD50,000 to JD600,000, and those of other publications from JD15,000 to JD300,000. The new capital must be raised within three months. Editors are required to have at least ten years' job experience. Lastly, the amendments canceled the requirement, found in the 1993 law, that the government reduce its shareholdings in the two major daily papers. This last move guaranteed that the government would retain its financial interest in those papers.

Reaction to the amendments was swift and angry. The heads of all of the country's professional organizations resigned, except, ironically, for the Jordanian Press Association. A protest held outside the prime ministry was broken up by police, and several persons were injured.

The provisions remained in force, and the government brought ten legal cases against papers for violating the new amendments. The first judgment was issued in September 1997, when the weekly al-Bilad was fined JD15,000 for publishing information about the security forces. The paper claimed that it ran the story about Jordan handing over a Palestinian to Israeli authorities based on a press release issued by Agence France Presse, and also claimed that the paper's management was never even informed about the charge against it until the court issued its judgment (Jordan Times 1997d).

Taken together, the regime's moves toward greater democratization since 1989 were quite breathtaking. The national mood from 1989-91 in particular was electric as numerous changes in the political climate were made. Jordan by the early 1990s enjoyed a reputation for stable democratic development, although the regime's moves to curb the press and the Islamist opposition revealed the limits to its tolerance.

Human Rights in Jordan Since Democratization

What can be said about the overall situation regarding human rights in Jordan? Human rights are respected in Jordan to a much higher degree than in surrounding countries in the region, and the era of democratization has included an increased awareness of the importance of human rights in Jordanian society. The government subscribes to several international human rights conventions, including the International Covenant on Civil and Political Rights, the International Covenant on Economic, Social and Cultural Rights, the Convention on the Rights of the Child, and the Convention Against Torture and Other Cruel, Inhuman or Degrading Treatment or Punishment. The National Covenant calls for respect for the United Nations Universal Declaration of Human Rights, which Jordan has signed. Beyond this, the king commissioned the creation of the Center for Studies on Freedom, Democracy and Human Rights in the Arab World.

Several human rights organizations exist within Jordan which press the government to abide by international human rights standards. These are a chapter of Amnesty International, a chapter of the Arab Organization for Human Rights (AOHR), the Jordanian Society for Human Rights, the Jordanian Human Rights Organization, and the Peace Center for Humanitarian Studies. The AOHR has been particularly active in monitoring allegations of human rights abuses, and has issued annual reports detailing Jordan's human rights record. It has also issued an October 1996 'emergency report' dealing with the August 1996 riots. It also assisted in the Daqamisa trial (see below).

Human rights activists press for real safeguards for human rights in Jordan. One area of concern has been how political detainees are treated while in government custody. Allegations of ill-treatment of detainees have continued even into the era of democratization. In the two years after January 1992 alone, the government detained over 800 suspects for reasons of security (Amnesty International 1994a, p.9). These persons were held in detention not by the Public Security Directorate (national police), but the General Intelligence Directorate (known in Arabic as the *Mukhabarat*). A civilian agency established in 1964, the Mukhabarat is headed by a military officer and reports directly to the prime minister and the king. The Mukhabarat has earned a feared reputation over the years, particularly for its ill-treatment of detainees. Its influence extends far beyond internal and external security since it also issues 'good conduct' papers for employment, residency permits, and other such documents for ordinary citizens. Mukhabarat informants, sometimes recruited under duress, report on the political activities of Jordanian students at home and abroad.

The Mukhabarat can still detain suspects indefinitely and incommunicado under the Code of Criminal Procedure. Even lawyers can be and have been denied access to suspects. Detention can be extended for 15 day periods by a public prosecutor. Mukhabarat officials can act as public prosecutors and thus can extend the period of detention themselves. Twenty-five men arrested for allegedly trying to detonate bombs and overthrow the government in 1994 were held incommunicado for up to six months (the case was referred to as the 'Afghans case', because some of the men had received military training while serving with the anti-Soviet Islamic resistance in Afghanistan). Most of the 800 detainees during the 1992-94 time period referred to above were released without formal charges being brought against them.

Torture has long been alleged to occur while suspects are held in Mukhabarat detention. This has included both physical and psychological torture. In 1992, the Mukhabarat instituted a system of regular medical examinations of detainees conducted by its own doctors. It does not allow independent examination of detainees. As in regular prisons, the Mukhabarat allows visits by representatives of the International Committee of the Red Cross. The Mukhabarat is not alone in facing charges of ill-treatment; a man arrested by the Public Security Directorate in December 1996 died while in custody after rough treatment.

More recently, the Mukhabarat has tried to change its image to fit the era of democratization and human rights. It moved from its former imposing building in Amman (known as the 'Palestinian hotel' given the large numbers of Palestinian political activists who had been detained there over the years) to a new, less visible facility on the western outskirts of the city. In 1996, the Mukhabarat also became the first Arab intelligence agency to establish a web site on the internet. The slick site offers information about the agency, Jordan, links to other Jordanian sites, even the Mukhabarat's address, telephone, and fax numbers. Yet some Jordanians claim that the Mukhabarat became even more active in spying on citizens during the era of democratization than before.

The judiciary's readiness to intervene in cases of Mukhabarat torture was demonstrated in two high-profile security cases in March 1995. Illustrating the degree to which the civil judiciary maintains its independence from the government, the Court of Cassation reversed the January 1994 convictions by the State Security Court of ten persons in the Liberation Party/al-Mu'tah University case discussed above. Three men had been sentenced to death. The defendants had appealed against the verdict to the Court claiming that their confessions had been secured by Mukhabarat torture. In March 1995 the Court of Cassation overturned the December 1994 conviction of 18 men convicted by the State Security Court in the 'Afghans case'. The Court also overturned a June 1995 death sentence returned by the regular criminal court because the only real evidence in the case, the defendants' confessions, was allegedly obtained following their ill-treatment.

The rising number of executions in Jordan since the onset of democratization has worried some foreign human rights organizations such as Amnesty International, even though execution is a common practice regionally. The number of persons executed has risen from four in 1990, to seven in 1991, and 12 in 1993 (Amnesty International 1994b, p. 9). Ten persons were executed in 1996. Persons have been sentenced to death by a variety of courts, including regular courts, martial law courts, and the State Security Court. Crimes have ranged from spying to selling land to Israelis (most of these sentences were in absentia) to simple murder. It is worth stating, however, that most persons executed in recent years were convicted of murder, not political crimes. Additionally, legal due process has generally been followed in these cases and some capital sentences were even commuted by royal decree.

Press freedom and freedom of speech continue to be some of the main testing grounds for the limits of human rights in Jordan. Journalists who have been accused of insulting the king or royal family have even been tried before the State Security Court. A celebrated case in 1996 involved a well-known Islamist politician, Layth Shubaylat, who criticized government policy. Shubaylat had earlier incurred the government's wrath in 1992 when as a parliamentarian he had been at the forefront of a probe into corruption. He and another Islamist were arrested on charges of possessing weapons and attempting to overthrow the government, charges that many believed were unfounded. He was sentenced to death in October 1992, but was pardoned by the king within days and released. Shubaylat was convicted a second time by the State Security Court in March 1996, this time for allegedly slandering King Husayn in a statement he had made following the king's attendance at the funeral of Israeli Prime Minister Yitzhak Rabin in November 1995. The court sentenced him to three years imprisonment, but he was once again pardoned by the king, in November 1996.

The May 1997 amendments to the Law on Press and Publications were bitterly denounced by both journalists and human rights activists, including foreign organizations such as Human Rights Watch, the Committee to Protect Journalists, and Article 19. In September 1997, the government detained Ibrahim Ghawsha, local spokesperson for the Palestinian organization Hamas, for two weeks following remarks he made in the wake of a Hamas suicide bombing in Jerusalem. Government security forces prevented activists from the Arab Organization for Human Rights from visiting Ghawsha's family during his incareration.

Another aspect of human rights in Jordan concerns the rights of women and children. Both official and unofficial social discrimination against women is common in Jordan. Jordanian society generally considers a woman's welfare to be the responsibility of either her husband or her male relatives. Her ability to function independently in society or receive equal economic rights suffer as a result. Several barriers confront women in the workplace. The government's social security benefits are higher for men than for women, and government pensions are paid to the family of a deceased male civil servant but not to the family of a deceased female civil servant. In terms of official status, Jordanian mothers cannot pass along Jordanian citizenship to children born to non-Jordanian husbands. A woman also needs her husband's permission to apply for a passport. Lastly, the Islamic courts that deal with personal status issues for the Muslim majority in Jordan do not grant equal credence to a woman's testimony as a man's, nor do Islamic inheritance laws recognize gender equality.

A situation that has begun receiving attention is that of violence against women. The reported cases of rape in Jordan is low in comparison to Western societies. In 1991, the number of rape cases per 100,000 citizens in Jordan was 0.5, compared to 37.6 in the U.S. and 15.7 in Sweden (Jordan: Keys to the Kingdom, p. 39). Far more common are acts of domestic violence directed against women: men assaulting wives and daughters, brothers assaulting sisters, and so forth. The government offers to place women threatened with death in protective custody. In addition to rape and domestic abuse, so-called 'honor killings' take place in Jordan. In such instances, a male relative murders a woman whom he suspects has engaged in some type of illicit sexual behavior that has stained the 'family's honor'. The Public Security Directorate issued a study in September 1997 detailing crimes against women. It indicated that 16 of the 39 murders of women in Jordan in 1996 were 'honor killings' (*Jordan Times* 1997c). The police also claim that such killings have been on the increase in the past two decades. Men who commit such killings are treated more leniently under the law than 'regular' murderers. They receive prison sentences instead of the death penalty and usually serve only about two years. By contrast, women cannot invoke the 'honor killing' defense in killing a male caught in adultery. Recently, attention has also been focused on the problem of violence against female domestic workers from Sri Lanka and the Philippines.

An August 1997 seminar on the security of Jordanian women and children discussed not only crimes against women, but against children as well. Jordan ratified the Convention on the Rights of the Child and forbids the employment of children under the age of 16. Penalties for sexual abuse of children are harsh. Like violence against women, however, child abuse often goes unreported and unpunished.

Workers enjoy a number of official rights according to Jordanian law. The law allows both public and private sector employees to join unions. Unions must be registered by the government and the umbrella organization to which all unions belong, the General Federation of Jordanian Trade Unions, is subsidized by the government, which oversees the election of its officers. Unions cannot strike without government authorization. Consequently, strikes are rare events. Legislation mandates a 48-hour work week for most employees, weekly time off, and minimum wages for specific occupations. Jordan has no overall minimum wage requirement.

Ethnic and religious minorities fare relatively well in Jordan. At some six per cent of the population, Christians are the largest minority group.

Most Christians are Arabs, although Armenians and others are also present. Christians are well represented in society, including government, despite the fact that Islam is the official religion in Jordan. Christians serve in the bureaucracy and military, have seats reserved for them in parliament, and are subject to their own personal status courts (for marriage, divorce, inheritance, etc.) separate from Islamic courts. Some religions are not granted official status by the government, however, and thus cannot register property in their names. These include the Baha'i faith as well as certain Protestant Christian sects. In practice, though, adherents to these faiths face no active interference in worship or daily life. Ethnic minorities similarly face no significant hardships even in a country that prides itself on its Arab heritage. The Circassians and Chechens have in fact occupied a disproportionately large number of high-level political posts, and like Christians, have special seats reserved for them in parliament.

For Palestinians and bedouins origin has affected their political and socio-economic life most profoundly. Many Jordanian citizens and passport holders are of Palestinian origin (Brand 1995). Estimates of the numbers of Palestinians in Jordan have ranged from between some 40 per cent to over 60 per cent of the population. Most of these are refugees from the 1948 and 1967 Arab-Israeli wars and their descendants. Because of the political tensions between the Palestinian national movement and the Jordanian government since the 1960s, the regime has been suspicious of politically-active Palestinians. Palestinians have risen to such top civil positions as prime minister and chief-of-staff of the army. Palestinians are also well represented in the economy, media, and universities. The bedouin, descendants of nomadic and semi-nomadic pastoralist tribes, have been by contrast well represented in the military and security forces and have seats reserved for them in parliament. Until the 1970s, they were subject to special laws as well. Key posts in special security forces like the Mukhabarat, the Public Security Directorate's Desert Police, and special units of the army like the Royal Guards are heavily if not exclusively made up of East Bank Jordanians.

The government has adopted some measures on paper to protect the human rights of the disabled. In March 1993, King Husayn signed the Law for the Welfare of Disabled Persons. This law guarantees the disabled the right to work and bans the practice of denying them life insurance. Additionally, portions of the 1996 Jordanian Labor Law and the National Building Code make reference to the disabled and their accessibility to employment and public buildings. However, the disabled are not seen in public very often. Both social stigma and a lack of concrete governmental measures have hindered significant progess in terms of accessibility.

Wheelchair-bound persons still experience extreme difficulties in negotiating streets and buildings in Jordan.

Into the 21st Century

Jordan's march toward democracy and respect for human rights since the late 1980s has been profound; real change has occurred. Yet the limits on political rights on the eve of the 21st century are illustrated in the government's response to several serious political issues that faced the country in 1996 and 1997.

The first was the severe rioting that broke out in August 1996. On 13 August, the government of Prime Minister `Abd al-Karim al-Kabariti raised the price of bread some 50 per cent overnight in order to cut down on deficit spending and meet austerity targets established by the International Monetary Fund. Since bread is the staple food for poor Jordanians, the doubling of this subsidized item provoked widespread anger among a populace anxious to see the economic 'peace dividend' anticipated in the wake of the 1994 Jordanian-Israeli peace treaty. Demonstrations and the burning of buildings occurred in the the southern cities of al-Karak, al-Tafila, and Ma`an, and even in part of the capital, Amman. Police, the para-military Desert Police, and army troops were called in and a curfew imposed in al-Karak. The king, appearing in uniform and grim-faced, addressed the nation on television and vowed to suppress the rioters with force. He later blamed domestic forces allied with Iraq for instigating the disturbances

The government detained hundreds in the wake of the disturbances, targeting persons associated with the Jordanian Communist Party, the pro-Iraqi Jordanian Arab Ba`th Socialist Party, and the leftist Jordanian Democratic People's Party—the three parties whose formation the government had tried to prevent in 1992. According to official government sources, security and intelligence forces detained 572 persons, of whom 521 were later released (U.S. State Department 1997, p.3). Charges against the remaining were withdrawn following a royal amnesty in November. Some detainees claim that they were tortured while in detention.

The repression continued on other fronts. Attempts by the Islamist and secular opposition to hold a march to protest the rise in food prices were rebuffed by the government. Fourteen journalists were charged with violating various laws while reporting on the disturbances (the state-owned Jordanian Television was not allowed to cover the riots in al-Karak). And while the Arab Organization for Human Rights (AOHR) was granted access to some of the detainees several weeks after the disturbances began, the public freedoms committee of the Jordanian parliament was denied such access until mid-October. The AOHR's annual report on Jordan later stated that the country witnessed 'grave violations' of human rights during 1996 (Star 1997).

A second issue indicating the fragility of Jordan's march toward expanded democratization and human rights was revealed in the government's trial of Ahmad al-Daqamisa, a soldier in the Jordanian army. On 13 March, Daqamisa shot and killed seven Israeli schoolgirls and injured six at an island on the Israeli-Jordanian border frequented by Israeli tourists. He was arrested and interrogated by a military investigatory commission at Mukhabarat headquarters before his case was referred to a military court. Daqamisa's case became a referendum on Jordan's peace treaty with Israel. While King Husayn denounced Daqamisa and publicly asked why his fellow soldiers had not shot him dead during the onslaught, many flocked to Daqamisa's defense not out of sympathy with his deeds but out of frustration with the king's insistence upon normalizing relations with Israel and out of fear that Daqamisa would be denied a fair trial. As with the case of detained Hamas spokesperson Ibrahim Ghawsha (see above), security forces blocked pro-Daqamisa activists from entering the accused's home village to express solidarity with his family. The AOHR, the Jordanian Lawyers Association, and the Islamic Action Front Party all volunteered to form a legal defense team for Daqamisa. Daqamisa was eventually sentenced to life imprisonment in July 1997. The case was clearly one where the government's agenda and that of the opposition were at odds, and one where the government was not above eclipsing certain freedoms to prevent a demonstration of popular sympathy with the killer.

Conclusion

A poll released in June 1997 by the University of Jordan's Centre for Strategic Studies (CSS) revealed that respondents rated Jordan's democracy at a 4.88 on a scale of one to ten, with one representing the beginning of democracy and ten representing full democracy (*Jordan Times* 1997b). These results approximated those collected by the CSS in 1993 and revealed that the public's perceptions had not changed much since then. Respondents also believed that political parties exerted little influence over political decisions, and felt that parliament was not always effective.

The public's scepticism rests upon the perceived failure of this new era to have effected any real change in people's lives. Forces committed to democracy have not been able to alter the fundamental feature of Jordanian political life: the presence of an authoritarian regime that is able to determine just how far democratization and human rights will go. Moreover, the public has not perceived political parties to have had any effect upon the system. Leftist parties have failed to garner significant public support just as support for the Islamist opposition has begun to dwindle. But the 1993 elections demonstrated the continued strength of 'tribalism' in Jordanian politics.

Democracy has similarly not been able to alter the all-important exogenous factors that reverberate inside the Jordanian political system. Jordan's peace treaty with Israel and the country's new political orientation have met with dissatisfaction among many who feel that parliament, parties, professional organizations, and the like are unable to affect the country's foreign policy decisions. Some Jordanians believe the regime will resort to repressive measures to ensure that popular anger against normalization with Israel does not cross a certain threshold. In fact, the civil liberties committee of the Jordanian parliament issued a report in September 1995 noting that the Jordanian- Israeli peace treaty has 'visibly affected the ceiling of public freedoms' in Jordan (Congressional Research Service, 1996, p. 5).

The course of democracy and human rights in Jordan is not merely a function of the regime and international relations, however. The history of Jordanian politics reveals a long tradition of 'opposition' forces trying to carve out a greater degree of democracy. The legacy of these forces has been profound and their ability to influence the future of democratization in the country is at least theoretically strong. Yet their effectiveness has been hampered by several factors. The first of these has long been the regime's ability to coopt opposition figures into the governing process. The king has a long tradition of pardoning political opponents and then appointing them to positions in his government. Beyond this, the opposition has not always been able to transform itself into a significant force on the popular level. The opposition of the 1930s and 1940s were largely intellectuals and leading tribal *shaykhs* whose ideas and agendas were far removed from those of the masses. This was also true of the leftist, pan-Arab, and later Islamist opposition politicians of the 1950s-1990s.

Independent social forces can influence the future course of democracy and human rights in Jordan. Some powerful social institutions in the country, like tribes have once again been coopted by the regime in a most effective manner. King Husayn has promoted himself as the father of a united Jordanian family and the shaykh of a singular Jordanian tribal unit. Social scientists studying the Middle East have recently focused much attention upon the role that social elements like unions, professional organizations, and other expressions of socio-political independence can play in deepening democratization and 'wrest(ing) expressional and operational "territory"' (Brand 1995b, p. 152) from the state. Even here, though, business leaders, unions, professional organizations, and journalists have long found their independent spheres of action subject to considerable governmental influence.

There is no doubt that the state of democratization and human rights in Jordan in 1997 is better than any time since the mid-1950s. It is also clear that this trend has not emerged simply because of royal fiat, to be curbed by future royal whim. Opposition parties and an emerging civil society can strengthen the course of democratization. Yet the continued success of this democratic experiment will ultimately depend upon its ability to 'work' for ordinary citizens in tangible ways.

References

Amawi, Abla (1994), 'The 1993 Elections in Jordan', *Arab Studies Quarterly* Vol. 16, No. 3, pp. 15-27.

Amnesty International (1994a), *Jordan. Human Rights Reforms: Achievements and Obstacles*, Amnesty International: London.

_____(1994b), *Jordan. Executions on the Rise*, Amnesty International: London.

_____(1995), *Jordan. Legal Safeguards Needed to Eradicate Torture*, Amnesty International: London.

Brand, Laurie A. (1995a), 'Palestinians and Jordanians: A Crisis of Identity', *Journal of Palestine Studies* Vol. 24, No. 4, pp. 46-51.

_____ (1995b), '"In the Beginning was the State...": the Quest for Civil Society in Jordan', in Norton, Augustus Richard (ed.) *Civil Society in the Middle East*, E.J. Brill: Leiden, New York, Cologne.

Jordan. Keys to the Kingdom (1995), Jordan Media Group: Amman.

The Jordan Times (Amman) (1997a), 'Press and Publications Law Boasts Stiffer Penalties on Newspapers and Journalists'.

_____ (1997b), 'Jordanians Rate Democracy at Middle of Road, Losing Faith in Press: Poll,' 5-6 June.

_____ (1997c), 'Crimes Against Women, Children Highlighted by Police Report,' 2 Sept.

_____ (1997d), 'First Paper Convicted Under New Press Law,' 4-5 Sept.

Library of Congress, Congressional Research Service (1996), *Jordan: U.S. Relations and Bilateral Issues*. CRS Issue Brief, Library of Congress: Washington.

The Star (Amman) (1997), 'Human Rights Activists Call on Government to Close Bread Riots Chapter', 27 Feb.

United States Department of State (1997), *Jordan Country Report on Human Rights Practices for 1996*, Washington, D.C.

6 Egypt: Human Rights and Governance

MAMOUN FANDY AND DANA HEARN

In 1952, the Egyptian Revolution dramatically cast aside centuries of foreign domination and established a popular revolutionary republic. Riding the crest of this wave of change, Gamal Abd' al-Nasser projected his charismatic, proudly independent presence throughout the Arab world. His disruption of elite hegemony, implementation of socialist reforms, embrace of pan-Arabism, and non-aligned foreign policy won the support of the masses in Egypt and other Arab states who hoped for humane politics and greater political participation. Beneath this idealistic image, however, less than ideal means were employed to safeguard the new regime's hold on power. Both accommodative and coercive tactics were used to neutralize opponents; the latter tactics severely tarnished the state's human rights record. Anwar Sadat assumed power following Nasser's death in 1970 and was credited with moving Egypt away from Nasser's socialist legacy toward more liberal economic policies and a multiparty system. When critical voices began targeting Sadat himself, he cracked down on his opposition and jailed thousands of intellectuals and activists. The alienation and anger this generated among the populace was dramatically revealed in 1981, when he was assassinated by Islamist opponents. His successor and the current president, Hosni Mubarak, proceeded cautiously during his first term, wary of the fate of his predecessor. As the following report reveals, however, Egypt's human rights record remains far from satisfactory. Nominal guarantees and lofty ideals aside, formal structures and informal practices uphold a framework of repression.

A Political Framework

Because the examination of Egypt's human rights record tends to gravitate towards state-centered analysis, an overview of formal political arrangements provides an appropriate starting point. While these highly visible, clearly defined arrangements provide only one part of the human rights story, they are nonetheless a central feature of the political context in which it unfolds. Nominally a multi-party democracy based on the division of executive, legislative, and judicial power, the political system is designed to incorporate Western models of governance along with Islamic principles. The permanent constitution, issued in 1971 and amended in 1980, establishes the basic framework of this system, delineates citizens' rights, and defines the role and jurisdiction of state authorities. It declares the Arab Republic of Egypt a 'democratic, socialist State based on the alliance of the working forces of the people,' designates Islam as the state religion and Islamic jurisprudence as the main source of legislation, and identifies the populace as the central 'source of authority' (Egyptian Constitution, Art. 1-3). Although these lofty, abstract ideals have limited bearing on actual political arrangements, they underlay the ideological and organizational narrative of the state.

The executive branch, headed by the President of the Republic, is the official nexus of political, coercive, and economic power. According to constitutional provisions, the president must be nominated within the legislative People's Assembly and then win majority approval in a national plebiscite. There are no restrictions against re-election. A single presidential term lasts for six years, theoretically allowing Egyptians to reevaluate their support for the president based on his performance in office. The president is constitutionally bound by the rule of the law and separation of executive, legislative, and judicial powers. Nominal checks on executive power aside, however, the president enjoys extensive autonomy from other state authorities and the general populace. Aided by his appointed cabinet ministers, he defines and directs domestic and foreign policy, serves as commander-in-chief of the military and police, is chairman of the Judicial Council, and has the authority to dissolve the People's Assembly and call for re-elections.

Occupying an intermediate position between the executive and legislative branches, the Consultative Council, or *Shura*, is an advisory body for the president and People's Assembly. Adopting an Islamic name for this political forum is an attempt by the state to appease its Islamic opponents and to create the illusion of a state faithful to its Muslim tradition. The Council consists of 264 members, two-thirds of whom are elected by popular vote and one-third of whom are appointed by the president. Members serve six year terms and can be reelected or reappointed. Appointed members are central to the expansion of presidential power. The president usually appoints prominent figures who lack popular constituencies and thus remain within the presidential orbit. Theoretically, the president and People's Assembly should seek Council members' opinions regarding domestic and foreign policy issues, proposed constitutional amendments, and socio-economic development plans. In reality, however, the *Shura* Council merely provides further religious legitimization for the policy positions of the executive. It also provides another avenue of controlled political participation.

As the main legislative body and symbolic center of multi-party participation, the People's Assembly (PA) is touted as a link between state and society and a bulwark against unrestrained executive power. Of the 454 members, 444 are directly elected, and ten are appointed by the president. They serve five-year, renewable terms and are responsible for passing legislation, approving the national budget, levying taxes, and approving government programs. Despite these seemingly broad powers, the PA is merely another instrument to be manipulated by the executive branch. Moreover, its membership composition exposes the shallow depths of the multi-party framework. The ruling National Democratic Party (NDP) currently holds 417 seats, while six are occupied by the *Wafd* Party, five by *Al-Tagalmu*, one by the liberal *al-Ahmar* Party, one by the United Nasserite Party, fourteen by independents, and ten by presidential appointees.[1] While the state allows certain opposition groups to participate in the electoral system, it ensures that the NDP retains an overwhelming political and economic advantage. Faced with restraints on free expression and limited access to resources, opposition parties are able to muster little more than a token presence in the People's Assembly. Other opposition groups, such as the Muslim Brotherhood and Islamic Group, lack even token inclusion. Because the state determines which groups constitute legitimate parties, it can cautiously choose its own political competitors.

Finally, the Egyptian Constitution also provides for an independent judicial system based on Islamic, French, Dutch, and English law. The country is partitioned into twenty-six *muhafizats*, or governates, each of which has its own primary and summary tribunals.[2] At the top of the judicial hierarchy, the Supreme Constitutional Court determines the constitutionality of laws and interprets legislation. The constitution likewise establishes State Security Courts, a State Council to rule in administrative disputes, and a Socialist Public Prosecutor charged with safeguarding society's political and economic interests. Article 166 asserts that, 'no authority may intervene in the cases of justice affairs,' and, indeed, the court system enjoys considerable independence relative to the *Shura* Council, PA, and other government institutions.

Not to be outdone, the state can circumvent judicial autonomy by trying opponents in military tribunals. These tribunals exist outside of the regular court system and are not subject to provisions regarding due process, fair trial, and public disclosure of information. Moreover, even in the regular courts, the president may choose not to take judges' rulings seriously. The Higher Administrative Court in Cairo has the authority to rule whether voting irregularities occur in PA elections, but it lacks the power to remove an elected member (*U.S. Dept. of State 1996*). The Constitutional Court declared several PAs null and void due to election violations, yet two continued to function, and one was dissolved only one year before its term was completed. While the judiciary system has thus remained faithful to the rule of the law, its rulings are implemented at the discretion of the state.   As evident from this cursory overview, Egypt's governmental framework is fraught with contradictions.   Despite constitutional assertions to the contrary, the executive branch, and specifically the president, dominate the formal political and economic arenas.   Since this disjuncture between political ideals and actual arrangements is mirrored in Egypt's human rights record, it provides an appropriate prelude to the report which follows.

Egyptian Human Rights: Commitments and Realities

On the surface, Egypt's constitutional guarantees and ratification of international agreements suggest a national commitment to the preservation of human rights. The Egyptian Constitution purports to safeguard the right to freedom and personal safety, the right of assembly, the right to commute, and the right of residence (*Egypt. Org. of Human Rts.* 1996). Moreover, as a ratifying party to the *International Covenant on Civil and Political Rights* and the *International Covenant on Social and Economic Rights*, Egypt is ostensibly bound by a globally recognized, comprehensive human rights framework. Mirrored in the government's official policy positions, these outward commitments appear to safeguard citizens against rights violations.   Even a cursory look beyond these external ideals, however, yields a vastly different image of reality. Formal executive, legislative, and judicial measures as well as informal practices on state and non-state levels go far to undermine the basic principles of human rights.

An overview of Egyptian political history reveals implementation of emergency law as a continual threat to constitutional and international guarantees. Following the Arab defeat in the war of 1967, the Egyptian executive assumed exceptional powers under the precept of national security. Although Sadat lifted emergency law in May 1980, it was quickly restored following his assassination and remains in place at present. Government preoccupation with the preservation of internal order and state-defined national interests thus continues to supercede secondary concerns for human rights. Expansion of executive powers and broad impunity for coercive security apparatuses are at once consequences of this situation and causes behind its perpetuation. As citizens attempt to exercise their political, social, and economic rights, they confront the realities of state censorship, intimidation, and violence. The Egyptian Organization of Human Rights thus claims that authorities have accepted the Emergency Law 'as a second constitution for the country, with all that this entails in terms of allowing the executive to place restrictions on fundamental rights and freedoms'(*Ibid.*).

Aside from the overarching Emergency Law, additional legislative and judicial measures also undermine constitutional and international guarantees. Amendments to existing legislation have circumscribed freedom of the press and expanded government control over professional associations, political groups, and private mosques. Judicially, military courts provide an instrument for implementing state policies without the hassles of due process. Against this restrictive backdrop, the press, professional and student organizations, opposition groups, and individual citizens find their activities closely scrutinized and regulated by the state's executive, legislative, and judicial branches.

Why are such measures necessary from the state's perspective? Faced with economic troubles and challenges to its legitimacy, the Egyptian government seeks to curtail potential threats to its power. Perceived as a central component of such threats, Islamist groups are frequently the target of restrictive and even violent measures. Human rights violations are thus couched within the language of domestic security, wherein the government affects a protective role and purports to defend the country from Islamic radicals. Yet apart from the violent extremism of certain Islamist groups, the state is also averse to more benign expressions of popular discontent. Religious and secular groups alike are subject to institutionalized and informal limitations of human rights. These limitations undermine rights to life, personal safety, and freedom; due process and fair trial; and freedom of expression and peaceful assembly.

The Rights to Life, Personal Safety, and Feedom

Rights to life and personal safety, the most basic of human entitlements, are not unconditionally protected by the Egyptian state. National as well as international human rights organizations have documented increasingly violent government measures to suppress domestic opposition, particularly that linked to Islamist activity. As the state's primary coercive instruments, security apparatuses have thus acquired expanded powers and the ability (or even obligation) to violate human rights with impunity.

In response to escalating attacks by Islamist groups against Christian citizens, policemen, and government officials, the state has sought to violently crush militant activity. The resulting cycle of attack and retaliation has failed to eliminate Islamist opposition, thus driving the government to adopt increasingly repressive tactics. While the state's efforts to prevent extremist violence are arguably directed at defending innocent citizens' rights to life and safety, they have resulted in widespread human rights violations. Indiscriminate use of firearms, arbitrary arrest, torture during detention, and collective punishment threaten the lives and safety of countless citizens who are innocent of anti-state violence.

Because detention by government security forces frequently carries the added threat of physical endangerment, the rights to freedom, life, and personal safety are closely interlinked. Under the Emergency Law, state security forces are granted considerable license to arbitrarily arrest and detain citizens. According to the Egyptian Organization for Human Rights (EOHR), government efforts to stem Islamist activity has often led to illegal detention for long periods, recurrent detention, and continued detention after sentence completion or court-ordered release. State Security Investigation (SSI), the Interior Ministry's main security apparatus, regularly holds suspects incommunicado for days or weeks prior to court proceedings or official imprisonment. If released from prison after sentence completion or by court ruling, detainees are frequently returned to SSI offices. After those held incommunicado by SSI have been released according to official prison records, they are again eligible for arrest and detention. After being held temporarily by SSI, they are thus transferred back to prison. This practice of recurrent detention allows the Interior Ministry to circumvent court-ordered releases and hold political opponents for extended periods.

Because those held by SSI are considered 'disappeared persons' rather than registered detainees, security forces can abuse their rights with impunity. According to Middle East Watch (MEW), this has resulted in systematic, government-sanctioned use of torture during SSI interrogation and detention. While the Interior Ministry categorically denies all such allegations, national and international human rights organizations cite overwhelming evidence to the contrary. MEW, in its various reports on Egypt, has documented numerous cases of torture conducted by SSI officials for the purpose of collecting information, eliciting confessions, and punishing or intimidating those critical of the state. Victims are subjected to various forms of physical and psychological abuse, including beating and kicking, electric shocking, suspension from bound wrists, and threatening family members.

Torture, while technically illegal in Egypt, continues due to a failure to enforce existing laws and international commitments. In terms of national provisions, the Egyptian Constitution prohibits 'any assault on individual freedom,' and the Penal Code mandates hard labor and/or imprisonment for public employees who use torture to elicit confessions. Egypt has also ratified the *Convention Against Torture and Other Forms of Cruel, Inhuman or Degrading Treatment or Punishment.* State security courts have drawn on these laws and commitments to order inquiries into torture allegations and acquit defendants whose confessions were forcefully extracted. Human rights monitors and lawyers have likewise filed numerous reports of torture with Egypt's Justice and Interior Ministries.

In the absence of follow-up action by the state, however, reports and court rulings do not result in tighter enforcement of anti-torture provisions. The Justice Ministry, while officially responsible for investigating torture allegations, adheres closely to the government's policy of denial. Failure of the Prosecutor General to actively investigate complaints is coupled with institutionalized obstacles to proving claims of abuse. Most significantly, torture generally occurs at locations which are not under court or Justice Ministry supervision, such as the Interior Ministry's SSI offices. When reports are filed in prisons, they are slow to reach the Medical Examination Office, allowing time for the physical evidence of torture to fade.

The state's failure to acknowledge mounting evidence of security forces' use of torture has fueled criticism at home and abroad. In response, the Mubarak government has reiterated previous denials, criticized the motivations of human rights organizations, and attempted to discredit the alleged victims. EOHR, Amnesty International, and MEW's efforts to expose state-sanctioned torture were countered by state claims that human rights activists were merely attempting to destabilize the government and tarnish Egypt's international image. Moreover, Egyptians who filed abuse reports were dismissed as violent Islamist extremists undeserving of activists' attention. When the Egyptian Cabinet did address the issue of torture during a 1992 meeting, ministers' central concern was deflecting public allegations rather than investigating their validity.

Given the vast disparity between Egypt's legal framework and actual practice, citizens' rights to life, personal safety, and freedom are far from secure. Threatened by Islamist groups and others critical of its economic or political performance, the state has adopted increasingly coercive measures. Its determination to eliminate all opposition has resulted in arbitrary use of force, indiscriminate arrests, excessive detention policies, and torture. Such practices, while not officially sanctioned by the state, are facilitated by the broad powers granted to security forces, passivity on the part of the Justice Ministry, and emergency legislation. By condoning (or even ordering) these developments, the government places its myopic security interests above general rights to life, personal safety, and freedom.

The Right to Due Process and Fair Trial

The rights of due process and fair trial, like the rights of life, safety, and freedom, are ostensibly protected under Egyptian and international law. Once more, however, practice imperfectly reflects official ideals. The regular court system adheres to the law, guarantees the right of appeal, and serves as an arena for lawyers to freely argue their clients' cases. Increasingly, however, the state has circumvented judicial obstacles to executive autonomy by utilizing military courts and legislation designed to combat terrorism. The primacy of national security, as enshrined under emergency law, offers government officials a detour for bypassing due process and fair trial.

Although Egypt's Law of Criminal Procedure purports to sanctify due process, legislative amendments qualify its application. These amendments authorize officials to hold anyone suspected of terrorist activity in precautionary custody without specific legal grounds for up to six months. Moreover, EOHR cites instances when the length of precautionary custody was illegally extended, thereby violating both the spirit of due process and the letter of the law.

Drawing again on its emergency powers, the state can bring alleged terrorists to trial in military rather than civilian courts. Because defendants are denied the right of appeal, court judges have broad license to disregard the law when issuing rulings and sentences. They thus serve as instruments of executive power rather than as guardians of an independent judiciary. As an early indication of the courts' coercive potential, military judges sentenced thirty-nine Islamist militants to death between December 1992 and November 1993. Use of military trials subsequently expanded; 143 civilian defendants were tried in 1995. While the government defends these measures under the pretext of domestic security, they reflect a more general pattern of combating political opposition via suppression of human rights. As a testament to the dangers of this trend, military courts are increasingly being used to try political opponents not charged with terrorist acts. Moreover, the absence of due process and fair trial sharply curtails citizens' ability to challenge other human rights violations committed by the state.

The Right to Freedom of Expression and Association

While the government justifies suppression of Islamist militancy as part of its obligation to protect society, restrictions on freedom of expression and association reveal state intolerance of even non-militant challenges. Faced with criticism from various angles, the government seeks to limit the public space afforded individuals, secular and religious groupings, and the press. Legislative and executive measures are employed to obstruct channels of political activity, thereby limiting citizens' ability to check state power.

In its efforts to silence opponents and preempt public criticism, the state severely limits citizens' freedom of association. Executive and legislative measures are used once again to justify violations of international and constitutional guarantees, as the government narrowly defines the parameters of peaceful assembly and organization. Within these parameters, religious, political, professional, and academic groups have limited space to express critical positions, direct their own affairs, and participate in the political process.

Given the government's determination to crush Islamist opposition, efforts to restrict freedom of association often target bases of organized Islamist support. These bases not only include unlicenced political organizations and militant groups, but also legalized parties and community spaces such as private mosques. Whereas the state violently confronts illegal and militant groups, it undermines more moderate power bases via legislative restrictions. Leaders and journalists of the Labor Party, a legal party allied with the Muslim Brotherhood, have thus been subject to detention and interrogation in accordance with emergency law and Law 93. Already denied official inclusion within the political system, the Muslim Brotherhood and other unlicenced parties were banned from informal participation in 1992, when the People's Assembly barred political activity by groups that lacked legal status and prohibited political alliances between such groups and legalized political parties. Moreover, government efforts to neutralize organized Islamist support extend beyond the formal political arena, as evidenced by plans to take control of private mosques and regulate topics covered in Friday sermons. The broad scope of these restrictions on freedom of association suggest that the state is increasingly unwilling to differentiate between militant Islamists, moderate Islamic organizations, and Islamic communities.

Although Islamist groups are the foremost targets in the government's campaign to stifle critical opposition, neither professional syndicates nor other non-governmental organizations escape restrictive measures. Under Egypt's Law 32 of 1964, the state has wide discretion to grant or deny private organizations legal status. By refusing to recognize human rights groups and other NGOs as legal organizations, the government undermines their legitimacy and threatens their ability to operate freely. As evidence of this threat, in 1995 the Justice Ministry issued a memorandum advising that all funding sources of unrecognized organizations be severed. Security forces have likewise intervened in the groups' internal affairs, at times preventing them from holding meetings or training courses.

Even legalized institutions such as professional syndicates are not beyond the reach of government control. Alarmed by the growing number of Islamist victories in syndicate elections, Mubarak pushed revised regulations through the People's Assembly in 1993. Since low voter turnout had facilitated past Islamist successes, the new law stipulated that fifty percent of Syndicate General Assembly members must vote in order to validate Syndicate Chief and Syndicate Council elections. Should participation fall short of this requirement, new elections are to be held in which 33 percent of members must vote. If a 33 percent quorum is not met after two elections, a panel of appointed judges and senior members is to administer the syndicate for six months. Amendments to this legislation were adopted in 1995, granting judicial committees the right to oversee syndicate elections, set nomination and election times, and announce election outcomes. While Mubarak asserts that these regulations will prevent a minority from imposing its dictatorship over the majority, most syndicate members oppose government appropriation of their administrative freedoms.

Although the government did make a token gesture of political openness by initiating a dialog with opposition groups in 1994, the talks ended in failure. By prohibiting the Muslim Brotherhood, Islamic Group, and professional syndicates from taking part in this exchange, the state quashed all prospects for meaningful communication and change. The exclusion of these key players led others, such as the liberal *Wafd* Party, to boycott the talks. Even those who did attend criticized the government for dominating the agenda and failing to address the real issues. Reflecting a continuation of the status quo, the empty dialog served only to heighten opposition groups' cynicism. The government refused to abandon its confrontational stance towards Islamists or reconsider the long-term dangers of political exclusion.

In addition to restricting the activities of formal groupings, the state is also intolerant of loosely organized forms of protest. This intolerance was dramatically revealed in 1995, when students at Ein-Shams University held peaceful marches to protest Israel's participation in the Cairo International Fair. After security forces broke up the initial marches, students attempted once more to hold peaceful demonstrations. The security forces then violently intervened and placed many students under arrest. When students in other universities reacted to these events by staging demonstrations of their own, they too were forcefully suppressed.

Regardless of ideological, political, social or functional orientation, formal as well as informal venues of expression and association are thus subject to state restrictions. Emergency law and amendments to existing legislation provide an institutionalized framework for undermining constitutional and international guarantees. The government is once again able to frame its limitation of human rights in the language of domestic security and stability.

While these limitations undeniably tarnish Egypt's human rights record, they should not be equated with complete suppression of freedom of expression and association. As of 1991, 13,521 associations were registered with the Egyptian Ministry of Social Affairs (Al-Sayyid, 1995). In addition, Egypt has twenty-three trade unions, twenty-six chambers of commerce, and twenty-three professional associations (*Ibid.*). The Center for Human Rights Legal Aid, an organization which provides legal assistance to members of Islamist groups, is recognized as a corporation and thus bypasses the licensing requirements of private associations (*U.S. Dept. of State Rpt. 1997*). Mosques and churches, while not officially registered with the Ministry of Social Affairs, nonetheless serve as venues for political and social activities. Moreover, certain organizations which lack government recognition continue to operate openly. The Arab Organization for Human Rights, the Egyptian Organization for Human Rights, and Amnesty International's local branch have been unsuccessful in their ongoing efforts to obtain private licenses. Nonetheless, all three groups exercise significant freedom in carrying out their activities and leveling criticism against the state. The US Department of State (1997, p. 1242) goes as far as to claim that 'the EOHR and other human rights groups sometimes enjoy the cooperation of government officials. The Government allows EOHR field workers to visit prisons, to call on some government officials, and to receive funding from foreign human rights organizations.' While freedom of expression and association is by no means unbounded in Egypt, the number and scope of non-governmental organizations dispels notions of complete suppression and points to a gradual widening of political space.

Freedom of the Press

Although freedom of the press is closely linked to freedom of expression and association, it warrants special attention as an indicator of the state's wider efforts to constrain human rights, limit popular participation, and avoid accountability and transparency. A free press is capable of exposing and questioning government actions within a public arena and could thus undermine the Egyptian state's control and ideological credit. To stem this potential threat, Nasser and Sadat both imposed restraints on journalistic freedom. Despite his supporters' claims to the contrary, Mubarak has preserved the repressive legacy of his predecessors and erected new barriers to freedom of the press. Nonetheless, recent developments reveal a selective opening of political space.

Historical Backdrop: The Press under Nasser and Sadat

A cursory overview of the Nasser and Sadat eras reveals a history of state control over the media. In an effort to silence their opponents, both leaders imposed laws which prevented the emergence of a free press and created institutions to ensure their enforcement. Prior to the 1952 Revolution, most Egyptian newspapers were controlled by foreign families. During the early years of Nasser's rule, four of the six major papers were shut down, and the regime established its own publishing house, daily newspaper, and biweekly military magazine. Because the regime's newspaper, *Gomhoria*, and magazine, *al-Tahreer*, were heavily subsidized, the voice of the state dominated the national press. These early limitations on journalistic freedoms were expanded following the nationalization of the Suez Canal and the tripartite attack in 1956. In 1960, new press laws placed the National Union (NU) in charge of licensing all newspapers and awarded it ownership rights over all major publications. These powers, in addition to the authority to choose newspapers' boards of directors, were later transferred to the Arab Socialist Union (ASU). In order to further consolidate its control over the press, the regime established a new censorship office within the Interior Ministry and created the Ministry of Information.

Upon assuming power, Sadat touted his commitment to political and economic liberalization. Rhetoric aside, the new opening was limited to those who supported Sadat's regime and criticized Nasser. Government censorship thus remained in place, and all newspapers were subject to review before going to press. Although Sadat officially abolished this system of prior censorship in 1974, his actions quickly dispelled any illusions of expanded freedom. On the same day as he 'abolished' censorship, he also dismissed the editor-in-chief of *al-Ahram*, Mohammed Hassanian Haykal, due to his critical stance on the state's foreign policy. Sadat went even further in 1975, when he decreed a new policy for regulating the press. This decree created additional institutions to restrict journalistic freedom, including the Supreme Press Council, a body entrusted with the authority to license newspapers and design and enforce an ethical code for journalists.

In 1976, attempting to stave off pressure for a multiparty system without lifting the 1953 ban on political parties, Sadat announced that three forums for expressing political opinions would be permitted within the framework of the ASU. Based on the existing left, center, and right platforms, these groups were afforded some leeway for free expression in 'party' newspapers. The leftist paper, *al-Ahaly*, was openly critical of government policies. By 1978, Sadat found this criticism intolerable and announced that he would hold a referendum to ask the Egyptian people if 'atheists' (a code word for leftists) should be barred from the political arena. Given the disregard of democratic standards, Sadat 'won' an overwhelming majority. The central component of the referendum, 'The Law of Shame' prohibited blasphemy, the publication of false news that could inflame public opinion, or criticism of the government. Indeed, the prohibition against blasphemy and the official position of the state against books deemed offensive to Islam later led to the arrest of author Ala Hamid and may be responsible for inciting some extreme Islamists to gun down the liberal author Farag Fauna. The law of shame was not directly responsible for this, but it created an atmosphere and a context which was conducive to violence. Moreover, it established an extrajudicial court of values and granted the Socialist Public Prosecutor wide jurisdiction to investigate political offenses. Despite these increasingly restrictive measures, criticism of Sadat's policies mounted. Thus, in 1981, he ordered a crackdown on all opposition parties and dissident journalists. This led to the arrest of 3,000 people, including many members of the press, as well as the closure of seven publications and dismissal of sixty-seven journalists from their positions. Sadat's initial relaxation of journalistic restrictions, like his brief foray into political liberalization, was thus dramatically reversed during the course of his rule (see Nasser, 1979;1990).

Institutionalized Repression: A Lasting Legacy and New Developments

After his death, Sadat left behind a legacy of institutions and amendments designed to curb freedom of the press. Mubarak chose to preserve this legacy, as evidenced by the continued role of the Supreme Press Council and *Shura* Council in regulating and censoring media outlets. Established in 1975, the Supreme Press Council remains the government body responsible for the press in Egypt. It not only controls regulation and licensing of newspapers, but also allocates newsprint, sets prices, determines the amount of advertising, and grants permission for journalists to work for non-Egyptian media or overseas. This far-reaching authority is coupled with that of the *Shura* Council, a government body established in 1980 and currently dominated by Mubarak's National Democratic Party.

In addition to holding ownership rights for 51 percent of the national press, the *Shura* Council appoints board chairmen and editors of Egyptian newspapers. Together, the two institutions safeguard the state's dominant position in the national media (see Khalil, 1993; Isa, 1987).

Constitutional guarantees aside, Egypt's legal framework merely facilitates the regulatory and restrictive measures of the Supreme Press Council and *Shura* Council. As stipulated by Article 48 of the Egyptian Constitution, 'freedom of the press and of printing, publishing and the information media is guaranteed,' and 'administrative censorship, cautioning, suspension or prohibition of the publication of newspapers are not permissible.' Within the same article, however, provisions are set forth which qualify these freedoms by allowing for limited censorship during a state of emergency or a time of war. Since Egypt has been ruled by emergency law for nearly fifty years, these constitutional 'exceptions' effectively nullify all promises for freedom. The government is thus able to draw on emergency law stipulations permitting censorship and confiscation of published materials under the pretext of national security.

The Penal Code further limits journalistic freedoms and includes a separate section which addresses 'crimes of the press.' Under the code's provisions, the state prohibits publications which instigate hatred of the ruling system, humiliate civil authorities, humiliate the armed services or parliament, excite public opinion by propaganda, transmit false news, attack any of the three monotheistic religions, or propagate atheism. Moreover, Articles 179 and 188 stipulate punitive measures to be carried out against journalists who insult the Egyptian president or publish false information, and any written material which is used to commit or incite crimes against the government is subject to confiscation.[3]

Law 93, an amendment passed in 1995, reflected the government's efforts to extend Penal Code restrictions. While it was ultimately overturned via court ruling, the measure was indicative of the state's continued insistence on far-reaching control. Known as the 'Press Assassination Law,' it mandated fines and/or imprisonment for anyone who published 'untrue or malicious news, information or rumors, sensational propaganda, papers which are fake, forged, or attributed falsely to others' with the intent to 'disturb the public peace, harm the public interest, hold in contempt the state organizations or civil servants or arouse panic among people.'[4] Journalists who directly targeted or threatened national interests were subject to a minimum penalty of five years imprisonment or a fine of LE 10,000 to LE 20,000 (*Al-Ahram*, 1-7 June 1995, p. 2). In addition, the law permitted detention of suspected journalists prior to interrogation and afforded no protection to those who unknowingly published false information. This stipulation canceled Article 135 of the Criminal

Procedures Law, which prohibited detention of journalists while investigations were pending. Given its highly subjective language, Law 93 granted the state wide discretion to tighten its control over the Egyptian press and use legal measures to suppress critical voices.

In addition to his efforts to strengthen the restrictive regulations of his predecessors, Mubarak considers new 'anti-terrorism' amendments an integral part of his campaign to suppress Islamist groups. Issued in 1992, these amendments are ostensibly designed to combat violent extremism. In the provisions' language and application, however, 'terrorism' is broadly defined to include any form of 'intimidation or terror' which harms people, spreads panic, or obstructs the work of authorities.[5] The law extends the death penalty not only to those who join a group guilty of terrorism, but also to anyone who knowingly or unknowingly supplies such a group with 'funds and information.' Further, anyone whose speech, publications, or recordings promote disruption of social peace or prevent authorities from doing their work is eligible for five years' imprisonment. While some of these activities were already punishable under the Penal Code, the anti-terrorism amendments are notable for prescribing harsh punitive measures.

Egyptian journalists view the new laws as particularly threatening, since they can now be charged with 'terrorism' based solely upon their writing. In an incident that underscored this threat, Mahmoud al-Maraghi, the editor of *al-Arabi*, was accused of promoting terrorism after running an interview with Ayman al-Zawahri, a leader of Egypt's Islamic Group. Since *al-Arabi* is a Nasserist paper, and the Islamists regard Nasserites as enemies, this charge was clearly unfounded. Al-Maraghi, like other opposition journalists, was merely addressing vital issues which concern the wider Egyptian public. By charging that his writings posed a threat to society, the state sought to avoid these issues and silence critical voices.

The Opposition Press

Within the overarching framework of institutionalized regulation and repression, Egypt's opposition press and national press face additional constraints. The opposition press, consisting of all newspapers owned by political parties other than the National Democratic Party, must cope with special logistical and financial limitations on its freedom. In addition to government regulations which impose constraints on newspaper licensing and ownership, opposition parties lack their own publishing houses and distribution companies. As a result, most newspapers are printed and distributed through the government-owned print shops of *al-Ahram* and *al-Akbar*. While the managing editor of *al-Ahram* stressed that these were purely commercial arrangements, Adel Hussein, the former head of the Socialist Labor Party's *al-Sha`ab*, disagreed. He maintained that 'when the government gets nervous, *al-Ahram* gets nervous,' thereby placing the opposition press in an extremely vulnerable position. Moreover, he asserted that even in the absence of direct censorship, the government is able to 'manipulate the media by different means.[6] Clearly, state surveillance and regulation of opposition papers is facilitated by the parties' dependence on the government for publication and distribution.

State control over advertising is yet another means of manipulating the opposition press. Because advertisements for the extensive public sector are printed in pro-government publications, opposition papers are deprived of a vital source of funding. In order to cover production costs, opposition parties are thus forced to issue weekly rather than daily papers and/or maintain higher newsstand prices than their competitors. Given the financial burdens associated with a narrow advertising base, the ability of the opposition press to influence public opinion is significantly weakened. The state's predominant position in the Egyptian economy thus provides an additional tool for limiting journalistic freedom.

Even beyond censorship and financial constraints, opposition journalists must also face government intimidation and harassment. Although Mubarak initially avoided Sadat's coercive tactics in dealing with the opposition press, his approach became increasingly aggressive. By his second and third terms, he surpassed Sadat in trying journalists before military courts and allowing police to intimidate journalists with impunity. As an example of the regime's coercive policies, EOHR notes the arrest of ten journalists for 'inciting' a strike at the Helwan steel factory in August 1989. In addition to being detained, several were subjected to physical torture. A more recent case, the six month imprisonment of *al-Sha`ab* journalist Abdel Sattar Abu Hussein in 1994, is representative of the government's wider campaign to silence its critics. Charged with 'endangering state security' by reporting on upcoming training exercises between Egyptian, American, French, and German forces, Abu Hussein noted that the government's *al-Ahram* published the same news story two days after his interrogation. Additional charges were levied against him for his coverage of alleged involvement in arms sales by former military generals and alleged management corruption at Military Factory 81. Following detention and interrogation by the State Security Investigation (SSI), Abu Hussein was tried before a military court and sentenced to a military prison. While he was not physically tortured, he saw others tortured before him, was forced to live in an unsanitary environment, and received insufficient food and water. His case, although one of the most visible instances of harassment and intimidation of opposition journalists, was not an isolated incident. As the experiences of Abu Hussein and others reveal, there is not always a clear distinction between the suppression of journalistic freedom and violation of targets' rights to personal safety and due process.[7]

Beyond professional and legal attacks against individual journalists, opposition newspapers are also faced with the threat of government closure. The state revoked the license of *Sautal-'Arab* in 1989 and *Misr al-Fatah* in 1992, forcing both newspapers to shut down. In the case of *Sautal-'Arab*, reports of Israeli reconnaissance flights over Saudi Arabia, coupled with earlier criticism of Saudi Arabia's human rights record, led to the publication's closure. According to Editor-in-Chief Abdul Azeem Manaf, the Saudi Arabian government pressured the Ministry of Social Affairs into withdrawing the parent organization's permission to operate, thereby canceling its right to publish a paper. The closure of *Misr al-Fatah* was likewise implemented by undermining the organization holding the newspaper license. In response to the paper's criticism of Western strikes against Iraq, Egyptian foreign policy, and Saudi Arabian and Egyptian human rights abuses, the government orchestrated a split in the *Misr al-Fatah* party and masterminded the installation of new, pro-government leaders. The Political Parties Committee recognized the new leadership, and the Supreme Press Council ordered the government-controlled print shops to stop printing the party's paper. Although the courts eventually overruled the new leadership's authority and reversed the paper's closure, implementation of this ruling was obstructed by the state's bureaucratic maneuvering and manipulation of the legal system.

The tactics used to undermine *Sautal-'Arab* and *Misr al-Fatah*, while not frequently employed, serve as a warning to all opposition journalists. As evidence of the continued credence of this warning, the opposition paper *al-Dastoor* was shut down in March 1998. In this case, the publication was targeted due to its critical position on Egyptian business practices. The incident thus reflected a sharp disjuncture between the state's cautious willingness for economic opening and stubborn insistence on political closure.[8]

The National Press

The national media, while not targeted in the same fashion as the opposition press, is subject to different constraints on journalistic freedom. Although the national press is not merely an instrument of government propaganda, it does reflect the state's position on major issues and seeks to mobilize public support for state policies. Because the editors of national papers are dependent on the government for their positions and income, their journalistic freedom is sharply curtailed. If state officials are displeased with an editor's performance, they can deprive his paper of public sector advertising and/or refuse to renew his editorship. Given the state's sway over editors' decisions, censorship often takes the form of insisting upon a pro-government slant.

State ownership and control of the national press induces self-censorship at all levels of reporting and publication. Although self-imposed limitations on journalistic freedoms are difficult to document, all editors and journalists must keep criticism within 'acceptable' bounds and tailor their reporting to satisfy state requirements. Certain sensitive topics, such as Egyptian human rights abuses or criticism of the Saudi Arabian government are carefully avoided, and direct criticism of the Egyptian president is strictly prohibited. Editors for papers which are distributed in the Gulf states and benefit from Gulf advertisements censor their publications for domestic and foreign markets. The managing editor of *al-Ahram*, while denying that criticism of Saudi Arabia was forbidden, acknowledged that 'cosmetic' changes were sometimes made to avoid offending valuable Saudi patrons. To ensure continued political and economic support the national press has little alternative but to adopt self-censorship. Should it fail to do so, the state assumes the task and imposes limitations from above.

The Expansion of Political Space from Above and Below

Aided by the extensive institutional, coercive, and financial instruments under its control, the state is thus able to impose severe restraints on freedom of the press. Despite the bleak implications this holds for human rights guarantees in general, the government is unable to assert complete hegemony or remain completely unresponsive to demands for change. The Egyptian populace employs creative means of expanding political and economic space. Even within the national press, journalists find ways to circumvent state restrictions and cautiously test the limits of freedom. Publications issued by the Ahram Center for Political and Strategic Studies have traditionally cloaked critical analysis and debate in the language of objective scholarship and policy advice (Baker, 1990, p. 179). Likewise, the *Economic Ahram*, a specialized economics journal, mounted a sustained challenge to the key aspects of the official definition of the economic realities that Egyptians faced during the seventies and early eighties (*Ibid.*, p. 206). Technical language and statistical analysis were used to blunt sharp criticism of government policy, and the writers' professed concern for national interests afforded them greater leeway to express independent views. Although the journal's attacks against the Camp David Accords ultimately led Sadat to curtail its freedom, it was a forerunner of later efforts to creatively assert independence from the state.

Journalists' use of creative means to circumvent state restrictions is indicative of a wider pattern in Egyptian society. Informal family and community networks provide channels for contesting ideals, rights, and the allocation of resources (Singerman, 1995). By helping people to meet their social and financial needs, these networks reduce society's dependence on the government and mitigate the effect of institutionalized human rights restrictions. Rather than exist in isolation from the state, they incorporate political and public sector officials. In addition to fulfilling individual and collective needs, informal networks thus enhance the public's capacity to communicate with the state and make demands on state resources.

Beyond creative strategies and informal avenues, the state has been reluctantly responsive to some calls for reform. Despite his misguided policies of political exclusion and continued adherence to coercive, repressive tactics, Mubarak has tolerated the selective expansion of popular freedoms. As evidence of this cautious opening, 160 newspapers are now published in Egypt, and the government added six new television channels to the two Cairo-based channels which it originally broadcast. While these new media outlets exist within a state-dominated framework, they nonetheless indicate a slight widening of the accepted limits of free expression.

Conclusion

On the surface, Egypt's constitutional guarantees and ratification of international agreements suggest a national commitment to the preservation of human rights. In reality, however, Egypt's human rights record mirrors a wider pattern of disjuncture between political ideals and actual practice. Nominal guarantees and lofty principles aside, formal structures and informal practices uphold a framework of political exclusion and repression.

Faced with a crisis of popular legitimacy, the government seeks to silence voices which undermine its tenuous hold on ideological credit. Islamist groups, considered the state's most threatening challengers, bear the brunt of these efforts. Drawing on emergency laws and anti-terrorism amendments, the state has increasingly resorted to coercive tactics and flagrantly undermined the rights to life, personal safety, and freedom. These human rights violations are couched within the language of domestic security, wherein the government affects a protective role and purports to defend the country from Islamic radicals. Yet apart from the violent extremism of certain Islamist groups, the state is also averse to more benign expressions of popular discontent. Religious and secular groups alike are subject to institutionalized and informal limitations of human rights. These limitations undermine the rights to due process and fair trial, freedom of expression, and freedom of association.

Freedom of the press warrants special attention as an indicator of the state's wider efforts to constrain human rights, limit popular participation, and avoid accountability and transparency. A free press is capable of exposing and questioning government actions within a public arena and could thus undermine the Egyptian state's control and ideological credit. To stem this potential threat, Nasser and Sadat both imposed restraints on journalistic freedom. Although Mubarak has preserved the institutionalized framework of this repressive legacy, recent developments reveal a selective opening of political space. As a further indication of this trend, numerous associations are registered with the Ministry of Social Affairs, and non-registered human rights organizations are able to operate openly. Nonetheless, freedom of the press, like human rights in general, remains hostage to an overbearing, powerful state.

Notes

1. Egyptian State Information Service Home Page, (http://www.sis.gov.eg/egyptinf/), 15 April 1998.
2. *Ibid.*
3. Interview with Magdi Ahmed Hussien, Cairo, July 1996.
4. *Ibid.*
5. Article 86 (bis), Article 89 (b), Article 89 (f) Article 102, and Article 102 (bis).
6. Interview with Magdi Ahmed Hussien, Cairo, July 1996.
7. Interview with Abdul attar Abu Hussien, 29 September 1995.
8. Interview with Khalid Khodier, Washington Bureau Chief for the Egyptian news agency MENA, Washington DC, 13 March 1998.

References

al-Ahram (June 1-7, 1995),'Regulating Democracy,' p. 2.
Al-Sayyid, Mustapha Kamil (1995), 'A Civil Society in Egypt?,' in R. Augustus (ed.), *Civil Society in the Middle East*, Vol. I, ed. Augustus Richard Norton, E.J. Brill, Leiden.
Baker, Raymond (1990), *Sadat and After*, Harvard Univ. Press, Cambridge, MA.
Egyptian Organization for Human Rights, (1994), *Human Rights Watch World Report*, Washington, D.C.

`Isa, Salah (ed.) (1987), *Al-`idwan `ala Hurriat al-Sahafa wal Sahafieen* [Attacks on Journalists and Freedom of the Press], Malfat al-Ahaly, Cairo.

Nasser, Munir K. (1979), *Press, Politics and Power: Egypt's Heikal and al-Ahram*, Iowa State Univ. Press.

Nasser, Munir K. (1990), *Egyptian Mass Media under Nasser and Sadat*, AEJMC.

Khalil, Abdalla (1993), *Al-Qawaneen al-Muqaida lil Huquq al-Madania wal Siyasa fi al-Tashre'a al-Misri* [Laws Restricting Political and Civil Rights in Egyptian Legislation], EOHR Publications, Cairo.

Singerman, Diane (1995), *Avenues of Participation*, Princeton University Press, Princeton.

U.S. Department of State (March 1996), *Egyptian Human Rights Practices, 1995*, Washington, D.C.

U.S. Department of State (1997), *Country Reports; Egypt, Human Rights Practices 1996*, Washington, D.C.

7 Democratization, Liberalization, and Human Rights: Challenges Facing the Gulf Cooperation Council[1]

ROLIN G. MAINUDDIN

Two of the major forces sweeping the world in the 1990s are democracy and religious resurgence. The collapse of the Soviet bloc was followed by democratic experiments in former Soviet countries. Beginning with southern Europe and Latin America in the 1970s, and eastern Europe in the 1980's, the events marked, what Samuel Huntington of Harvard University called, the 'third wave' of democratic transition(Huntington, 1993, pp. 21-4). Soon thereafter, Mark Juergensmeyer of the University of California, Santa Barbara, warned that secular governments will have to reckon with emerging religious forces in the post-Cold War period (Juergensmeyer, 1994, pp. 15, 33, 195-97). Beginning with the 1979 Islamic Revolution in Iran, in particular, the rising tide of Islamic rejuvenation in the Muslim world has drawn international attention.

Within the aforementioned global context, this chapter ascertains the 'mini-wave' (Ibrahim, 1995, p. 37) of political change and its two attributes: democratization (regime change) and liberalization (interest articulation) (Huntington, 1993, p. 34; Brynen and others, 1995, p. 3; Almond and Powell, 1966, p. 73). The objective is to understand the challenges of democratization and liberalization in the Gulf Cooperation Council (GCC) countries through case studies of Bahrain, Kuwait, and Saudi Arabia. Although the task is undertaken primarily from a Western, secular vantage point, it does not neglect the Islamic perspective. Furthermore, this work briefly examines the implications of the aforementioned two processes for human rights practices. In grappling with the domestic challenges facing the Gulf monarchies, one needs to consider the interaction between global and regional milieus.

The External Environment

The GCC ruling elites face three interacting, concentric dilemmas involving the security, political, and religious domains. The first scenario involves the security dilemma. Islam is an important aspect of social and political life in the Persian Gulf sheikhdoms.[2] The Gulf monarchies, particularly Saudi Arabia, project themselves as the fountainhead and bastion of Islam. But when faced with threats from their two powerful and ambitious Muslim neighbors (Iraq and Iran), the Gulf leaders must rely on countervailing security cooperation with non-Muslim, Western countries (Mainuddin et al., 1996, p. 43).

Cooperation with the West was inevitable following the August 2, 1990, Iraqi invasion of Kuwait. The Gulf sheikhdoms, with the exception of Saudi Arabia, surreptitiously deployed Western combat planes on their soil. Bahrain housed FA-18 attack aircraft, AV-Harrier jets, A-6 bombers, and EA-6 electronic jamming planes. Oman took in F-15 fighters; F-16 fighter jets were stationed in Qatar and the United Arab Amirates.

Although General H. Norman Schwarzkopf was the overall commander of the anti-Iraqi coalition during the 1991 Operation Desert Storm, joint Arab-Islamic forces operated separately under Saudi Lieutenant General Khalid bin Sultan al-Saud. Comprised of troops from the GCC countries, Egypt, Syria, Morocco, Bangladesh, and some Afghan volunteers, the Arab-Islamic contingent was designed to give the Muslim world a semblance of operational autonomy. By the same token, Kuwaiti forces were orchestrated to be the first to enter and liberate Kuwait City. Yet, the reality was that Desert Storm was primarily implemented by American, British, and French troops.

After Desert Storm, however, the August 1992 allied no-fly zone operation against Iraq did not win public support from Arab leaders in the region. In the face of a strong 'fellow Muslim' sentiment, the Pentagon denied Saudi Arabia's direct involvement in the air strike (Mainuddin et al., 1996, p. 44).

Even before the 1990 Operation Desert Shield was implemented to protect Saudi Arabia, military weakness forced Kuwait to seek Western protection in the latter phase of the Iran-Iraq War. Iran's 'tanker-war' lead Kuwait to abandon its earlier nonaligned posture. In fact, during 1987-88, the U.S. Navy escorted Kuwaiti oil tankers through the Persian Gulf. Lacking adequate military capabilities, the GCC countries were not able to defend themselves; nor could they safeguard Arab and Islamic interest worldwide (Mainuddin et al., 1996, pp. 42-3). For example, the Gulf sheikhdoms were too weak to intervene militarily to prevent 'ethnic cleansing' of Muslims in Bosnia. It fell to the United States and other major Western powers to end such atrocities in former Yugoslavia.

The second scenario pertains to the political dilemma. Western security protection carries with it the expectation of a transition to democracy. But, as Western democratic values are embraced by the Gulf population, they threaten the very institution of monarchy in the GCC countries. After the 1990 invasion by Iraq, the Western powers were involved in liberating Kuwait primarily to ensure a continued supply of oil from Kuwait's Rumaila oil field. Even though the U.S. did not intervene to promote democracy, that objective had always been an intricate part of American foreign policy (Mazarr et al., 1993, pp. 14, 81; Robinson, 1996, pp. 11, 112-14). During the Kuwait crisis, the U.S. alone sent 500,000 troops to the Gulf. The deployment precipitated demands for democracy in Kuwait and Saudi Arabia (Huntington, 1993, p. 286). Winds of political change in those countries spread to other Gulf monarchies. 'Petition fever' not only became pervasive in Kuwait and Saudi Arabia, but also had a ripple effect in Bahrain and Qatar (Gause, 1994, p. 98). With the continued American presence, through troop rotation and joint exercises, liberal forces within the sheikdoms are likely to be more stalwart in pressing for political change.

In the tradition of tribal leadership, the GCC countries are ruled by the predominant families. Al-Khalifa, al-Sabah, and al-Thani families are at the helm of power in the amirates of Bahrain, Kuwait, and Qatar, respectively. The al-Said family reigns in the Sultanate of Oman; the al-Saud family controls the Saudi kingdom. In order to ensure survival of the regime, the Saudi Ministry of Defense and the internal security apparatus are in the hands of the royal family. The situation is similar in the United Arab Amirates (Anthony, 1981, p. 24 fn1). For these dynasties, power sharing is risky. Democratization and liberalization threaten their privileged positions. They would prefer the status quo of absolute monarchy over even a transition to constitutional monarchy.

The third scenario involves the religious dilemma, what Jerrold Green calls 'institutional Islam' versus 'popular Islam' (Green, 1985, p. 315). The ruling families have used Islamic symbols to consolidate and perpetuate their political power (Piscatori, 1983, pp. 59-63). By questioning the notion of 'Divine Rule,' the nonconformist[3] religious opposition (popular Islam) threatens the very legitimacy of the ruling dynasties (Al-Rasheed, 1996, p. 17; Dunn, 1995, p. 35). Close cooperation with the West and un-Islamic social behavior erode the royal families' images, particularly in the eyes of the coterie of religiously conservative professionals. In order to broaden their power base, these groups are astute in invoking Western principles of political freedom and democracy. What is ominous for the reigning dynasties is that these religious groups use Islam to discredit the monarchy. *Lajna al-Difa an al-Huquq al-Shari'a* (Committee for the Defense of Shari'a Rights) in Saudi Arabia was formed by six conservative Muslims. For the Saudi royal family, militant groups like the Movement for Islamic Change and Tigers of the Gulf raise the specter of a destabilizing, protracted armed conflict. The Damascus-based *al-Jabhah al-Islamiyyah li Tahrir al-Bahrain* (Islamic Front for the Liberation of Bahrain), with offices in Tehran and London, poses a similar threat for the al-Khalifa family in Bahrain (Bahry, 1997, p. 45).

The aforementioned dilemmas affect the ways the ruling families deal with the challenges of democratization and liberalization. However, Western and Islamic perspectives of these two issues differ.

Conceptual Montage

Democratization is the process of transition to democracy. It involves meaningful political participation by the people, through elections, in selecting or replacing their governmental representatives (Brynen et al., 1995, p. 3; Huntington, 1993, pp. 6-9). Liberalization is the granting of rights and liberties to the people. While rights entail government protection in ensuring certain benefits, liberties relate to a degree of freedom for political activism (Sorensen, 1993, p. 14; Brynen et al., 1995, p. 3; Huntington, 1993, p. 9).

Broadly speaking, the process of democratization involves three stages: ending authoritarian rule, installing democratic government by constitutional means, and developing institutions and culture necessary to sustain political change (Huntington, 1993, p. 35). While a focus on democratization is relevant in discussing the authoritarian regimes of the Gulf sheikhdoms, we must remember that democracy has different meanings in Islamic and Western traditions.

'Democracy' is derived from the Greek word *demokratia*. According to its Greek origin, *demos* means people and *kratia* refers to rule or authority. However, the fundamental notion of 'rule by the people' leaves open to interpretation three important issues. First, who should be the ruler? This pertains to legitimacy: selection process, duration of tenure, opportunity for renewal, and succession. Second, what authority should be vested in the ruler? This is associated with the concentration-dispersion continuum of power: defining the objectives, functions, and circumstances. Third, how does the ruler use his authority? This relates to the notion of justice: the welfare of the people, which is the substance of democracy (Dahl, 1989, pp. 3-5). Whereas the Western notion of democracy stresses the first two issues, the Islamic perspective focuses on the third.

Robert Dahl of Yale University views democracy as a collective process for making binding decisions (Dahl, 1989, p. 5). Western scholars also emphasize the need for institutionalized mechanisms for 'free, open, and fair' elections of political candidates competing for public office (Huntington, 1993, pp. 6-9). Huntington is aware that actual power may be in the hands of powerful interest groups, who are indifferent to the 'public good' (Huntington, 1993, p. 10). Dahl is optimistic, however, that Western democracy can incorporate the normative aspect of public welfare (Dahl, 1989, pp. 5-6).

Most Western scholars believe that the Western democratic experience provides the foundation for defining democracy. Focusing on the 'western experience' precipitates a debate however, as Giovanni Sartori notes, over whether the key concept is 'western' or 'experience' (Esposito and Voll, 1996, p. 17). The issue of a non-Western path to democracy is reminiscent of a debate in the development literature over associating development with westernization. Anthropologist Richard Shweder draws attention to 'divergent rationalities,' or differences in rational thought processes that are influenced by different traditions, cultures, and history (Sharabi, 1990, p. 19).

The essence of democracy is 'popular empowerment' (Esposito and Voll, 1996, p. 13). Ayatollah Khomeini's notion of *vilayat-e-faqih* (government by the Islamic jurist) in Iran essentially empowered the previously marginalized Islamic jurists. A seventy-three member Assembly of Experts amended the constitution, passed by a majority vote in a national referendum in December 1979, that established a twelve member Council of Guardians for religious review of legislation (Lorentz, 1995, pp. 17, 41). *Taqi al-Din al-Nabhani's Hizb al-Tahrir al-Islami* (Islamic Liberation Party) in Palestine explicitly advocated the supremacy of *shari'a* (Islamic law). Likewise, Egypt's Sheikh Omar Abdel Rahman, borrowing from Sayyid Qutb, stressed *hakimiyya* (God's governance). Western democracy is rejected by orthodox Muslims for emphasizing sovereignty of the people over God (Taji-Farouki, 1996, pp. 39-41; Sidahmed and Ehteshami, 1996, p. 9; Ismail, 1995, p. 102). By the same token, on March 29, 1992, in an interview with several Arab newspapers, King Fahd ibn Abdul Aziz al-Saud ruled out Western-style democracy for Saudi Arabia. Democracy, he elaborated, must be in conformity, politically and socially, with Islam. Earlier, in a speech at the beginning of the month, he declared shari'a the 'keystone' of Saudi society (Gause, 1994, p. 111).

Despite a lack of commitment to democracy by Muslim political leaders, Huntington does not rule out democracy in Muslim societies. While Islam incorporates some ideas compatible with democracy, he notes that a key impediment is the merger of religious and political communities in Islamic doctrine (Huntington, 1993, pp. 297, 307). To Western intellectuals, *din wa-dawla* (religion and state) combine the spiritual (associated with irrationality) with the political (associated with rational self-interest) realms (Eickelman and Piscatori, 1996, pp. 46, 56). In equating rationality with secularism, Western social science is not well-prepared for the mundane mix of religion and politics (Luckmann, 1991, pp. 167-68). Whereas Huntington finds *din wa-dawla* undemocratic, King Fahd, al-Nabhani, and Abdel Rahman view Western democracy as unacceptable precisely because of this intertwining in Islam. Yet, Khomeini, al-Nabhani, and Abdel Rahman differ from King Fahd by rejecting monarchy as Islam distinguishes between the *ulama* (religious scholars) and *umara* (princes) (Ismail, 1995, p. 104).

In establishing the Jamaat-i-Islami party in colonial India in 1941, Abul A'la Mawdudi implicitly gave support to the idea of compatibility of Islam with democracy. However, Muslims who accept democracy do so within the fundamental framework of *tawheed* (monotheistic God). In fact, tawheed, *risalat* (prophethood), and *khilafat* (leadership and succession) are the triad of an Islamic political system. The third concept, *khalifah*, has been interpreted by scholars as leadership either exercised under God's agent or as vested in the entire community (Esposito and Voll, 1996, pp. 23-6. Also, see Mawdudi, 1994, pp. 23-7, 52-8).

Although Islam does not advocate participation through multiparty, competitive elections, it urges community participation—what may be called 'inclusive participation'—through consensus building. Given the demographic size of modern nation-states, community consensus is not feasible in the GCC polities. There is not a large enough gathering place to hold all the citizens for direct involvement in decision-making. If democracy is to take hold in the Gulf sheikhdoms, it has to be representative democracy. The Islamic concepts associated with inclusive participation, however, are distant from the majoritarian or adversarial model of the Anglo-American system. Rather, the concepts of *shurah* (consultation) and *ijma* (consensus) are closer to the consensus model of Western democracy associated with Austria and Belgium in continental Europe (Esposito and Voll, 1996, p. 19). Nevertheless, it is important to stress that shurah and ijma relate to *ijtihad* (interpretation) within the framework of the Qur'an and Sunna.

In Islamic and Western societies the unit of focus is different. Whereas the West emphasizes protection of the individual, the Islamic tradition stresses social order. From the Western vantage point, liberty is the opposite of authority. A government must have the authority to govern. Instead of promoting the greater public good, there is always the danger that government will abuse its power against citizens. Political rights set limits to government's power over citizens. Political liberties enable individuals to legitimately articulate their concerns through non-governmental channels (Mill, 1985, pp. 59-60, 71).

While Islamic tradition allows *ikhtilaf* (disagreement), differences of opinion must not result in *fitnah* (disorder). Thus, concern over the latter can limit the former. The ruler can use the fear of disorder to restrict the range of political opinion (Esposito and Voll, 1996, pp. 41-4). However, there is nothing peculiarly Islamic about preferring social order over anarchy (Fuller and Lesser, 1997, pp. 45- 6). The fear of political unrest is paramount for the ruling families of the Gulf sheikhdoms. Understandably, they are more concerned about preserving monarchy than establishing democracy. It is not in their interest to promote individual rights or freedom of expression, because these only lead to further demands for political change.

Political Change

Muhammad Faour of the American University of Beirut does not foresee a transition to Western-style democracy in the GCC countries (Faour, 1995, p. 36). In fact, in order to limit power sharing, the Gulf monarchies find it prudent to argue that Western-style democracy is un-Islamic. Elections are not held in Bahrain or Saudi Arabia. While the amir of Kuwait has permitted voting in that country after the 1991 Gulf War, it is restricted to adult male natural born citizens (citizens by birth). Women do not have the right to vote. Until the 1996 election, naturalized adult male Kuwaiti citizens with less than 20 years in that status could not vote either (U.S. Department of State, 1997, pp. 1316, 1321). Although the process of inclusive participation has been mostly cosmetic, there has been some change (Mazrui, 1997, p. 125).

Bahrain

The ruling al-Khalifa family in Bahrain belongs to the Sunni Muslim sect. Sunnis are a minority; two-thirds of the population are Shi'ite Muslims. Thus, it was not surprising that civil unrest in the 1970s was mainly initiated by the politically and economically disadvantaged Shi'ite majority. Viewed as a security risk, the Shi'ites are routinely denied 'politically sensitive' jobs by the Bahraini Government. Parliament has been closed since 1975. Pro- democracy demonstrations initially erupted in December

1974. In clashes between police and demonstrators one police officer and nine civilians were killed.

On April 2, 1995, Sheikh Isa bin Salman al-Khalifa, the amir of Bahrain, met with twenty prominent Shi'ite leaders. While the meeting set the stage for future dialogues between the ruling elite and the Shi'ite opposition, it did not resolve differences between the two parties. Later that month, opposition leaders urged the government's continued engagement in talks for ending civil unrest. They also disavowed violence as a tool for achieving their political goals. Subsequently, in September 1996, leaders of the Shi'ite majority called on the Sunni minority government to restore the National Assembly. Earlier, in July 1992, over 200 Bahrainis signed a petition urging the amir to reopen parliament. It is noteworthy that the Bahraini Constitution mandates direct election of parliamentary officials by the people (Gause, 1994, p. 99). Instead of reopening parliament, the following December Sheikh Isa announced his intention to create a Consultative Council. By the end of the year, he had appointed thirty members to the Council, evenly proportioned between the Shi'ites and Sunnis. Ibrahim Hamidan, a Shi'ite and former Minister of Transportation, was designated president of the consultative body by the amir. The Council was comprised of a cross section of the middle class. About two-thirds were merchants and contractors; the remaining one- third included lawyers, doctors, religious judges, academicians, and a journalist. The Consultative Council had limited powers. Lacking the power to initiate bills, it was restricted to reviewing legislations sent by the Council of Ministers. Unable to make recommendations, its oversight power was limited to only questioning the ministers on public policy (Gause, 1994, p. 115).

In April 1996, the Islamic Front for the Liberation of Bahrain[4] called for a general civil disobedience campaign. Earlier, in January, civil unrest broke out in several Shi'ite villages. The following month, as part of a crackdown on the opposition movement, Bahraini authorities arrested forty-one people. This was a reversal of the April 1995 good-will gesture when the government released 120 political prisoners. Significantly, those arrested included Ahmad al-Shamlan and Sheikh Abdul Amir al-Jamri. Al-Shamlan, a renowned lawyer and writer, is a Sunni; al Jamri, a former member of the parliament, is a Shi'ite cleric. They highlighted the democratic element and broad-based support of the opposition movement.

Parliamentary democracy is not acceptable to the Bahraini Government. In February 1996, Bahraini officials even denied eight deputies entry to parliament because they had supported the opposition's demands for reopening parliament. The Shi'ite majority has been demanding better job opportunities. With the restoration of parliament, they envisioned greater opportunities for themselves through their elected representatives. With that constitutional route closed, they resorted to civil disobedience, demonstrations, and violence. The government responded with both legal and coercive measures. Convicted of killing a police officer, Isa Ahmed Hassan Qambar was executed in March 1996 by a Bahraini firing squad. That led to riots. Militants detonated nine bombs simultaneously in Manama in his remembrance. The following June, forty-four Bahrainis were arrested for plotting to overthrow the al-Khalifa dynasty and install a Shi'ite regime. Later in September, the state security court sentenced fifteen plotters to prison terms of six months to five years.

Kuwait

Kuwait, the only GCC country to take the election route, has so far avoided the violence witnessed in Bahrain. Founded in the 1960's, the *Majlis al-Um'ma* (National Assembly) in Kuwait had real legislative power. While tolerating debates in the Majlis, however, the monarchy did not find public criticism of government policies by Parliamentary leaders palatable. Facing an assertive representative institution and a burgeoning economic crisis, the ruling al-Sabah family took advantage of public sentiment for domestic unity during the protracted Iran-Iraq War. In July 1986, Jabir al-Ahmad al-Sabah, the amir, suspended the Majlis (Crystal, 1992, p. 105).

The war between Kuwait's neighbors, which began in 1980, ended in August 1988. About 30,000 Kuwaitis signed a petition the following year urging the amir to restore the assembly in the country. The amir was not moved by the petition drive; his government banned public gatherings of more than five people without prior authorization. Consequently, what emerged were the *diwaniyyas*: informal, family-based social gatherings of adult males to discuss political issues (U.S., Department of State, 1997, p. 1319). Under public pressure, in 1990 Sheikh Jabir created a seventy-five member National Council. Whereas two- thirds of its members were elected, one-third was appointed by the amir. While it served the amir in dividing the opposition, the Council's role was limited to inquiry and consultation (Gause, 1994, p. 90).

In the aftermath of the August 2, 1990, Iraqi invasion of Kuwait, many Kuwaitis demanded restoration of the National Assembly that had existed in the 1960s. In October of that year, at a meeting in Jedda, Saudi Arabia, Sheikh Jabir and Crown Prince Saad al-Abdullah al-Sabah promised 1,200 Kuwaitis political participation after liberation from Iraqi occupation. Perhaps, what tipped the balance was pubic opinion in the U.S. and other Western countries. The following year, opposition political leaders signed a petition reiterating their demand for a return to an elected National Assembly (Gause, 1994, p. 91).

To appease domestic and international public opinion, Sheikh Jabir reestablished the Majlis al-Um'ma and held an election on October 5, 1992. On the 17th of that month, Prince Saad, who is also the prime minister, named a sixteen member cabinet that included six opposition deputies. Four years later, on October 7, 1996, eligible Kuwaiti males participated in their second parliamentary election in the post-Gulf War period. During the 1996 election, the campaign centered on four major issues affecting the public: jobs, public services, consumer prices, and housing. An estimated 75 percent of the voters turned out to cast their ballots. That was lower than in 1992, when an estimated 85 percent of the electorate cast ballots.

Unlike the parliament of the 1980s, the Majlis al-Um'ma of the 1990s effects the political process very little. First, political parties are not legal in Kuwait. Comprised of independent candidates, the opposition is politically weak. Even though they had a thirty-one seat majority in the 1992 parliament, their diversity made it difficult for them to present a united front vis-a-vis the royalists. However, a loosely organized religious bloc captured seventeen seats in the 1996 election. Although that translates to a two seat decline from the 1992 parliament, the religious bloc, representing both Shi'ite and Sunni Muslims, is a significant faction of the opposition. Second, the Majlis cannot override decisions made by the amir, who is constitutionally empowered to bypass the legislature (U.S., Department of State, 1997, p. 1321). For example, Kuwait's 1991 defense pact with the U.S. did not need parliament's approval (Murphy and Gause, 1997, p. 64). The Majlis must operate within the framework set by the amir. Third, the royal family continues to control the key positions in the cabinet. Although the amir appointed opposition members to the posts of ministers of oil, commerce and industry, and justice in the 1992 cabinet, he kept control of the security apparatus and the ministry of foreign affairs within the ruling al-Sabah family. That strategic control did not change in the 1996 cabinet. Nevertheless, in February 1994 the Kuwaiti Government ratified, 'with reservations,' a 1979 U.N. Convention on the Elimination of All Forms of Discrimination Against Women. The provisions included equal opportunity and equal pay in employment, maternity leave, choice in marriage, and a co- educational system (*Chicago Tribune*, 1994, p. 5). The last provision was subsequently rejected by the parliament, however. Fear of sexual promiscuity from public intermingling of men and women is strong in Kuwait's traditionally Muslim society. Although the religious faction was not in the majority, in July 1996 the Assembly voted to ban co-education in colleges and vocational schools. Islamic political views influence the teachers' association and the Ministry of Education (Ghabra,

1997a, p. 60). The policy on co-education is unlikely to change in a society where women are still not eligible to vote. Even in ratifying the 1979 Convention, the Kuwaiti Government was not enthusiastic about voting and child-custody rights for women.

Women are not the only group that cannot vote. Until recently, naturalized Kuwaiti citizens also did not have the right to vote, and as in some other countries, *bedoon jinsiyya* (without nationality) or legal residents are not eligible to vote. Under Article I of the 1959 Citizenship Law, to be a citizen a person must prove one's own or one's patrilineage's continuous residence in Kuwait since 1920 (Human Rights Watch/Middle East, 1995, pp. 10, 15). Under a 1994 law, however, any male with a Kuwaiti biological father becomes a Kuwaiti citizen by birth. The 1994 law also granted voting rights to persons who had been naturalized citizens for 20 years (Ghabra, 1997b, pp. 370-71).

Saudi Arabia

In September 1993, King Fahd ibn Abdul Aziz al-Saud issued a decree in favor of limited political participation in Saudi Arabia. The decree raised expectations of advisory councils both at the central and regional levels. People expected the creation of a national council under the king and regional councils under the amir of each province. Indeed, there were reasons to hope for such changes. Earlier, on March 1, 1992, King Fahd had issued decrees, known as the 'Basic System of Government,' that decentralized political power and ensured certain individual rights. These decrees were the first attempt to codify Saudi law.

One of the provisions of the 1992 decrees established a *shurah* (Consultative Council) with the right to review, but not change, all national policy. In addition, the shurah can initiate legislation or propose amendments to existing laws. The shurah also has the right to question cabinet members and other government officials about legislative issues, and it can subpoena government documents for information. Another provision of the 1992 decrees created separate ten-member provincial shurahs to advise each of the provincial governors. In addition, the decrees gave the provinces greater authority over local development and financial matters. On December 29, 1993, the Consultative Council held its inaugural session with Justice Minister Ibrahim Jubair, King Fahd's appointee, serving as its speaker.

Saudi Arabia is far from a representative democracy. First, all sixty members of the shurah are appointed by King Fahd for a four-year term. Second, it only has an advisory role to the monarch and his cabinet. It reviews national policy and sends its recommendations to the king's cabinet. If the shurah and cabinet are in agreement, the measures are enacted with routine approval by the king. In cases of disagreement, however, the king is the final arbiter. Thus, the monarch holds the ultimate decision-making authority. Third, legislative initiatives or amendments must be supported by at least ten members or one-sixth of the shurah before being forwarded to the king's cabinet. Because the king appoints all the members of the Council, the one- sixth requirement is more ceremonial than substantive. Finally, deliberations in the shurah are not open to the public. Nevertheless, the maiden session of the shurah was monumental in bringing some semblance of inclusive participation to the desert kingdom. Significantly, the shurah did not include any members of the royal family. That in itself was an historic step taken by the ruling al-Saud family.

Interestingly, the third provision of the March 1992 Basic System changed the royal succession rules. Crown Prince Abdullah ibn Abdul Aziz al-Saud remains King Fahd's successor. Thereafter, however, the Saudi prince judged 'the most suitable' by a royal family consensus will succeed to the throne. Thus, grandsons of the late King Abdul Aziz will also be eligible to become king. Extending beyond the sons of the dynasty's founder, the decree incorporated the next generation of al-Sauds. This change was designed to ensure a continuation of the monarchy. The royal family is not contemplating any dramatic steps to facilitate democratization. As in Bahrain and Kuwait, the ruling family has closely guarded the key posts of internal security, defense, and foreign affairs.

Yet, the al-Saud family faces pressures for change. A fourth provision of the 1992 Basic System of Government introduced a 'bill of rights' to protect individuals against the abuse of authority. The consequence was to restrict the power of the *mutawein* (religious police), who assiduously enforce the strict Islamic social mores that prohibit alcoholic consumption and gender intermingling in public. Practically operating independently of the government, the mutawein had become a public opinion liability for the ruling elite. King Fahd banned the unauthorized search of private homes, and stripped the religious police of their power to arbitrarily arrest and harass people. Furthermore, he ordered a stop to police phone tapping and mail opening practices.

The Saudi ruling elite acknowledge individual rights, but it does not tolerate organized political opposition that threatens the very legitimacy of the al-Saud dynasty. Fearing political persecution of its members, the Committee for the Defense of Shari'a Rights announced relocation of its office to London in April 1994. Two months later, Mohammed al-Khilewi, a former First Secretary to the Saudi U.N. Mission, who was granted political asylum in the U.S., accused the Saudi Government of human rights abuses, corruption, and sponsoring terrorism. The same month, Ahmed Zahrany, Saudi Vice Consul in Houston, Texas, who sought political asylum in the United Kingdom, also rebuked the Saudi Government for human rights violations. Although denied by the Saudi Embassy in Washington, D.C., the allegations by two former Saudi officials did not help the already tarnished image of the Saudi royal family. In effect, al-Khilewi and Zahrany gave credibility to the Committee's allegations of human rights violations by the Saudi Government.

Six conservative Muslims formed the Committee for the Defense of Shari'a Rights in May 1993. In a meeting with its members, Prince Salman bin Abdel Aziz, brother of King Fahd, warned the Committee against 'disruptive' actions. When the Committee did not heed the warning, the Saudi Government tried to discredit the organization through Saudi Arabia's state religious agency. The Higher Council of Senior Ulama, a state-supported religious institution, castigated the dissident group for violating Islamic law. The government outlawed the organization the same month and dismissed four of the founders from government service. It closed the law offices of the remaining two founders. Later that May, it arrested a seventh person, who had served as the group's spokesperson.

What the monarchy finds most threatening is that the Committee, like the royalists themselves, invokes shari'a in its struggle for political rights and social justice. This invocation denies the ruling family the advantage of a religious monopoly in dealing with the political opposition. Even though the Committee is now London-based, its position derives from its founders' religious background. Given the important role of Islam in Saudi Arabia, the monarchy finds a religious based dissention even more threatening than secular political opposition. That explains why, even in the aftermath of the 1990 Gulf Crisis, the ruling elite still regards the Islamic Republic of Iran as a greater threat than secular Iraq (Abi-Aad and Grenon, 1997, pp. 65, 74; Braibanti, 1995, p. 61; Anthony, 1993, p. 117). During the 1987 *hajj* (pilgrimage), clashes between Iranian pilgrims and Saudi security forces had taken 402 lives. Consequently, in 1993, Saudi authorities prevented a demonstration by about 100,000 Iranian pilgrims.

Abdullah al-Masaari, the leader of the Committee, is familiar with Islamic legal scholarship. That makes it impractical for the establishment to dismiss him through religious repartees. On the contrary, al-Masaari was on the offensive in February 1996. Characterizing the Saudi dynasty as corrupt and autocratic, he made a clarion call for a truly Islamic government. While the Wahhabi alliance made the Saudi monarchy conservative (Elmusa, 1997, p. 348), it by no means holds the more orthodox views witnessed in Iran after the 1979 Islamic Revolution. Al-Masaari's call for an Islamic government endangers the very existence of the Saudi monarchy. Earlier, in September 1994, Saudi authorities arrested Salman al-Awdah and Safar al-Hawali, two Muslim clerics, for publicly criticizing the ruling dynasty. After escaping abroad in self-imposed exile, al-Masaari and Osama bin Ladin, another outspoken critic of the al-Saud family, had their citizenship revoked by the Saudi Government (U.S. Department of State, 1997, p. 1368).

Even though American troops add a sense of security from external threat, their presence feeds internal discontent. The June 1996 fuel truck explosion at the American military base in Khobar, near Dhahran, illustrates that volcanic sentiment. The vow by the Legion of the Martyr Abdullah al-Hazaifi to rid 'the holy Saudi land' of foreign troops adds a perilous twist for the al-Saud family.

Fearful of a religious threat to the monarchy, in April 1993 the Saudi Interior Ministry made it a requirement for Islamic civic or religious organizations to obtain official permission for soliciting funds. In addition to financial control, the monarchy has resorted to coercive tactics. In September 1994, the Committee for the Defense of Shari'a Rights claimed that Saudi authorities had made over 1,000 arrests in an anti-militant roundup. In 1993 al-Masaari was detained by the Saudi Government for six months for his role in establishing the Committee. In April 1995, London-based Amnesty International expressed grave concern over the dramatic increase in executions of prisoners in the Saudi Kingdom. During the first trimester of that year, 90 people were executed compared to 53 executions for the entire 1994. Under the shari'a penal code in Saudi Arabia, defendants do not have the right to a lawyer. Thus, they are denied the right to due process of law according to UN human rights standards as stated in the UN Covenant on Civil and Political Rights.

Conclusion

The GCC countries are not immune to global democratic and religious trends. Faced with ambitious regional Muslim neighbors, the ruling elite is forced to enter into security cooperation with major Western powers. With bilateral military arrangements with the West, the Gulf sheikhdoms face demands for domestic political changes. Western public opinion wants a transition to democracy in the Gulf monarchies, and Western human rights organizations criticize the Gulf sheikhdoms. These put pressure on Western governments to support and urge political change in the region. With increased exposure to the West, a segment of the professionals in the Gulf sheikhdoms has embraced Western ideas of democracy and liberty. The Shi'ites in the region are prudent in increasingly expressing their demands in democratic, rather than in sectarian terms. While some opposition organizations are secular in their views, others espouse a religious agenda. It is the latter group, invoking Islamic precepts, that poses a more serious challenge to the monopoly of power enjoyed by the ruling dynasties.

Islamic tradition strongly influences daily life in the GCC countries. Muslim interest groups view the monarchies as deviating from the path of Islam. Thus, they advocate a truly Islamic state based on the shari'a. The ruling elite has pursued the strategies of accommodation and confrontation, but only the al-Sabah family in Kuwait has gone so far as to allow parliamentary elections. The ruling families in Bahrain and Saudi Arabia have refused to move beyond appointing consultative bodies. Although limited, the step was significant for Saudi Arabia because the Saudi Consultative Council did not include any member of the ruling al-Saud family. Belonging to the minority Sunni sect, the al-Khalifa family in Bahrain is particularly vulnerable to a transition to majority rule.

The consultative bodies in Bahrain and Saudi Arabia are within the framework of an Islamic notion of consensus decision-making. Opposed to the Western adversarial model of democracy, the ruling families are more willing to experiment with a modified version of the consensus model. However, the reigning dynasties are not comfortable with Western procedural democracy. Even in Kuwait, which witnessed two elections in the post-Gulf War period, formal political parties are prohibited. Whether councils are appointed or elected, there is no significant separation of powers between the executive and legislative branches. Despite being the only GCC country to grant voting rights to its male citizens, real power sharing is limited in Kuwait. The legislative branch is clearly subordinate to the executive branch controlled by the monarch.

Inclusive political participation in Bahrain, Kuwait, and Saudi Arabia is limited to adult male citizens. With the increasing prominence of Islamic groups, voting rights for women do not have a high priority in these traditionally male-dominated Gulf societies. Kuwait has recently granted voting rights to some of its long-term male residents. In addition to undertaking administrative decentralization, Saudi Arabia has promulgated certain civil rights. However, those steps were also prompted by the desire of the al-Saud family to curb the power of the religious police that the government increasingly found intolerable. With regard to civil liberties, Saudi Arabia and Bahrain show a similar lack of tolerance.

The ruling elites in the GCC countries feel the changing wind sweeping the Persian Gulf. The Gulf dynasties are apprehensive about granting more civil liberties or civil rights. The ruling families have been willing to accept a degree of inclusive participation following Islamic tradition rather than Western-style democracy. The Gulf monarchies face a dilemma. By facilitating change, they loose their grip on power; by resisting change, they chance political upheaval, leading to their downfall. While resisting change, the ruling families have been pragmatic in making some limited concessions to the inevitable forces.

Notes

1.   The official name is the Cooperation Council for the Arab States of the Gulf. Founded on 25 May, 1991, the members are Bahrain, Kuwait, Oman, Qatar, Saudi Arabia, and the United Arab Amirates.
2.   In addition to amir (commander), sultan (imperial leader), and malik (king), the word sheikh is used in a generic sense to imply a 'ruler.' It is in that context that the work 'sheikhdom' is used in this chapter (Hottinger, 1981, p. 2; Esposito and Voll, 1996, pp. 25-6).
3.   The word 'nonconformist' is borrowed from Madawi al-Rasheed. Whereas 'radical' connotes deviant, 'fundamentalist' is a contested concept. While Bruce Lawrence of Duke University defends the latter term, John Esposito of Georgetown University rejects it. According to Lawrence, fundamentalists oppose modern world values through their adroit use of modern technology. Identifying three different interpretations, however, Esposito holds the term to be value-laden. Yet, taking a third perspective, two British scholars of Middle East origin view the word as a useful label (al-Rasheed, 1996, p. 17; Lawrence, 1987, pp. 32-4; Esposito, 1993, pp. 7-8; Sidahmed and Ehteshami, 1996, p. 5).
4.   The Islamic Front for the Liberation of Bahrain is a broad coalition of religious, nationalist, and Marxist opposition elements (Hiro, 1996, p. 260).

References

Abi-Aad, Naji and Michel Grenon (1997), *Instability and Conflict in the Middle East: People, Petroleum and Security Threats*, St. Martin's Press: New York.

Almond, Gabriel A. and G. Bingham Powell, Jr. (1966), *Comparative Politics: A Developmental Approach*, Little, Brown and Co.: Boston.

Al-Rasheed, Madawi (1996), 'Saudi Arabia's Islamic Opposition,' *Current History*, Vol. 95, No. 597, pp. 16-22.

Anthony, John D. (1981), 'Transformation amidst tradition: the UAE in transition,' in Chubin, Shahram (ed.), *Security in the Persian Gulf*, Vol. 1: *Domestic Political Factors*, International Institute for Strategic Studies, Allanheld, Osmun and Co.: Montclair.

Anthony, John D. (1993), 'Iran in GCC Dynamics,' *Middle East Policy*, Vol. 2, No. 3, pp. 107-20.

Bahry, Louay (1997), 'The Opposition in Bahrain: A Bellwether for the Gulf?' *Middle East Policy*, Vol. 5, No. 2, pp. 42-57.

Braibanti, Ralph (1995), *The Nature and Structure of the Islamic World, Position Paper One*, International Strategy and Policy Institute: Chicago.

Brynen, Rex; Bahgat Korany; and Paul Noble (1995), 'Introduction: Theoretical Perspectives on Arab Liberalization and Democratization,' in Brynen, Rex, Bahgat Korany, and Paul Noble (eds.), *Political Liberalization and Democratization in the*

Arab World, Vol. 1: Theoretical Perspectives, Lynne Rienner Publishers: Boulder.

Crystal, Jill (1992), *Oil and politics in the Gulf: Rulers and merchants in Kuwait and Qatar*, Cambridge University Press: New York.

Dahl, Robert A. (1989), *Democracy and Its Critics*, Yale University Press: New Haven.

Dunn, Michael C. (1995), 'Is the Sky Falling? Saudi Arabia's Economic Problems and Political Stability,' *Middle East Policy*, Vol. 3, No. 4, pp. 29-39.

Eickelman, Dale F. and James P. Piscatori (1996), *Muslim Politics*, Princeton University Press: Princeton.

Elmusa, Sharif S. (1997), 'Faust without the Devil? The Interplay of Technology and Culture in Saudi Arabia,' *The Middle East Journal*, Vol. 51, No. 3, pp. 345-57.

Esposito, John L. (1993), *The Islamic Threat: Myth or Reality?* Oxford University Press: New York.

Esposito, John L. and John O. Voll (1996), *Islam and Democracy*, Oxford University Press: New York.

Faour, Muhammad (1995), *The Arab World after Desert Storm*, United States Institute of Peace Press: Washington, D.C.

Fuller, Graham E. and Ian O. Lesser (1997), 'Persian Gulf Myths,' *Foreign Affairs*, Vol. 76, No. 3, pp. 42-52.

Gause, F. Gregory, III (1994), *Oil Monarchies: Domestic and Security Challenges in the Arab Gulf States*, Council on Foreign Relations Press: New York.

Ghabra, Shafeeq N. (1997a), 'Balancing State and Society: The Islamic Movement in Kuwait,' *Middle East Policy*, Vol. 5, No. 2, pp. 58-72.

Ghabra, Shafeeq N. (1997b), 'Kuwait and the Dynamics of Socio-economic Change,' *The Middle East Journal*, Vol. 51, No. 3, pp. 358-72.

Green, Jerrold D. (1985), 'Islam, Religiopolitics, and Social Change, A Review Article,' *Comparative Studies in Society and History*, Vol. 27, No. 2, pp. 312-22.

Hiro, Dilip (1996), *Dictionary of the Middle East*, St. Martin's Press: New York.

Hottinger, Arnold (1981), 'Political Institutions in Saudi Arabia, Kuwait and Bahrain,' in Chubin, Shahram (ed.), *Security in the Persian Gulf*, Vol. 1: *Domestic Political Factors*, International Institute for Strategic Studies, Allanheld, Osmun and Co.: Montclair.

Human Rights Watch/Middle East (1995), 'The Bedoons of Kuwait: Citizens without Citizenship,' Human Rights Watch: New York.

Huntington, Samuel P. (1968), *Political Order in Changing Societies*, Yale University Press: New Haven.

Huntington, Samuel P. (1993), *The Third Wave: Democratization in the Late Twentieth Century*, University of Oklahoma Press: Norman.

Ibrahim, Saad E. (1995), 'Democratization in the Arab World,' in Schwedler, Jillian (ed.), *Toward Civil Society in the Middle East?* A Primer, Lynne Rienner Publishers: Boulder.

Ismail, Salwa (1995), 'Democracy in Contemporary Arab Intellectual Discourse,' in Brynen, Rex; Bahgat Korany; and Paul Noble (eds.), *Political Liberalization and Democratization in the Arab World*, Vol. 1: *Theoretical Perspectives*, Lynne Rienner Publishers: Boulder.

Juergensmeyer, Mark (1994), *The New Cold War? Religious Nationalism Confronts the Secular State*, University of California Press: Berkeley.

'Kuwait, With Reservations, Nixes Sex Discrimination' (1994), *Chicago Tribune*, 6 March, p. 5.

Lawrence, Bruce B. (1987), 'Muslim Fundamentalist Movements: Reflections toward a New Approach,' in Stowasser, Barbara F. (ed.), *The Islamic Impulse, Center for Contemporary Arab Studies*, Georgetown University: Washington, D.C.

Lijphart, Arend (1977), *Democracy in Plural Societies: A Comparative Exploration*, Yale University Press: New Haven.

Lijphart, Arend (1984), *Democracies: Patterns of Majoritarian and Consensus Government in Twenty-One Countries*, Yale University Press: New Haven.

Lorentz, John H. (1995), *Historical Dictionary of Iran*, The Scarecrow Press: Lanham.

Luckmann, Thomas (1991), 'The New and the Old in Religion,' in Bourdieu, Pierre and James S. Coleman (eds.), *Social Theory for a Changing Society*, Westview Press: Boulder.

Mainuddin, Rolin G. (1995), 'The New World Order Transition in the Third World: Implications for the Nation-State,' *Journal of Third World Studies*, Vol. 12, No. 1, pp. 233-46.

Mainuddin, Rolin G. (1996), 'Is Islam A Threat to the West? A Review Article,' *Journal of Third World Studies*, Vol. 13, No. 1, Spring.

Mainuddin, Rolin G., Joseph R. Aicher, Jr., and Jeffrey M. Elliot (1996), 'From Alliance to Collective Security: Rethinking the GCC,' *Middle East Policy*, Vol. 4, No. 3, pp. 39-49.

Mawdudi, Abul A'la (1994), *Towards Understanding Islam*, Translated and edited by Khurshid Ahmad, American Trust Publications: Lahore.

Mazarr, Michael J.; Don M. Snider; and James A. Blackwell, Jr. (1993), *Desert Storm: The Gulf War and What We Learned*, Westview Press: Boulder.

Mazrui, Ali A. (1997), 'Islamic and Western Values,' *Foreign Affairs*, Vol. 76, No. 5, pp. 118-32.

Mill, John S. (1985), *On Liberty*, Himmelfarb, Gertrude (ed.), Penguin Books: New York.

Murphy, Richard W. and F. Gregory Gause, III (1997), 'Democracy and U.S. Policy in the Muslim Middle East,' *Middle East Policy*, Vol. 5, No. 1, pp. 58-67.

Piscatori, James P. (1983), 'Ideological Politics in Sa'udi Arabia,' in Piscatori, James P. (ed.), *Islam in the Political Process*, Cambridge University Press: New York.

Robinson, William I. (1996), *Promoting Polyarchy: Globalization, US Intervention, and Hegemony*, Cambridge University Press: New York.

Sharabi, Hisham (1990), 'The Scholarly Point of View: Politics, Perspective, Paradigm,' in Sharabi, Hisham (ed.), *Theory, Politics and the Arab World: Critical Responses*, Routledge, Chapman and Hall: New York.

Sidahmed, Abdel S. and Anoushiravan Ehteshami (1996), 'Introduction,' in Sidahmed, Abdel S. and Anoushiravan Ehteshami (eds.), *Islamic Fundamentalism*, Westview Press: Boulder.

Sisk, Timothy D. (1992), *Islam and Democracy: Religion, Politics, and Power in the Middle East*, United States Institute of Peace Press: Washington, D.C.

Sorensen, Georg (1993), *Democracy and Democratization: Process and Prospects in a Changing World*, Westview Press: Boulder.

Taji-Farouki, Suha (1996), 'Islamic State Theories and Contemporary Realities,' in Sidahmed, Abdel S. and Anoushiravan Ehteshami (eds.), *Islamic Fundamentalism*, Westview Press: Boulder.

U.S. Department of State (1997), *Country Reports on Human Rights Practices for 1996*, Washington, D.C.

8 Turkey

PAUL J. MAGNARELLA

Turkey stands as the only democratic state with a predominantly Muslim population. Although most of Turkey's territory lies in the Middle East, its political leaders have created a West European-style constitutional republic with a pro-Western foreign policy. Turkey boasts a democratically elected parliament and an independent judiciary. It is a member of the North Atlantic Treaty Organization, the Council of Europe, the European Union (associate member), and the Conference on Security and Cooperation in Europe. Turkey is also an American ally and has often been a major recipient of United States foreign aid.

Despite these achievements, Turkey is currently a major target of domestic and international criticism over its human rights practices. Critics have focused their concern mainly on the following allegations: 1) torture and the suspicious deaths of prisoners while in detention; 2) disappearances and extra-judicial killings of opposition politicians, human rights activists, journalists, and Kurdish nationalists; 3) government infringements on the freedoms of speech, press and association; 4) denial of due process to persons under the jurisdiction of state security courts and in the state of emergency region; 5) the destruction of Kurdish villages in the Southeast by the Turkish military; and 6) suppression of Kurdish cultural expression.[1] The United States, the Council of Europe's Parliamentary Assembly, and the Conference on Security and Cooperation in Europe have all urged Turkey to improve its human rights record.

This chapter examines the issue of human rights in Turkey from legal, political, and cultural perspectives and offers information gathered by the author during a fact-finding trip to Turkey in April, 1994. In addition to presenting a general background to Turkey's human rights problems, the article focuses on the legal bases for human rights abuses and the special situation of the Kurds.

Political and Legal Background

After World War I, Mustafa Kemal Atatürk provided the charismatic political leadership to construct the modern Turkish Republic on the crumbled foundations of the multi-ethnic Ottoman Empire. As head of a one-party political system, Atatürk, with the support of his Republican Peoples Party (RPP), embarked on the ambitious agenda of remaking multi-ethnic Anatolia and Eastern Thrace into a modern 'nation-state.' Although Turkey's population was predominantly Muslim, it was, and continues to be, ethnically diverse, consisting of such peoples as Abkhasians, Albanians, Arabs, Armenians, Assyrians, Azeris, Bosnians, Chechens, Circassians, Georgians, Greeks, Gypsies, Kurds, Laz, Turks, and others.[2]

In the post-World War I Treaty of Lausanne (1923), Turkey recognized the distinct ethnic status of only Christian Armenians, Christian Greeks, and Jews, in order to appease the victorious Western powers, who apparently cared little about the Muslim minorities (B. Lewis, 1961, pp. 348-51). In the process of nation-building, the Turkish governing elite categorized all Muslims as ethnic Turks. Use of their languages in public discourse, educational institutions, broadcasts, and publications was prohibited. Turkism, the ideology that all citizens (with the exception of Jews and Christians) were ethnically Turks and should learn true Turkish (their languages were supposedly substandard variants of Turkish) was deeply inculcated in much of the population through compulsory public education. The existence of Muslim ethnic minorities was officially denied. The government did not tolerate non-Turkish cultural expression, regarding it as a danger to the indivisibility of the state. 'The Turkish Republic has consistently been concerned to promote linguistic and cultural homogeneity' (Barchard (1985, p.13).

The strongest resistance to these cultural restrictions has come from the Kurds, a people speaking an Indo-European language (Kurdish) and claiming Turkey's Southeast as part of their traditional homeland. Approximately 40 percent of their estimated 8.5 million to 12 million population in Turkey resides in the central and western parts of the country (Gunter, 1990, pp. 6-7). While many of these Kurds have been Turkified and integrated into Turkish society, a large proportion of those residing in the remote Southeast have not.

The leaders of the new Turkish state had inherited the long statist tradition of the Ottoman Empire. Atatürk and his closest supporter and successor, Ismet Inonu, had been products of the Ottoman tradition of elite-directed military and bureaucratic reform aimed at strengthening the state's defenses and preventing secession (Pevsner, 1984, p. 6). The six principles of Kemalist ideology—republicanism, secularism, statism, populism and reformism—provided for loyalty to a unified nation defined in terms of ethnic Turkism (Karpat, 1959, pp. 251-348).

Having accused Islamic-Ottoman institutions and culture of causing the fall of the Ottoman Empire, Atatürk embarked on a vigorous program of secularization, abolishing the offices of Caliphate and Sultanate, disestablishing Islam as the official religion, replacing Islamic law with European legal codes, and substituting Latin letters for the Arabic script. Atatürk's principle of populism involved substituting Turkish national and state identity for Islam.

Atatürk died in 1938, and former general Ismet Inonu succeeded him. He saw his RPP suffer defeat in Turkey's first open and honest multi-party election in 1950. Over the years, Turkey's electoral system had progressively evolved. During the early years of the republic the voting franchise had been limited to males over eighteen years of age, and the national electoral had been indirect. Men voted for secondary electors who selected the actual deputies to the unicameral assembly. In 1934 women received the right to vote and to run for national office. In 1950 and thereafter elections were based on fully direct suffrage. All votes became equal; citizens cast secret ballots; and election officials counted the ballots publicly. From 1950 to 1994, citizens twenty-one years of age or older were eligible to vote, the exceptions being military personnel below the rank of officer, persons convicted of serious crimes, and persons banned from the process by military governments. In 1995, the minimum voting age was reduced to eighteen. (For a more detailed description of the systems of government and politics in Turkey prior to the 1980 coup, see Magnarella, 1983.)

The political divisions manifested during Turkey's subsequent multi-party eras grew out of the country's diverse sociocultural and economic composition. The elitist RPP had been supported by secularists, ardent Turkish nationalists, the urban elite, civil bureaucrats, military leaders and large landowners. During its period of rule, the Democrat Party (DP) appealed to the disinherited and the RPP's own disenchanted. It eased legal restrictions on Islamic religious expression and directed more economic benefits to small businessmen and farmers, who comprised about 70 percent of the population. These constituencies returned the DP to power in the 1954 and 1957 elections. Significantly, unlike Atatürk and Inonu, neither the DP president nor prime minister had previously been generals. Consequently, they lacked the confidence and support of the military, whose fixed salaries were actually diminishing owing to the high inflation created, in part, by liberal government spending. After the government had repeatedly called on the military to quell 'illegal' demonstrations of political protest by university students in Ankara and Istanbul, the generals decided civilian politics had failed.

Headed by General Cemal Gursel, the military carried out a bloodless coup on May 27, 1960 and drove the Democrats out of office (Weiker,

1963). The ruling junta, known as the National Unity Committee (NUC), appointed a committee of liberal law professors to write a new constitution that would both act as a legal obstacle to future political abuses and institutionalize the military's involvement in politics. The resulting document created a bicameral parliament and made members of the NUC senators for life. It also created a National Security Council, comprised of the armed forces chiefs, who would assist the cabinet in making decisions concerning national security and coordination. In addition, the constitution provided for a constitutional court; it legalized free trade unions with the right to strike and bargain collectively; and granted autonomous status to radio and television stations and to the universities. The constitution also guaranteed the freedoms of conscience, political belief, assembly, and press as well as the right to form political parties. This, Turkey's most liberal constitution ever, went into force in 1961 after winning acceptance in a national referendum. (For a comparison of Turkey's 1924, 1961, and 1982 constitutions, see Tamkoç 1983.)

That same year the NUC lifted its ban on political parties and allowed national elections as well as the renewal of civilian rule. During the 1960s, the military, with its establishment of the Military Mutual Assistance Association (known as OYAK), became intimately involved in the Turkish and international economies. OYAK controlled a huge investment fund accumulated through obligatory and voluntary contributions of military personnel and investment profits. It invested heavily in the automobile, truck, and tire manufacturing industries; petrochemical, cement and food processing industries; and retail and service industries. As a result of OYAK investments, the economic security of thousands of active and retired armed forces officers and enlisted personnel became dependent upon the profitability of large domestic and international capitalistic enterprises. The Turkish military, through OYAK became partners with foreign and domestic firms and shared with them the same concerns for profits, political stability, and labor compliance. Consequently, the military's corporate interests expanded into the areas of labor law, trade unionism, monetary policy, corporate taxation, investment banking, the media, and other related matters (Ahmad, 1977, pp. 280-81; Ergil, 1975, p.12-15).

For the rest of the 1960s various civilian government coalitions tried to cope with the country's growing economic and demographic problems: high rates of inflation and unemployment, labor-management strife, violent strikes and lockouts, small business bankruptcies, anti-government demonstrations, clashes between right- and left-wing students, and rapid urbanization. Believing the civilian politicians were unable to cope with these crises, the praetorians forced the government to resign and replaced it with a series of 'above party' governments from 1971 to 1973. During this period, the military also declared martial law in most major cities and over a dozen provinces. It prohibited strikes and lockouts; banned radical political publications; arrested thousands of people, including labor activists, leftists, religious activists, and intellectuals; and shut down radical political organizations, such as the pro-Islamic National Salvation Party and the pro-Marxist Turkish Workers Party. These suppressive measures, however, only temporarily lowered the country's level of agitation.

From 1973 to 1980 another series of fragile and ineffective coalition governments confronted the same problems of the 1960s, with the addition of widespread political terrorism. The situation was aggravated by an economic decline in Western Europe that put a halt to the flow of Turkish workers going abroad and reduced the remittances of those already there. In addition, the U.S. embargo on military aid to Turkey, because of the latter's 1974 Cyprus intervention, caused serious reductions in the defense budget (Magnarella, 1982).

On September 12, 1980, the military marched into this chaotic scene and took control of the government once again. In order to bring about stability, protect Atatürk's heritage and safeguard its own economic interests, it declared martial law throughout the country, dissolved parliament, banned all political parties and political activity, and arrested thousands of suspected terrorists and criminals, along with political activists, intellectuals and labor leaders. The new junta, called the National Security Council (NSC), ruled the country for the next three years and three months as the most repressive of Turkey's praetorian governments. It came down especially hard on members of leftist trade unions and Kurdish nationalists (Barchard, p. 13, 1985; van Bruinessen, 1984). Ruling by decree, the NSC permanently terminated all existing political parties and arrested several of their leaders. It outlawed all but one moderate labor confederation, strictly limited the right to strike, and decreed that henceforth labor unions could not engage in political activity. The NSC placed the universities and radio and television stations under direct government supervision and sharply curtailed freedom of the press. Any criticism of the coup, the NSC or its actions constituted crimes.

The NSC replaced the 1961 constitution with a much less liberal document that created a unicameral parliament and a strong presidency. According to the new constitution, presidential actions are largely immune from the checks of other governmental branches. For example, Article 105 states: 'No appeal shall be made to any legal authority, including the Constitutional Court, against the decisions and orders signed by the President of the Republic on his own initiative.' Note that up to this point in Turkey's history, only one president had not been a retired general or admiral.

Article 125 states: 'The acts of the President of the Republic in his own competence and the decisions of the Supreme Military Council are outside the scope of judicial review.' Parliament (Grand National Assembly) elects the national president, who holds office for a single, non-renewable seven year term. The constitution also provides for a prime minister, who heads the council of ministers. With the acceptance of the new constitution in the November 1982 referendum, General Kenan Evren, the head of the NSC, automatically became president. Multi-party national elections followed, and civilian politicians, with the advice of military leaders, have governed the country since 1983.

Turkey's 1982 Constitution and Turkish Constitutionalism

The 1982 constitution stresses the concept of an indivisible, unified state and the reforms of Atatürk. For example, the preamble (which Article 2 incorporates into the constitution) states in part:

> [N]o protection shall be afforded to thoughts or opinions contrary to Turkish national interests, the principle of the existence of Turkey as an indivisible entity with its state and territory, Turkish historical and moral values, or the nationalism, principles, reforms and modernism of Atatürk, and that as required by the principle of secularism, there shall be no interference whatsoever of sacred religious feelings in state affairs and politics... .

Article 14 not only reemphasizes indivisibility, but apparently prohibits any kind of regional autonomy arrangement for a large, distinctive ethnic population, such as the Kurds:

> None of the rights and freedoms embodied in the Constitution shall be exercised with the aim of violating the indivisible integrity of the State with its territory and nation, ... of placing the government of the State under the control of an individual or a group of people, or establishing the hegemony of one social class over others, or creating discrimination on the basis of language, race, religion or sect, or of establishing by any other means a system of government based on these concepts and ideas. (Art. 14).

Several provisions of the constitution guarantee the rights of thought, speech and the press:

Article 25. Everyone has the right to freedom of thought and opinion. No one shall be compelled to reveal his thoughts and opinions for any reason or purpose; nor shall anyone be blamed or accused on account of his thoughts and opinions.

Article 26. Everyone has the right to express and disseminate his thoughts and opinion by speech, in writing or in pictures or through other media, individually or collectively. This right includes the freedom to receive and impart information and ideas without interference from official authorities.... The exercise of these freedoms may be restricted for the purposes of preventing crime, punishing offenders, withholding information duly classified as a state secret, protecting the reputation and rights and the private and family life of others, or protecting professional secrets as prescribed by law, or ensuring the proper functioning of the judiciary... .

Article 28. The press is free and shall not be censored. The establishment of a printing house shall not be subject to prior permission and to the deposit of a financial guarantee.
. . .
Anyone who writes or prints any news or articles which threaten the internal and external security of the State or the indivisible integrity of the State with its territory and nation, . . . shall be held responsible under the law relevant to these offenses.

With Article 28, the constitution also provides the legal basis for criminalizing speech that criticizes governmental actions (if the speech is deemed to threaten the security of the state) or advocates a cultural rights policy for non-Turkish minorities, such as the Kurds (if it is deemed to threaten the indivisible integrity of the state with its territory and nation).

Based on his own analysis of Turkish history, this writer concludes that the principles of constitutionalism that provide the Turkish politico-legal system with its essential structure and bases for action, consist, in part, of the following:

1) *Statism and authoritarianism.* The state, through the government in power, closely directs the country's economy, society and culture. 'In Kemalist Turkey, reform and centralization by a cohesive center was the ideal aim of statecraft, as it had been in Ottoman Turkey. In the multiparty period [from 1946] this tradition persisted in the form of 'bureaucratic

paternalism' and military imposition of reform' (Pevsner, 1984, p. 9). The Turkish political scientist, Metin Tamkoç has written: 'Modernization of Turkey was initiated under the authoritarian regime of Atatürk. His authoritarian political system was the product of the traditional political culture and patrimonial infrastructure' (Tamkoç, 1983, pp. 26-27). '[In] Turkey there is no room for an 'opposition group.' The governing elite do not tolerate opposition to their authority or their policies' (*Ibid*). The ruling elites have also shown little tolerance for criticism. For example, in her statement to the U.S. Commission on Security and Cooperation in Europe, Lois Whitman, Deputy Director of Helsinki Watch, said police had harassed, detained, interrogated, and beaten scores of journalists for their writings. Some have been tried and sentenced, having been convicted under the very broad anti-terror law of such offenses as criticizing or insulting the president, public officials, Atatürk, or the military, or of printing anti-military propaganda (*Human Rights in Turkey,* p. 20).

2) *Military involvement in government, the economy and society.* The military elite, seeing themselves as the guardians of the state and Atatürk's heritage, intervene frequently in the economy and government, either through authoritarian advice or coups. The noted Turkish political journalist, Mehmet Ali Birand (1987, p. 2), has written that the Turkish armed forces are perceived to have the legitimate right and duty to intervene in politics and government in the name of the nation. He adds that through coups and military rule, the generals 'have stamped their imprint on every aspect of Turkish society for the foreseeable future' (*Ibid*.; For discussions of this theme, see also Tamkoç, 1976 and Hale, 1994).

3) *Atatürk's principle of populism.* Populism stands against class-based politics and for an indivisible, unified state based on one people and one language. A component of populism is Turkification: the state, through ruling governments from Atatürk to the present, has tried to convert ethnically heterogeneous peoples into a homogeneous population of Turks. The process has involved rewriting history (e.g., the sun-language theory, which maintains that Turkish is the origin of all other languages) (Karpat, 1959, p. 55) and suppressing the cultural identity and expression of non-Turkish peoples within Turkey.

4) *Legalism.* The practice by both civilian and military governments to legalize all the above, so as to legitimize the state's often intimate involvement in the economy, society and culture; the political and legal consequences of military intervention; and the related processes of Turkification and suppression of non-Turkish culture.

All of these principles have had serious consequences for human rights.

Charges of Torture and Death While in Custody

Despite the Constitution's ban on torture, the Government's cooperation with unscheduled foreign inspection teams, and public pledges by successive governments to end the practice, torture continues to be widespread. In December, 1992, the European Committee for the Prevention of Torture stated that over a three year period it had found abundant proof that 'torture and other forms of severe ill-treatment of persons in police custody remains widespread in Turkey and that such methods are applied to both ordinary criminal suspects and persons held under anti-terrorism provisions' (Cited in *Amnesty International Report* p. 290, 1993). The Turkey's Human Rights Foundation (THRF) reported 530 credible applications for treatment during 1997 (*U.S. State Dept. Rpt. 1997*). In January 1997, the United Nations Special Rapporteur on Torture and other Cruel, Inhuman, or Degrading Treatment or Punishment reported that he continued to be concerned by the apparently widespread practice of torture in Turkey.

According to the U.S. Department of State's 1997 report, human rights observers report that because the arresting officer is also responsible for interrogating the suspect, some officers may resort to torture to obtain a confession that would justify the arrest. Many detainees state that prosecutors ignore their claims of abuse during interrogation. Commonly employed methods of torture alleged by the THRF's torture treatment centers include: high-pressure cold water hoses, placing large ice blocks on the chest and stomach, electric shocks, beating on the soles of the feet, beating of genitalia, hanging by the arms, blindfolding, sleep deprivation, deprivation of clothing, systematic beatings, and vaginal and anal rape with truncheons and, in some instances, gun barrels. Other forms of torture were sexual abuse, submersion in cold water, use of truncheons, hanging sandbags on detainees' necks, forcing detainees to stand on one foot, releasing drops of water on detainees' heads, oxygen deprivation, sitting on detainees' laps, riding on their shoulders, and withholding food. Human rights attorneys and physicians who treat victims of torture say that most persons detained for or suspected of political crimes usually suffer some torture during periods of incommunicado detention in police stations and gendarmerie stations before they are brought before a court. Turkish government officials admit that torture occurs, but they deny that it is systematic; they explain that it is closely tied to the fight against terrorism. Many cases of torture, however, occur in western Turkey, outside the zone of conflict.

In response to international criticism concerning torture, parliament passed special legislation to bring Turkey's criminal procedures in line with its obligations under the European Convention for the Protection of Human Rights and Fundamental Freedoms and to sharply reduce, if not eliminate, torture and deaths of persons in custody.

Changes in Criminal Procedure

On November 18, 1992, the Turkish parliament passed the bill entitled 'Amendments to the Code of Criminal Procedure and the Law on Establishment and Prosecution Procedures of the state security courts.' In a Turkish Embassy (Washington, D.C.) press release dated December 1, 1992, the Turkish government claimed that this piece of legislation, known in Turkey as CMUK, 'brings Turkish law into conformity with international standards in the vital areas of detention periods, arrest procedures and interrogation practices.' The law contains many positive, human rights elements, but its restrictions have raised concerns among Turkish lawyers and human rights NGOs. Following is a summary of the law's main articles.

Taken together, Articles 12, 20, and 22 institute a Turkish version of the U.S. Miranda rule. Article 12 requires the police to inform anyone taken into custody of the crime with which he/she will be charged and of his/her rights to remain silent and to have a lawyer present during all interrogations. Article 20 states that a defendant has the right to meet in private with his/her lawyer and to communicate with him/her freely. Article 22 requires the local bar association to assign a lawyer to any indigent defendant who requests one. Article 22 also states that the Ministry of Finance will allocate a fund to the Union of Bar Associations to meet lawyers' fees. If the court finds the defendant guilty, the Union of Bar Associations has the right to charge the defendant for court costs and lawyer's fees. Article 15 stipulates that a defense lawyer must be assigned to any defendant who is either under 18 years of age, deaf, dumb, or too impaired to defend him/herself. In such cases, no request for a lawyer is necessary. Article 13 prohibits the use of torture, force or violence, ill-treatment, drugs, or false promises during interrogation and detention. This article also establishes an exclusionary rule by stipulating that any statements extracted by unlawful methods will not be considered evidence for a conviction, even if the defendant consents.

Although the police and, in rural areas, the gendarmerie have the authority to take persons into custody, Article 5 states that only a judge has the power to issue an arrest warrant. The defendant, if present, and his lawyer as well as the prosecutor have a right to be heard by the judge before he/she issues the warrant. Article 5 stipulates that the arrest warrant should state, as explicitly as possible, the defendant's identity and the reasons for the arrest, including the acts attributed to him/her, the time and place of the acts, and the laws deemed to have been violated.

According to Article 6, a person arrested on a warrant issued in absentia, must be brought before a judge within 24 hours for a judicial determination concerning continued detention. Article 9 allows the arrestee to have a defense lawyer present at this appearance. Article 9 additionally states that the maximum period of police custody before the initial appearance before a judge is 24 hours in the case of crimes attributed to an individual and, if the prosecutor so orders in writing, up to four days for crimes attributed to three or more persons. A judge may double these times upon the written request of the prosecutor. The maximum detention periods for crimes falling under the jurisdiction of the state security courts are 48 hours in the case of crimes attributed to an individual and 15 days for crimes attributed to three or more persons. These periods may be doubled in state of emergency areas (see below).

Article 4 restricts the conditions of prolonged pre-trial detention and may promote the right to a speedy trial. If a defendant can prove his/her identity and residence, the court will not order detention if punishments for the crime(s) in question require imprisonment for six months or less. For crimes requiring imprisonment for up to seven years, the court will release the defendant if his/her trial has not been concluded within two years of arrest. For more serious crimes, the judge will release the defendant on bail (the amount to be determined by the judge) if his/her trial has not been concluded within two years of arrest.

Significantly, however, Article 31 states that none of the above articles, with the important exception of Article 13 (unlawful means of interrogation) apply to persons and crimes that fall under the jurisdiction of state security courts (see below). In March, 1997 CMUK was amended to grant immediate attorney access to persons arrested for common crimes, and after 4 days of detention to persons detained under the anti-terrorism law or for other 'security' crimes. However, private attorneys and human rights monitors reported uneven implementation of these reforms, claiming that in some cases police officers postdate the day of detention to comply with the new law (*U.S. Dept. of State Rpt. 1997*).

In an interview given to the author on April 22, 1994 in Ankara, Turkey, Mr. Sami Kahraman, Secretary General of the Ankara Bar Association, claimed that CMUK was working effectively. He explained that most members of the Ankara Bar served a 15-day duty period each year on a rotating basis. When the police arrest someone requiring a lawyer under CMUK, the station notifies the Bar Headquarters (located on the fifth floor of the main court building), which then assigns a on-duty lawyer from its computerized list. There is no charge to an indigent defendant for such representation. The Bar reimburses lawyers according to a schedule from funds supplied by the Ministry of Finance. Mr. Kahraman said that the bar associations in other major Turkish cities, such as Istanbul and Izmir, had established similar procedures and were experiencing the same success. He also said that the Ankara police had invited Bar lawyers to give them talks about the new law. Consequently, the Ankara Bar was actively involved in education programs for the police. Mr. Kahraman explained that the major shortcomings of CMUK were that it did not apply equally to the state security courts, to so-called 'terrorist' crimes (see below), or to the state of emergency area of the Southeast. But, he concluded, the law is a very positive beginning.

However, interviews conducted by the author with representatives of various independent human rights organizations in Ankara, such as the Contemporary Jurists Association, Human Rights and Solidarity for Oppressed People Association (an Islamic organization), and the Turkish Human Rights Association turned up less sanguine assessments. All agreed that CMUK moved in the right direction, but certainly had not eliminated the pattern of torture in Turkey's police stations and prisons. It appears that although Turkey passes much of the necessary human rights legislation and ratifies many of the key human rights conventions, its implementation of them leaves much to be desired. Some of the most serious infringements of human rights have been legalized by the state security courts and the anti-terrorist law.

State Security Courts and the Anti-Terrorism Law

Turkey currently has eight state security courts composed of both civilian and military judges and prosecutors. They have jurisdiction over civilian cases involving acts prohibited by the anti-terrorism law, drug smuggling, membership in illegal organizations, and the dissemination of ideas prohibited by law as damaging the indivisible unity of the State. These courts may hold closed hearings and may admit testimony obtained during police interrogation in the absence of counsel. Persons accused of crimes falling under the jurisdiction of these courts may be detained twice as long before arraignment as other defendants. Defense lawyers generally have access to the prosecutor's files after arraignment, but in cases involving the anti-terrorism law and other crimes, such as insulting the president and defaming Turkish citizenship, defense attorneys may be denied access on national security grounds.

The most important offenses over which state security courts have jurisdiction are those defined by the Law to Fight Terrorism (entered into force April 12, 1991). This law defines terrorism as 'any kind of act done by one or more persons belonging to an organization with the aim of changing the characteristics of the Republic as specified in the Constitution, its political, legal, social, secular and economic system, damaging the indivisible unity of the State with its territory and nation by means of pressure, force and violence, terror, intimidation, oppression or threat.' [Article 1. (1)] It defines a terrorist as:

> Any member of an organization, founded to attain the aims defined in Article 1, who commits a crime in furtherance of these aims, . . . or any member of such an organization, even if he does not commit such a crime, shall be deemed to be a terrorist offender.'

In addition, Article 2 (1) states,

> 'Persons who are not members of a terrorist organization, but who commit a crime in the name of the organization, are also deemed to be terrorist offenders... .'

Over the past several decades, Turkey has certainly been plagued by acts of terrorism, both by officials and private citizens. Among the non-governmental organizations engaging in terrorism are: the Kurdish Workers' Party (PKK), the Revolutionary Left (*Devrimci Sol*), and the Turkish Peasants' and Workers' Liberation Party (TIKKO), the Turkish Communist Workers Movement (TKIH), and the Turkish Revolutionary Communist Union (TIKB). These groups murdered or assassinated 331 persons during the 500-day period from November 21, 1991 to April 5, 1993 (*500-Day Report,* p. 24). Their targets were soldiers, police officers, mayors and prosecutors, village guards, and persons accused of being police agents or state supporters. Most were killed by the PKK. The danger of the Article 2 definition of terrorist is that overly zealous state security court prosecutors too frequently attach it to persons who share some of the cultural and political goals of terrorist groups, but not their methods (see below).

Turkish authorities have alleged that a wide range of political activity, such as speeches, petitions, and peaceful demonstrations are 'separatist' in nature. Consequently they have frequently indicted journalists, Kurdish nationalists, and even former members of parliament for statements which allegedly amount to 'propaganda against the indivisible unity of the State' and violate Article 8 (1) of this law:

Written and oral propaganda and assemblies, meetings and demonstrations aimed at damaging the indivisible unity of the Turkish Republic
with its territory and nation are prohibited, regardless of the methods,
intentions and ideas behind such activities. Those conducting such
activities shall be punished with a sentence of between 2 and 5 years'
imprisonment and with a fine of between 50 million and 100 million
Turkish liras. [Art. 8(1)]

In its 500-day report, THRF maintains that during the period most of
the 62 journalists and writers who had been tried, heavily fined and
sentenced to from six to 41 months in prison had been convicted of the
crimes of 'making or disseminating separatist propaganda' (a violation of
Article 8(1) above), or of 'insulting the state' or 'insulting Turkey's
security forces' (violations of Article 159/1 of the Turkish Penal Code)
(*500-Day Report,* pp. 40-43). Such oppression is not confined to press
journalists. On February 11, 1994, two civilian television journalists were
sentenced to two months imprisonment by a military court because they
had interviewed conscientious objectors, even though they had not
endorsed the objectors' views (Litherland, 1994). On April 21, 1994, this
writer was among a handful of people allowed to attend the military trial
of Mr. Aytek Özel, one of the conscientious objectors interviewed. At the
trial, held in Ankara's Mamak Military Prison complex, Özel, a former
president of the Association Against War, was found guilty of 'causing the
public to be opposed to the military,' and was sentenced to one year, fifteen
days in prison and fined 210,000 Turkish Liras. The defendant claimed that
his only crime was being against war.

Unlike similar sentences for ordinary crimes, 'Sentences imposed
under [the Law to Fight Terrorism] cannot be commuted to a fine,
converted to other measures or suspended' (Article 13). The permissible
detention periods for crimes under this law are longer than those for
ordinary crimes: 'People detained for offenses under this law shall be
presented before a judge within 48 hours [of their arrest]; in case of
collective crimes, within 15 days excluding the time it takes to bring the
suspect from the place of detention to the nearest court' (Article 11).
During detention, defendants do not have the right to meet privately with
their attorneys: 'The defendant in pre-trial detention or convicts may have
contact with a lawyer under the supervision of a detention center or prison
official.' Art. 10(b).

According to Turkish government figures obtained by the U.S.
Department of State at the end of 1993, 3,792 persons were being detained
under this law, and 811 persons were serving sentences for violations of its
provisions (*U.S. Department of State Rpt. 1994*). The legal bases for

human rights abuses are compounded where the state security courts and anti-terrorism law are combined with the laws pertaining to a state of emergency region.

State of Emergency Region

Since 1987, the southeastern provinces with the heaviest concentration of Kurdish people have constituted a state of emergency area and have been governed by a special governor with special powers and immunities. The legal bases for this arrangement rest primarily on the Turkish Constitution and two laws: the State of Emergency Law and the Emergency Regional Governance Law.

In 1983 the Turkish parliament passed the State of Emergency Law, which empowered the Council of Ministers assembled under the chairmanship of the President to declare a state of emergency 'whenever there appear serious indications resulting from widespread acts of violence which are aimed at destroying the free democratic order or fundamental rights and freedoms, or violent acts causing serious deterioration of public order.' Art. (1)(b). According to the Turkish Constitution, 'During the state of emergency, the Council of Ministers meeting under the chairmanship of the President of the Republic, may issue decrees having the force of law on matters necessitated by the state of emergency' (Art. 121). Significantly, there can be no judicial reviews of such decrees. Even the Constitutional Court may not review decrees having the force of law issued under a state of emergency or martial law.

Once such a state of emergency has been declared, 'All citizens between 18 and 60 years of age, who are resident within a state of emergency region . . . are obligated to perform the duties imposed on them under the state of emergency.' Art. 8(1). Measures which authorities may take in the state of emergency area include:

'Prohibition of people from residing in certain localities in the con-cerned region; . . . evacuation of certain areas and transfer of people to other areas.' Art. 9(a).

'Demolition of unsafe buildings, destruction of real estate and personal property which threaten health . . .' Art. 9(f).

'Imposition of a limited or full curfew.' Art. 11(a);

'Prohibition of any kind of assembly or procession or movement of vehicles in certain places or within certain hours.' Art. 11(b).

'Authorization of officials to search persons, their vehicles or property and to seize goods deemed to have evidentiary value.' Art. 11(c).

'Prohibition of the publication, importation or distribution of publications and confiscation of books, magazines, newspapers, brochures, posters and other publications that have been banned.' Art. 11(e).

'Control and, if deemed necessary, restriction or prohibition of every kind of broadcasting and dissemination of words, writing, pictures, films, records, sound and image bands.' Art. 11(f).

'Control and, if deemed necessary, restriction or prohibition of the exhibition of all kinds of plays and films.' Art. 11(h).

In addition, 'the custody periods prescribed in the Code of Criminal Procedure (Art. 128) may be doubled upon a written request made by the Public Prosecutor to a judge' (Art. 26). This means that persons detained for offenses under the anti-terrorism law should be presented before a judge within 96 hours of their arrest for individual crimes, but within 30 days in the case of collective crimes. This provision appears to run counter to Turkey's obligations under the European Convention for the Protection of Human Rights and Fundamental Freedoms. In *Brogan v. United Kingdom* (1988), a case involving U.K.'s 1984 Prevention of Terrorism Act, the European Court of Human Rights held that U.K. authorities, who had detained four Northern Ireland suspected terrorists for periods ranging from four days and six hours to six days and sixteen hours before bringing them before a judicial authority, had breached Article 5(3) of the European Convention, which requires detainees to be brought 'promptly' before a judge.

Significantly, the Turkish state of emergency law prevents anyone from using the courts to stop the governor or those acting under his authority from carrying out measures deemed to violate human rights: 'The issuing of stay orders against the administrative acts of governors performed in accordance with the authority vested in them shall be prohibited' (Art. 33).

Subsequently, in 1987, the President and Council of Ministers decreed that, 'A State of Emergency Regional Governance shall be established covering the southeastern provinces of Bingol, Diyarbakir, Elazig, Hakkari, Mardin, Siirt, Tunceli and Van.'[3] The decree provides that the emergency area governor shall have all private and public security forces in region at his disposal, [Art. 2(b)], and that 'he may order the temporary or permanent evacuation of villages, winter stations for flocks and arable fields in areas within his territorial jurisdiction to make necessary arrangements for the general security and may order the re-settlement or unification of inhabitants in such places.' Art. 2(h).

The decree also makes the governor immune from legal liability: 'No action shall be brought in any court of law in connection with the exercise of powers conferred on the State of Emergency Regional Governor by this Decree' (Art. 7). This last article apparently runs counter to Turkey's obligations under the European Convention for the Protection of Human

Rights and Fundamental Freedoms, which holds: 'Everyone whose rights and freedoms . . . are violated shall have an effective remedy before a national authority notwithstanding that the violation has been committed by persons acting in an official capacity' (Art. 13).

The primary reason for these measures has been the efforts on the part of the Kurdish Workers Party (PKK) to establish a separate state in the Southeast through a campaign of terrorism directed at both Turkish security forces and civilians. According to the Turkish Government, from 1984 through November 1997, 26,532 PKK members, 5,185 security force members, and 5,209 civilians have lost their lives in the fighting (*U.S. Dept. of State Rpt. 1997*). In an effort to deny the PKK logistical support, the Government has rationed food and other essentials in various southeastern provinces and has forcibly evacuated and destroyed from 2,300 to 3,000 villages, displacing over one million people (*Ibid.*). In November of 1997, the European Court of Human Rights found Turkey in violation of Article 8 (right to respect for home) in the case of three southeastern applicants whose homes were burned down by security forces in 1993. The Court attached particular weight to the fact that the public prosecutor did not carry out any meaningful investigation into the matter. The applicants were awarded court costs and expenses with damages to be determined at a future date.

Although human rights violations in Turkey affect a wide variety of people in different occupations and regions, the Kurdish case is especially egregious and demands particular attention.

The Case of the Kurds

Most of today's approximately twenty million Kurds live in the mountainous region where Turkey, Iraq and Iran converge. They may be descendants of Indo-European peoples who settled the region about 2,000 BC. Although their homeland has historically been known as Kurdistan, land of the Kurds, they have never had a unified state of their own. They became Muslims in the seventh century A.D., and were parts of the Ottoman and Persian Empires for centuries prior to World War I (van Bruinessen, 1978).

The 1920 Treaty of Sevres, between the victorious World War I Allies and the Ottoman Sultan, designated the Kurdish occupied southeastern area of Turkey as an autonomous region and granted the Kurds the right to opt for independence within a year. However, when the government of Atatürk renegotiated the terms of this agreement in the Treaty of Lausanne (1923), autonomy and independence for the Kurds was dropped (Shaw & Shaw, 1977, v. 2 pp. 365-366).

'The official ideology of the Republic of Turkey since the mid-1920s has sought to deny the existence of Kurdish people in the country. . . . Both Turks and Kurds were taught that they were descended from the pure Turkish race' (Gunter, p. 43, 1990). Kurds were referred to as 'mountain Turks' (G. Lewis p. 97, 1974).

From 1922 to 1938 there were three major Kurdish revolts against Turkey's policies of Turkification and secularization (Olson, 1989). Turkish forces crushed all three. Until the 1970s, the Kurds were largely quiescent despite the fact that Turkish law prohibited Kurdish speech in public and Kurdish cultural organizations, and public prosecutors considered references to Kurds or Kurdish in the press to be illegal attacks on the integrity of the republic.

During the 1970s and 1980s, however, a number of pro-Kurdish organizations began to vigorously advocate Kurdish cultural and political rights. The most prominent of these, the Kurdish Workers Party (PKK), sought to create a secessionist Kurdish state though violence and terrorism (Gunter, 1990, pp. 57-95). In 1984 the PKK launched a violent guerrilla campaign in the southeastern provinces. This led to a major counter-offensive by Turkish military forces, large-scale arrests of suspected Kurdish leaders, and imposition of martial law. A state of emergency replaced martial law in July, 1987, but the violence continued unabated.

Even purely cultural efforts by Turkey's Kurds have been thwarted by officials applying Article 8(1) of the anti-terrorism law. For example, on June 22, 1992, as required by law, the founding officers of the newly organized Kurdish Cultural Foundation applied to Istanbul's Court of First Instance for registration as a foundation. The organization's stated purpose was to promote research and publication on Kurdish language, literature, history, geography, folklore, music and ethnography. The Court subsequently denied registration to the organization claiming it was based on a race and thereby violated Article 14 of the Constitution(see above) (*500-Day Report* p. 45).

The Kurdish Institute, founded as part of the Mesopotamian Culture Center, to research Kurdish language history and culture, opened in Istanbul on April 18, 1992. On November 15, 1992 the police, following the directive of the state security court's Prosecutor's Office, raided it, detaining three persons and seizing documents, publications, films, photographs and computer disks (*Ibid.*). In subsequent years, this Center and its branches have experienced similar police raids and police harassment (*U.S. Dept. of State Rpt. 1997*). Such state actions are premised on the allegation that these cultural organizations, activities, and materials threaten the indivisibility of the Turkish state.

One of the most notorious cases is that of cultural anthropologist Ismail Besikçi, a Turk, who has researched and written on Kurdish culture, society and history. He had served ten years in prison between 1971 and 1987 for his publications, which courts had ruled constituted separatist propaganda (*U.S. Dept. of State Rpt. 1997*). In 1993 he was again indicted on two counts of disseminating separatist propaganda through two of his recent books. He was tried and convicted in the Ankara Security Court under the Law to Fight Terrorism and sentenced to 20 months and fined 42 million Turkish Liras on each count (*Ibid.*).

The state and military actions described above have generated support for the PKK. Mary Sue Hafner, General Counsel to the U.S. Commission on Security and Cooperation in Europe, remarked that while there is no doubt that the PKK is a terrorist organization, it is equally true that such anti-state movements feed on government human rights violations, unemployment, and poor living conditions (*Human Rights in Turkey*, 1993, p. 26). She advised the Turkish government to address the underlying political, economic, and cultural conditions that have made many Kurdish citizens sympathetic to the PKK's initial goal of establishing a separate Kurdistan or current goal of gaining regional autonomy within Turkey (*Ibid.*). Similarly, Lois Whitman has stated that based on interviews with Kurds and others in Turkey's Southeast, Helsinki Watch believes that the continuing pattern of abuse by Turkish security forces, their shooting of unarmed and nonviolent demonstrators, the failure to investigate assassinations, and the excessive detention and torture of Kurds have contributed to support for the PKK (*Ibid.* pp. 27-28).

Local and foreign human rights activists have accused Turkey of seeking only a military solution to the Kurdish issue and not a negotiated political one. This accusation appeared valid when on March 2, 1994 the Turkish Parliament, under apparent pressure from the military, voted to strip six Kurdish deputies of their parliamentary immunity to allow an investigation into their alleged separatist activities.[4] Five were members of the pro-Kurdish Democracy Party (DEP). In June the Constitutional Court banned the Democracy Party, stripping its 13 deputies of parliamentary membership. On August 3, 1994 state security court prosecutors accused the arrested deputies of acting as part of the political wing of the banned PKK and asked for the death sentence. The former deputies denied the charges.[5] Subsequently, a number of these former deputies were convicted under Article 168-1 of the anti-terrorist code and received sentences ranging up to 15 years.

Their arrests had stirred up international outrage. Former French foreign minister Roland Dumas agreed to participate in their defense (International News [radio] Paris, March 8, 1994). The president of the 32-state Council of Europe Parliamentary Assembly, Spain's Miguel Angel Martinez, publicly expressed the assembly's concern that such events could occur in a member country of the Council of Europe, 'which is based on democratic values including freedom of expression and the rule of law' (*Mideast Mirror* March 8, 1994). Danielle Mitterrand, wife of France's President, and 12 Nobel Peace Prize winners called for the United Nations to appoint a special envoy to investigate the plight of Turkish Kurds (Hepburn, 1994). Western criticism over the affair became so intense that the morale of Turkish diplomats was adversely affected (*Ibid.*).

The 1995 Constitutional Changes

In early 1995, when the Turkish government, then headed by Prime Minister Tansu Çiller, was negotiating Turkey's entrance into a customs union agreement with the European Union (EU), the EU Parliament informed Turkey that it had to amend its constitution to make it more democratic and demonstrate greater respect for human rights (Reuters, July 10, 1995).   Subsequently, Çiller submitted a package of proposed constitutional amendments to parliament and succeeded in getting most of them passed on July 23, 1995 by a 360-32 vote (Agence France Presse, July 23, 1995).   One group of new amendments facilitates greater citizen political participation by allowing associations (Art. 33), trade unions (Art. 52, repealed), foundations and vocational institutions (Art. 69 & 135), and cooperatives (Art. 171) to establish ties with political parties.   Amended Article 67 lowers the age for voting and party membership from 21 to 18, and permits both university faculty members and students to join political parties.   Article 75 increases the number of parliamentary seats from 450 to 550. With respect to labor rights, Article 53 allows certain categories of civil servants the right to form unions and to bargain collectively, but not to strike.

Çiller's success was viewed positively by the EU, the Council of Europe and Amnesty International, although they all stressed that more had to be done. Critics pointed to the necessity of amending the infamous Article 8 of the anti-terrorism code of 1991 as well as Article 13 of the Constitution, upon which it is based. Critics charge that these and related articles in the criminal code do not meet standards for free expression as set in the European Convention for the Protection of Human Rights and Fundamental Freedoms, which Turkey has ratified and has promised to respect. Article 10 of that Convention reads, in part, as follows:

Everyone has the right to freedom of expression. This right shall include freedom to hold opinions and to receive and impart information and ideas without interference by public authorities and regardless of frontiers... .

The exercise of these freedoms . . . may be subject to such formalities, restrictions or penalties as are prescribed by law and are necessary in a democratic society, in the interests of national security, territorial integrity or public safety... . [Council of Europe, 1992]

Anti-Terrorism Code Article 8

Parliament did not amend Article 13 of the Constitution, which allows for restriction of all fundamental rights and freedoms. Article 13 reads, in part, as follows:

Fundamental rights and freedoms may be restricted by law, . . . with the aim of safeguarding the indivisible integrity of the state with its territory and nation, national sovereignty, the Republic, national security, public order, general peace, the public interest, public morals and public health... .

The general grounds for restriction set forth in this article shall apply for all fundamental rights and freedoms.

Turkish authorities have alleged that a wide range of cultural expression and cultural analysis found in speeches, books, newspaper articles, petitions, and peaceful demonstrations are 'separatist' in nature. Consequently, Turkish prosecutors have frequently indicted journalists, authors, scholars, Kurdish nationalists, and even former members of parliament for making statements which allegedly amounted to 'propaganda against the indivisible unity of the State' and violated various articles of the criminal code and Article 8. In the four years following the adoption of the 1991 anti-terrorist law, Article 8 was used to convict 2,752 persons--mostly professors, writers, journalists, union leaders, and entertainers. (Rouleau, 1996).

In its survey entitled 'Attacks on Journalists in 1995,' the Committee to Protect Journalists claimed that Turkey led all countries in the numbers of journalists it imprisoned in both 1994 and 1995 (Haq, 1996). In her statement to the U.S. Commission on Security and Cooperation in Europe, Lois Whitman, Deputy Director of Helsinki Watch, said police had harassed, detained, interrogated, and beaten scores of journalists for their writings. Some have been tried and convicted under the very broad anti-terror law of such offenses as criticizing or insulting the president, public officials, Atatürk, or the military, or of printing anti-military propaganda (*Human Rights in Turkey*, 1993, 20). Article 8 stated that:

> No one shall, *by any means or with any intention or idea,* make written and oral propaganda or hold assemblies, demonstrations and manifestations against the indivisible integrity of the state of the Turkish Republic with its land and nation. Those carrying out such activity shall be sentenced to imprisonment from two to five years and fined from TL 50 to TL 100 million. [emphasis added]

Under Article 9 of the same law, the state security courts are responsible for applying Article 8, and they had chosen to interpret it as if it were a strict liability crime in which the real intention, whether innocent or not, of the defendant was immaterial. This resulted in severe restrictions on the freedoms of speech, expression, press, association and assembly. In October of 1995, Nadire Mater reported that there were 177 authors serving prison terms for 'crimes' related to promulgating Kurdish separatism, and 5,600 other cases involving violations of Article 8 were being heard by state security courts (Mater, 1995).

In 1995 state security courts predominantly handled cases under the anti-terror law and section 312 of the Criminal Code, which prohibits 'incitement to racial enmity.' Those accused of crimes falling under the jurisdiction of these courts can be detained twice as long before arraignment as other defendants. The heavy caseload often means that cases drag on for years. According to credible press reports, during 1995, 1,443 publications (56 books, 784 journals, 602 newspapers, and 1 bulletin) were confiscated on court order (*U.S. Dept. of State Rpt. 1996*).

Legislative reforms in 1991 had partially removed the ban on the use of the Kurdish language, but Kurdish-language broadcasts are still illegal. Pro-PKK 'Med TV' now broadcasts from England daily and can be received by satellite dish in Turkey's Southeast.

Thanks to Prime Minister Çiller's efforts, Turkey's parliament did amend Article 8 on October 27, 1995. The rewording of the law (in part) is as follows:

> No one may engage in written and oral propaganda *aimed at* disrupting the indivisible integrity of the State of the Turkish Republic, country and nation. Meetings, demonstrations, and marches *with this aim* may not be engaged in. Those who engage in such deeds will be sentenced

to from one to three years in prison and given a heavy fine of from TL 100 million to TL 300 million. [emphasis added]

The revised law contains a number of significant changes. For one, it replaces the phrase *'by any means or with any intention or idea'* with the more specific phrase *'with this aim.'* Hence, it should transform a strict liability crime, in which intent was irrelevant, into an intent crime, where the *mens rea,* or specific criminal intent, of the defendant is a necessary element of the crime to be proven by the prosecution, thereby making convictions more difficult.

The revised law also reduces prison sentences of from two to five years to from one to three years. This reduction reclassifies the penalty from one of 'criminal imprisonment' to one of simple 'imprisonment,' thereby allowing the courts to suspend the execution of punishments or commute them to fines.

Some Results of and Reactions to the Legal Amendments

Although many of Turkey's European critics were still not satisfied with Turkey's legal liberalization, the EU did approve Turkey's accession to the Customs Union by a vote of 343 to 149 on December 13, 1995. Hence, Çiller's government had achieved its immediate goal.

A temporary article accompanying the amendment to Article 8 called on the courts to reexamine the files of persons previously convicted under the old Article 8 to determine whether application of the new amendment might result in an acquittal, reduced sentence or conversion of sentence into a fine. As of January 8, 1996 the courts had ruled that 141 prisoners should be released and seven acquitted. Many journalists and publishers were among those who benefitted. According to human rights monitors in Turkey, however, about 100 persons remained in prison for things they had written or said, and thousands were being tried (Marcus, 20 Feb. 1996).

In August of 1996, the International Federation of Human Rights maintained that in Turkey 'no less than 152 laws have as their sole object the control of freedom of opinion and expression' (Agence France Presse, 7 Aug. 1996). The Federation described the modification of Article 8 as 'cosmetic,' and called for its total abolition. It also called on Turkey to immediately permit an inspection by a special UN rapporteur on freedom of expression. The organization, Reporters Without Borders, dubbed the amendment to Article 8 a false reform, a 'cosmetic measure aimed at enabling ratification of the customs union by the European Parliament' (Reuters World Service, Oct. 31, 1995).

In a dramatic challenge to the state security courts and as a test of the limits of free speech allowed by amended Article 8, approximately 1,080 of Turkey's leading figures (including writers, journalists, artists, entertainers, trade unionists and lawyers) listed themselves as the 'publishers' of a book entitled *Freedom of Expression and Turkey*, which contains writings by authors who had previously been convicted of writing 'separatist propaganda' under the old Article 8. Some of the articles discussed the campaign of Kurdish rebels to create a separate Kurdish state or an autonomous region in Turkey's Southeast. Others, including the one by Yasar Kemal (Turkey's best known writer internationally) critiqued Turkey's military response to the insurgency, which had taken the lives of 20,000 people over a 12 year period. The 73 year old Kemal had received a 20 month suspended sentence for writing the essay reproduced in this book.

In December of 1995, 99 of the 'publishers' were charged with violations of Article 8 (producing 'separatist propaganda'), Article 312 ('provoking enmity') and another article prohibiting the publication of criminal works. Istanbul's state security court rejected the defendants' argument that the three laws unconstitutionally limited debate of controversial issues and violated Turkey's international human rights commitments. (Marcus, 7 Dec. 1995).

Conclusion

Turkey faces the dilemma of reconciling two opposed objectives: its own acceptance as a truly liberal democracy and the continuation of its historic constitutional principles of Turkism, statism, and authoritarianism. As part of the policy to achieve the first objective, Turkey made many positive moves in the human rights area. It became a party to an impressive number of international human rights conventions (see Table 1.2). Turkey must now live up to these international obligations. When it does not, members of the international community, especially other States Parties to international human rights treaties, have the right to object and demand explanations and remedies.

As part of its effort to promote human rights, the government established a Parliamentary Human Rights Commission in 1990 and a Human Rights Ministry in 1991. On April 21, 1994, this writer interviewed Mr. Sabri Yavuz, President of the Turkish Parliament's Human Rights Commission, in Ankara. The writer was impressed with Mr. Yavuz's verbal commitment to human rights and especially with his statement that 'even a terrorist is a human and must be treated as a human once he is taken into custody.'

Turkey also has an active number of human rights lawyers and non-governmental organizations, even though many of their members have been attacked and killed by unknown assailants believed to be operating in complicity with Turkish security forces (*500-Day Report,* pp. 46-49). Many of these lawyers, especially those who are members of the Contemporary Jurists Association, represent human rights victims for little or no fee. These lawyers are becoming more aware of their ability to petition international human rights bodies on behalf of their clients when justice fails locally. In April, 1994 officers of the Turkish Human Rights Association presented this writer with a copy of their association's just-published book containing the major international human rights instruments in Turkish (Gemalmaz 1994). Both the general secretary of the Ankara Bar Association and an officer of the Contemporary Jurists Association told this writer that their organizations were about to complete manuals, to be distributed to members, explaining how to file a petition with the European Human Rights Commission.

According to Turkish government sources, in July 1994, there were approximately 300 individual petitions by Turkish citizens against Turkey before the European Human Rights Commission, and thirty cases against Turkey in the European Court of Human Rights. These figures became available when confidential letters between Turkey's foreign minister, justice minister and interior minister were leaked to the press (*Turkish Daily News* July 19, 1994). In his letter, Foreign Minister Hikmet Çetin, reacting to continuing criticism from the West, informed the other ministers that the large number of petitions filed against Turkey reflected the poor quality of justice in the state of emergency region. He warned that if the quality of justice does not improve, 'the European Court of Human Rights will take the place of Turkish judicial organs in relation to events that take place in the Southeast . . . .' (*Ibid.*)

The European Court may very well rule that parts of Turkey's state of emergency legislation conflict with the European human rights convention. Because Turkey is under a solemn obligation to honor the judgments of the European Court, the legal changes necessary to promote human rights may come from that direction.

The Turkish government must act soon, before an irreparable fissure separates Turks from Kurds. One observer has noted that the government's fight against the PKK 'has turned into a fight against the Kurdish nation and against human rights' (Marcus, 1994). Omur Lutfu Coskun, chairman of a parliamentary commission to study causes of and solutions to the problems in the Southeast, warned listeners at a press conference that despite PKK terrorism, 'sensitivity [on the part of the government and military] is necessary so as not to regard all the region's people as potential criminals' (*Daily Briefing*, April 19, 1994). One Turkish journalist concluded that 'the southeastern problem is the litmus test for democracy in our country' (Candar 1994).

For legal remedies to become effective, most Turks may have to be reeducated to tolerate and appreciate cultural differences, to value and accept cultural pluralism as a normal characteristic of modern, liberal democracies. As positive moves in this direction, Turkey, within the last few years, has made human rights education in primary schools mandatory; it is an elective in high schools. The government has also begun to provide human rights training for the police and military. The military has begun to emphasize human rights training for its officers and noncommissioned officers, which human rights NGOs reported led to a reduction in human rights violations in 1997 (*U.S. Dept. of State Rpt.* 1997).

Turkey's current (1997-98) government has stated that human rights are at the top of its agenda. In July of 1997, Prime Minister Mesut Yilmaz appointed an activist State Minister for Human Rights, who also is coordinator for the High Council for Human Rights. The Council, comprised of undersecretaries from the Justice, Interior, Education, Health, and Foreign Affairs Ministries (along with representatives of the security forces), meets weekly to review aspects of the human rights situation and to advise the Government on steps for improvement. The Minister and the Council have invited an active dialogue with the increasingly important NGOs that work for human rights reforms both in Ankara and in the Southeast (*U.S. Dept. of State Rpt. 1997*). Many Turks and friends of Turkey sincerely hope that these educational, legal and administrative measures will function effectively to establish Turkey as a model for human rights in the Middle East.

Notes

1. Charges and criticisms are contained in the reports of Amnesty International, Helsinki Watch, and the Human Rights Foundation of Turkey (see especially its *500-Day Report (21 November 1991- 5 April 1993)* [Ankara] (1993), hereinafter referred to as the *500-Day Report*), and U.S. Department of State, *Turkey: Country Reports on Human Rights Practices, 1993, 1994 , 1995, 1996, 1997* (Washington, D.C.).

2. In his 5 April 1993 statement before the U.S. Commission on Security and Cooperation in Europe, Turkish historian Heath Lowry said that when the 600 year old Ottoman Empire came to an end in 1923, 'there were somewhere between 35 and 45 different ethnic groups represented in what was to become the boundaries of the new Republic of Turkey.' *Human Rights in Turkey* (1993, p. 32). For ethnographic descriptions of many of these peoples, see Andrews (1989); Magnarella (1981; 1979).

3. Decree 285 having the Force of Law on the Establishment of the State of Emergency

Regional Governance. Published in the Official Gazette on 14 July 1987. (Article 1). Batman and Sirnak were added by Decree 246 dated 18 May 1990.

4. 'Indictment Read as DEP Trial Begins in Ankara,' *Anatolia* [in English, radio] 1610 GMT (3 Aug. 1994), Reported in *Daily Briefing* FBIS-WEU-94-150, at 39-40 (4 Aug. 1994).

5. In an interview published in a Berlin newspaper, Kemal Bilget, deputy chairman of the DEP stated that 'the DEP has nothing to do with the PKK. The PKK is an illegal organization that pursues an armed struggle. We, on the other hand, are a legal organization that struggles on a democratic basis; . . .' The Junta Constitution Continues to Be Valid in Turkey,' *Neues Deutschland,* 14 April 1994, p. 7. Reported in *Daily Briefing,* FBIS-WEU-94-075, at 36 (19 April 1994).

References

Agence France Presse (23 July 1995), 'Turkey Overhauls Constitution in a Move Likely to Appease West,' Lexis-Nexis News File.

Agence France Presse (7 Aug. 1996), 'Turkey: TFHR Details Turkish Torture, Murder, Detention,' FBIS-WEU-96-154.

Ahmad, Feroz (1977), *The Turkish Experiment in Democracy 1950-1975*, Westview, Boulder.

Anatolia [in English, radio] (15 April 1994) 'Commission Urges Tolerance with Southeast Problem,' 1425 GMT, reported in *Daily Briefing* (19 April 1994), FBIS-WEU-94-075, p. 35.

Andrews, Peter A. (1989), *Ethnic Groups in the Republic of Turkey,* L.Reichart, Weisbaden.

Barchard, David (1985), *Turkey and the West*, Routledge and Kegan Paul, London.

Birand, Mehmet Ali (1987), *The Generals' Coup in Turkey,* Brassey's, London.

Brogan v. United Kingdom. European Court of Human Rights, 1988. Ser. A No. 145-B, 11 EHRR 117.

Candar, Cengiz (3 July 1994), 'Southeast 'litmus Test' for Democracy,' *Nokta* [in Turkish] p. 10, reported in *Daily Briefing* (11 July 1994), FBIS-WEU-94-132, p. 44 .

Çevik, Ilnur (July 30, 1994), 'Dangerous Turn of Events for Turkey,' *Turkish Daily News*, p. A3.

Council of Europe (1992), *Human Rights in International Law: Basic Texts,* Council of Europe Press, Strasbourg, Fr.

Dahlberg, Robin et al. (1989), *Torture in Turkey: The Legal System's Response. Report of the Committee on International Human Rights of the Bar of the City of New York*, New York.

Ergil, Dogu (1975), 'Class Conflict and Turkish Transformation (1950-1975),' *Studia Islamica,* vol. 41, pp. 12-15.

Gemalmaz, Mehmet Semih (1994), *Temel Belgelerde Insan Haklarî* [Human Rights in Basic Documents], Kavram Yay., Ankara.

Gunter, Michael M. (1990), *The Kurds of Turkey,* Westview, Boulder.

Hale, William M. (1994), *Turkish Politics and the Military,* Routledge, London.

Haq, Farhan (14 March 1996), ' Media: Turkey Tops World in Jailing Journalists,' *Inter Press Service.*

Helsinki Watch (1989), *Paying the Price: Freedom of Expression in Turkey,* Washington, D.C.

Hepburn, Bob (17 April 1994), 'Turkey's Civil War Heating Up; Ankara Launches Crackdown against 'Kurdish Problem,'' *Toronto Star* p. C5.

Human Rights Foundation of Turkey (1993), *500-Day Report (21 November 1991- 5 April 1993)*, Ankara.

Human Rights in Turkey. Briefing of the [U.S.] Commission on Security and Cooperation in Europe 20 (5 April 1993), Washington, D.C.

Karpat, Kemal H. (1959), *Turkey's Politics*, Princeton Univ. Press, Princeton.

Kurkcu, Ertugrul (21 April 1994), 'Peace: a Rational End to the Southeast Conflict,' *Turkish Daily News*, p. B3.

Lewis, Bernard (1961), *The Emergency of Modern Turkey*, Oxford Univ. Press, London.

Lewis, Geoffrey (1974), *Modern Turkey* , Praeger, New York.

Litherland, Susan (11 Feb. 1994), 'Turkey-Human Rights: Government Criticized for Press Crackdown,' *Inter Press Service*, London.

Magnarella, Paul J. (1983), 'Turkey,' in G.E. Delury (ed.), *World Encyclopedia of Political Systems and Parties*, Vol. 2, pp. 1032-51.

Magnarella, Paul J. (1982), 'Civil Violence in Turkey: Its Infrastructural, Social and Cultural Foundations,' in Çigdem Kagîtçîbasî (ed.), *Sex Roles, Family and Community in Turkey*, Indiana Univ. Press, Bloomington, pp. 383-401.

Magnarella, Paul J. (1981), *Tradition and Change in a Turkish Town,* Schenkman, Cambridge.

Magnarella, Paul J. (1979), *The Peasant Venture*, Schenkman, Cambridge.

Marcus, Aliza (20 Feb. 1996), 'Turkish Writers Languish in Jail Despite Changes,' *Reuters World Service*.

Marcus, Aliza (7 Dec. 1995), 'Turkish Court Orders Trial of 99 Intellectuals,' *Reuters*.

Marcus, Aliza (Jan. 3, 1994), 'Turkey's Kurds Fight on Alone,' *The Nation* vol. 258, no. 1.

Mater, Nadire (26 Oct. 1995), 'Turkey-Human Rights: Infamous Article 8 Targets Dissident Writers,' *Inter Press Service*.

Olson, Robert (1989), *The Emergence of Kurdish Nationalism and the Sheikh Said Rebellion,* Univ. of Texas Press, Austin.

Ozkok, Ertugrul (13 July 1994), 'Çiller: I am Initiating a Debate on Kurdish Rights,' *Hurriyet* , (7 July 1994), p. 25. Reported in *Daily Briefing*, FBIS-WEU-94-134, p. 53.

Pevsner, Lucille W. (1984), *Turkey's Political Crisis*, Praeger, New York.

Reuters European Community Report (10 July 1995), Lexis-Nexis News File.

Reuters World Service (31 Oct. 1995), 'Press Watchdog Faults Turkey's New Free Speech Law.'

Rouleau, Eric (1996), 'Turkey: beyond Ataturk,' *Foreign Policy* No. 103, pp. 70-88.

Situation of Kurds in Turkey, Iraq and Iran, Briefing of the Commission on Security and Cooperation in Europe (17 May 1993), Washington, D.C.

Stanford, Stanford J. and Ezel Kural Shaw (1977), *History of the Ottoman Empire and Modern Turkey* , vol. 2, Cambridge Univ. Press, Cambridge.

Tamkoç, Metin (1983), *Inconsistency between the Form and Essence of the Turkish Political system*, Univ. of Utah Press, Salt Lake City.

Tamkoç, Metin (1976), *The Warrior Diplomats: Guardians of National Security and the Modernization of Turkey*, Univ. of Utah Press, Salt Lake City.

Turkish Embassy press release (1 Dec. 1992), 'Turkish President signs the Legal Reform Bill,' Washington, D.C.

U.P.I. (13 March 1996), 'Turkish Free-Speech Trial Adjourns'.

U.S. Department of State, *Turkey: Country Report: Human Rights Practices, 1993, 1994, 1995, 1996, 1997* (Washington, D.C.).

van Bruinessen, Martin (Feb. 1984), 'The Kurds in Turkey,' *MERIP Reports,* vol. 121, pp. 6-12.

van Bruinessen, M. M. (1978), *Agah, Shaikh and State: On the Social and Political Organization of Kurdistan*, Zed Books, London.

Weiker, Walter (1963), *The Turkish Revolution, 1960-61*, Brookings, Washington, D.C.

'Evren Says Çiller's Policy 'Impossible,'' *Yeni Günaydin*, 10 July 1994, p. 15. Reported in *Daily Briefing,* FBIS-WEU-94-134, p. 54, 13 July 1994.

'Indictment Read as DEP Trial Begins in Ankara,' (3 Aug. 1994), *Anatolia* [in English, radio] 1610 GMT , Reported in *Daily Briefing* (4 Aug. 1994), FBIS-WEU-94-150, pp. 39-40.

'The Junta Constitution Continues to Be Valid in Turkey,' (14 April 1994), *Neues Deutschland*, p. 7. Reported in *Daily Briefing* (19 April 1994), FBIS-WEU-94-075, p. 36.

'Ministers Respond to Çetin Letter on Rights,' (July 19, 1994), *Turkish Daily News*, pp. 1, A8. Reported in *Daily Briefing* (22 July 1994), FBIS-WEU-94-141, pp. 42-43.

'Roland Dumas to defend Turkish Kurd MPs,' (8 March 1994), International News [radio] Paris, Lexis-Nexis News Service.

'Treatment of the Kurdish MPs Draws Western Criticism,' (8 March 1994), *Mideast Mirror* vol. 8, no. 4, Lexis-Nexis News Service.

9 Human Rights within Israel

RUSSELL A. STONE [1]

Israeli society operates in an atmosphere of contradictions on human rights. Most international attention is focused on the controversial issue of Israeli actions and policies in the West Bank and Gaza, territories occupied by Israel following the 1967 war. International human rights organizations have been very vigilant and highly critical of Israel's human rights record in the territories. On the other hand, Israeli society itself (within the boundaries where Israel exercises sovereignty as an independent state) seldom draws international attention on human rights issues, despite a series of unique features and controversial issues confronting the country. This chapter deals with the topic of human rights *within* Israel. The chapter in this volume by Ilan Peleg focuses on the issues in the territories.

To be sure, a complete division of attention is impossible. The Supreme Court hears cases that relate to military policy in the territories as well as security-related actions within Israel (allegations of torture and permissible use of 'moderate physical pressure,' legality of collective punishment such as sealing or destroying houses), Israeli citizens express concern and demonstrate over their government's actions in the territories, and domestic (Israeli) human rights organizations watch over the situation in the territories as well as within Israel. However, this chapter focuses on a number of other issues in the structure and functioning of Israeli society that have important implications for human rights. These relate to some unique features of Israel itself.

Although Israel is a democracy, it operates without a formal constitution, and until recently it had little specific human rights legislation. As a relatively 'young' country, precedents set by the courts became important benchmarks for future decisions. Incomplete separation of religion and state means conflicts over religious issues can become matters of basic human rights. A strong egalitarian ethic has raised questions of gender equity within a human/civil rights context. The country is a party to a protracted conflict, and security concerns are ever-present. Censorship, state control of education, ethnic and religious minorities' rights, and needs for state security are all human rights topics of interest within Israel. Unlike the question of treatment of occupied peoples, which is perhaps unique to Israel and a few other 'problem spots' in the world, the human rights questions *within* Israeli society have relevance for comparison with many other countries in the Middle East and beyond.

This chapter on Israel will provide a brief review of: a) national history and governance, b) the nature of democracy in Israel, c) human rights legislation and policy, d) human rights in practice, and the international record, and e) organizations supporting human rights activities. Then we will consider three major human/civil rights issues facing the country, now and in the future.

The Historical and State Setting for Human Rights

The state of Israel was formally established on May 14, 1948 by the Proclamation of Independence from a "National Council" of political representatives of the Jewish community in Palestine and abroad. The council ruled through the period of war that broke out after independence was declared until elections to the first Knesset (parliament) were held in January 1949. Later in 1949 Israel was recognized by the United Nations, and the war ended in a series of armistice agreements with Egypt, Jordan, Syria and Lebanon that established the borders along cease-fire lines, defining the initial boundaries of the state. (Boundary issues came into question again when Israel occupied additional territory after the 1967 war. These issues have not yet been settled).

The First Knesset formalized a state framework with a democratic political structure headed by a president (fixed term, appointed by the knesset), and with a multi-party political system where parties compete in regular elections for seats in the Knesset. The Knesset forms the legislative branch of government. There is also an executive branch with government ministries, headed by a directly elected prime minister, who must have enough party support in the knesset to permit formation of a government. (All Israeli governments to date have been coalitions.) And, from a human rights point of view, the most important feature is an independent judiciary with judges appointed by the President for life (compulsory retirement at age 70). The court system consists of three levels: magistrates' courts, district courts (appellate plus original jurisdiction for serious civil and criminal charges), and a supreme court; plus special courts for municipal-level issues; and religious courts for matters of personal status such as marriage, divorce and religious conversion. There are separate religious court systems for Jews (rabbinical), Moslems (*sharia*) and Christians (ecclesiastical).

The Supreme Court is crucial to human rights decisions and issues in Israel. As the highest appellate court in the country, it hears appeals on matters of important principle, including cases where human rights are at issue. It has the power to override the actions of lower courts if they exceed their jurisdiction. As the High Court of Justice it also has original jurisdiction in petitions against the government, its ministers and all public officers and agencies. The High Court of Justice has jurisdiction in the occupied territories on issues involving actions of the Israeli armed forces and the military government. The court also interprets the application of the law of the land, including the important Basic Laws passed in the absence of a constitution (see legislation, below).

Democracy and Human Rights in Israel

From the outset Israel has defined itself as a democratic and a Jewish state. The "democratic" part of this formula has clear meaning, so the structure of Israeli democracy is not at issue. Elections are held at regular intervals and are always contested by a wide range of parties. All citizens, Arab and Jewish, female and male, have the right to vote. The number and ideological composition of political parties have varied over the years. Laws govern how political parties may be formed as well as minimum votes necessary for representation in the knesset. A recent electoral law changed the 'rules of the game' for election of the prime minister (direct election) and for rules governing parliamentary non-confidence. The impact of these changes has been controversial, but there is no internal disagreement over the legitimacy of how changes can be made. Rule of law is well established, with a clear and respected tripartite division of responsibility among legislature, executive and judiciary. The military and police are responsible to and subject to civilian control. Thus, all the formal structures for assuring preservation of human rights are in place and functioning . . . with one exception. There is no formal constitution.

Failure to enact a constitution during the first knesset and in all subsequent parliamentary sessions arises from the fact that Israel declared itself both a Jewish and a democratic state in the same Proclamation of Independence that assured freedom of religion. Arguments over how a Jewish state religion can coexist with democracy have resulted in numerous controversies, court cases, legislative battles and social debates over the years. Israel is not formally a theocracy. Both secular and religious (Jewish) political parties, and small Arab parties function within the political system. (There are no Moslem or Christian religious political parties, but in principle they could be formed. They have not, in light of the demographics and political history of Israel as a Jewish state with Moslem and Christian, mostly Arab/Palestinian, minorities.) However, compromise agreements reached early in the history of the state allocate certain rights to religious authorities, including control of personal status law (marriages and divorces), and rights of religious schools to receive state support. Following the precedent of the Ottoman *millet* system of separate jurisdictions for religious communities, confessional groups may establish their own religious courts for personal status issues as well as their own schools. Many political and legislative decisions over the years have been based upon compromises between secular and religious viewpoints, leveraged by religious party membership in most government coalitions. Defection by religious parties can result in a government losing its parliamentary majority. Thus, the interests of religious parties are constantly a part of the political scene, an active element in Israeli democracy.

Religious and secular interests have differed vehemently on the question of establishing a constitution from the very origin of the state. As human rights provisions are an integral part of a constitution, the religious/secular stalemate has affected the assurance of basic rights. The reason for religious opposition to a constitution is because most modern constitutions contain provisions for equality (including equality between the sexes) and separation of 'church' and state that appear inconsistent with *halacha* (Jewish traditional law). It was envisioned that granting basic freedoms could result in freedom to violate or ignore Jewish laws and traditions that the religious leadership intensely wished to observe, and to impose on the state. The parliamentary stalemate over the issue in the First Knesset resulted in a 1950 compromise agreement to establish a 'Constitution, Law and Justice Committee' that would propose piecemeal a series of "basic laws." The basic laws would be written as chapters of a potential constitution, but they would be enacted individually as they were completed. The compromise was intended to permit the knesset to adopt those parts of a constitution on which agreement could be reached, while deferring consideration of components over which religious and secular interests (among others) differed too strongly to achieve the necessary parliamentary support.

Legislation and Policy

The basic laws enacted so far, together with the Declaration of Independence and the Law of Return (which grants all Jews the right to immigrate and receive automatic citizenship), form the basis for constitution-like legislation. The Supreme Court has the jurisdiction to interpret this corpus of legislation and apply it to individual cases and issues. Because constitutional guidelines were so minimal at the outset of the state (and remain limited even today) the Supreme Court has important responsibility for interpreting the intent and applicability of existing laws and declarations.

When the State was established, the courts (and the law of the land) began operating under the very general human rights guidelines of the *Declaration of Independence*:

> The STATE OF ISRAEL will be open for Jewish immigration and for the Ingathering of the Exiles; it will foster the development of the country for the benefit of all its inhabitants; it will be based on freedom, justice and peace as envisaged by the prophets of Israel; it will ensure complete equality of social and political rights to all its inhabitants irrespective of religion, race or sex; it will guarantee freedom of religion, conscience, language, education and culture; it will safeguard the Holy Places of all religions; and it will be faithful to the principles of the Charter of the United Nations. (Knesset web site)

Over the years, these few words have been intensely studied and debated as the source for legislative and judicial interpretation. From 1953 the Supreme Court has held that the Declaration has 'persuasive power.' Beyond this, an early law stipulated that the laws in effect prior to independence would remain in effect to the extent that they did not contradict the Declaration of Independence or specific laws enacted by the knesset. Thus, Israeli jurisprudence began with a collection of precedents from Ottoman (Turkish) law and from British law in effect during the Mandate (1918-1948) - including English common law, Jewish religious law, and Ottoman criminal law. In the ensuing fifty years, some of this prior law has been superseded by specific legislation passed by the Knesset, and by precedent-setting interpretations of the courts.

Little of the accretion of legal and judicial precedent, however, had directly codified the assurance of human rights, until recently. The process of establishing Basic Laws (the building blocks toward a constitution) has moved very slowly. In the forty years through 1988 a total of nine Basic Laws was enacted—the first, codifying the structure of the Knesset took ten years to become law. All subsequent Basic Laws through 1988 dealt with the structure and functioning of various state institutions (the Lands Authority, the presidency, the government, the state economy, the military, the judiciary and the state comptroller). Perhaps the most controversial of these laws is the one on Jerusalem (1980) specifying its status as a united capital of the state of Israel.

Versions of a human and civil rights basic law were introduced into the fifth, seventh, tenth and twelfth knessets (1961-65, 1969-73, 1981-84 and 1988-92). Each failed to pass due to opposition from religious interests fearing any change in the status quo of religious rights and in the balance of power between secular and religious. (Sharfman, p.158-161). Finally, in 1992, after sustained pressure from pro-human-rights legislation advocates led by MK Amnon Rubenstein (*Shinui*), an envisioned human rights Basic Law was divided into portions, to be introduced into the knesset in parts, adopting for human rights legislation the same piecemeal approach that was accepted for the constitution as a whole, back in 1949. Two parts of the law were passed in 1992: *Basic Law: Freedom of Occupation,* and *Basic Law: Human Dignity and Liberty.*

Freedom of occupation was introduced first because the proposer felt that it would pass easily. There was consensus on the issue, supported by an early Supreme Court ruling. It was hoped that its passage would establish an example of successful human rights legislation, setting the stage for further measures. The *Basic Law: Freedom of Occupation* contains an 'entrenchment clause' stipulating that it can be changed or rescinded only by a majority vote of the knesset (61 members). In the same year the law on human dignity and personal freedom was passed. Though very general in nature, the latter does establish basic law on specific rights such as property, and general rights of the individual for respect and safety. It does not contain the 'entrenchment clause' found in some other basic laws, and therefore can be amended by a simple majority vote of knesset members present and voting (i.e., by less than half the total knesset membership). The Supreme Court has held that interpretation and implementation of these laws is subject to judicial review, but this holding remains controversial. Some observers believe the Knesset may pass a law restricting judicial review of these basic laws. One topic of contention has been the interpretation by Chief Justice Aharon Barak that the law implies the right of equality. This is opposed by religious interests because some gender discrimination is acceptable under *halacha*.

The freedom of occupation law came into immediate question. Based on it, the Supreme Court invalidated a previous statute prohibiting the import of pork. The court held that freedom of occupation allowed business interests to import whatever food they wanted, even if it was not *kosher*. The religious parties immediately objected to how the law was interpreted, and to the law itself because it permitted action that violated Jewish dietary rules. In 1994 a new *Basic Law: Freedom of Occupation* replaced the 1992 version. In it the stipulation was added that 'the purpose of this basic law is to protect freedom of occupation, *in order to establish in a Basic Law the values of the State of Israel as a Jewish and a democratic state*' (Knesset web page, italics added). The law further provides that freedom of occupation can be violated by a law 'benefitting the values of the State of Israel,' as defined above. Thus the religious parties established within a basic law that Israel was a Jewish as well as a democratic state; and, although the precedent was set for replacing a basic law over an issue of religion, the experience heightened opposition from religious parties to further human rights legislation.

Three other human rights basic laws are reported to be 'in process' in the knesset committee: *Rights in Justice* (due process); *Freedom of Expression, Assembly and Association*; and *Social Rights*. No action has been taken since 1994, and none is expected in the near future. Opposition to further human rights legislation comes from religious interests, as well as from secular legislators who are wary of the power of the court, which would be extended in matters of human rights if more basic laws are enacted and held to be subject to judicial interpretation. However, the legislation to date has been termed a 'constitutional revolution' by some interpreters, including Chief Justice Barak, as most of the items that would be part of a constitutional bill of rights have now become law (Hirschl, 1997; Lahav, 1993, p. 147; Barzilai, 1997, p.99).

Human Rights in Practice

Israel was established in a climate of conflict and war that affected early decisions regarding human rights. The government and courts recognized the necessity to limit civil rights in some cases in the interests of national security. The position of Arab/Palestinian citizens of Israel in the early years of the state brought into focus a number of issues on which civil and political rights were debated, and in many cases limited for reasons of national security. Definitions of citizenship rights, freedom of movement, property rights, and freedoms of expression, assembly, demonstration, and association, plus voting rights were all subject to limitations, particularly for Arab citizens, in the early years of the state. Most of these issues have been resolved over the years in the direction of individual freedom and equal rights. (For a discussion of the history and legal status of these limitations, see Hofnung, 1996, pp.17-184). However, the context for discussion and implementation of human rights in Israel has been significantly influenced by national security considerations as well as religious interests. For instance, a British Mandate era regulation (1945) permitting authorities to suspend human rights in time of emergency is still in force. Also, the report of the 1987 Landau Commission (headed by a Supreme Court justice) into allegations of torture by the General Security

Services (*Shin Bet*) asserted that the use of 'moderate physical pressure' was permissible in cases involving national security (within Israel as well as in the territories). A secret annex to the report stipulated what forms of torture were acceptable. The report has been adopted as legal precedent.

The 1996 U.S. State Department's review of human rights practices around the world indicates that within Israel, 'the Government generally respects human rights, and citizens enjoy a wide range of civil and other rights. Israel's main human rights problems have arisen from its policies and practices in the occupied territories.' Country reports from the major international human rights organizations (Amnesty International, Freedom House, Human Rights Watch, and the United Nations Center for Human Rights) also focus almost entirely on Israeli actions in the occupied territories and treatment of Palestinians (see Peleg chapter). Some internal issues are mentioned briefly by Freedom House (1966), and in more detail in the State Department's review. These include: the banning of ultra-nationalist political movements (Kach, Kahane Chai) for advocating violence; conditions in prisons; lengthy administrative detention, up to six months and renewable by law; censorship on security matters (more frequently applied to Arabic-language publications); equality of pay and employment opportunity for women; domestic violence (against women, and children); and jurisdiction by the Orthodox over marriage, divorce and burial for the entire Jewish sector.

Civil and Human Rights Organizations

A large number of civil and human rights organizations operate freely within Israel. They are mainly small voluntary organizations that focus on specific causes (children's rights, domestic violence, women's rights, rights for formerly nomadic Arab tribal people or Bedouin, rights for the disabled, etc.) The most prominent group is the Association for Civil Rights in Israel (ACRI). In a study of voluntary associations in Israel, Yishai (1991, p. 84) states that:

> the Civil Rights Association is one of the most structured, most effective public interest groups in the country. It was established in 1972 by prominent figures in the Israeli legal and judicial establishment . . . The association concentrates on specific complaints of a breach of civil rights, but it also acts as a lobby, trying to influence legislation and policy making. It deals extensively with freedom of faith, with inter-racial relations, and with all other issues pertaining to human rights in a democratic law-abiding society.

A recent annual report listed specific actions within Israel by the Association on more than 30 issues of human rights in six major categories:

1   Equality, including gender, discrimination against Arab citizens, lesbian and gay rights.
2   Religious pluralism and freedom of conscience, including rights of non-orthodox Jews.
3   Freedom of expression and responsibility for billboard messages
4   Freedom of information, including access to police, medical and government records.
5   Human dignity, including the right to privacy and dignity in burial proceedings.
6   Due process of the law, including criminal justice and complaints against the police.

(1996 - ACRI web site)

In addition, the Civil Rights Association undertakes human rights educational and public outreach activities, publishing materials, training teachers, programs in schools and youth groups, seminars for security forces (prison guards, police, military), publicizing and participating in human-rights-related events.

Recent books published by the Association (Gavison et al., 1991-92) and the Israel Defense Forces (Gavison, 1994) indicate that attention is paid to all the major categories of human rights issues globally recognized in documents such as the Universal Declaration of Human Rights. In addition to the categories listed above, their publications describe the basis for rights to: freedom of thought and conscience; life, safety and freedom; property rights; right to vote and be elected; freedom of movement and association; women's rights; rights of people with special circumstances; prisoners' rights; and rights in time of emergency. The Association receives financial support from the New Israel Fund, a philanthropic, social activist organization that supports more than 200 civic and human rights-related organizations in Israel.

The New Israel Fund works to strengthen democracy and advance social justice in Israel. Its primary strategy is building Israel's public interest sector. It nurtures the growing network of nonpartisan, nonprofit organizations that enable Israelis to advocate more effectively to improve their lives, the conditions in their communities, and the policies of their government. The New Israel Fund awards grants to citizens' initiatives working to strengthen democracy and support social justice in these areas: Civil and Human Rights, Improving the Status of Women, Jewish-Arab Coexistence, Religious Pluralism and Tolerance, Bridging Social and

Economic Gaps, Environmental Justice, and Government Accountability (NIF web page). ACRI is the largest recipient of NIF support, with funding totaling approximately 20 percent of NIF's annual allocation budget of more than $2.5 million in 1996.

Thus, Israel has a full range of organizations and a high level of activity devoted to protecting human rights and promoting the goals of special interest groups in a relatively open, democratic society.

Major Issues

Within a general context of positive support for and protection of human rights in Israel, three social issue areas are (and will continue to be) of particular interest and controversy. These are: issues of religion within the Jewish community; minority rights; and gender issues— women's rights.

Religion and Personal Freedom

Ironically, issues surrounding religion and human rights focus on controversies *within* the Jewish sector in Israel. Other religious groups, primarily Moslem, plus small numbers of Christians and other religions, enjoy legislatively-assured freedom of religious belief and practice. Religious institutions (mosques, churches, religious endowments—*waqf*) are protected, and religious courts, such as *sharia* courts for Moslems, administer personal status law, including marriage, divorce and burial.

However, religious pluralism is problematic within the Jewish community. Only the Orthodox stream of Judaism has official status. Conservative, Reform and Reconstructionist Judaism, the predominant orientations among religious Jews throughout the rest of the world, have no official recognition. Their congregations have no rights and only minimal state funding within Israel. Furthermore, secular (non-religious) Jewish Israelis are forced to make use of orthodox rabbis and institutions in matters of personal status. There is no provision for 'civil' marriage or divorce, for example. This issue may reach a crisis point in the near future. An estimated 100,000 immigrants from the former Soviet Union are not eligible to be married in Israel. Because their mothers are (or may be) non-Jewish, their status as Jews has been questioned by the Orthodox rabbinate.

Recent (1997) Supreme Court rulings stipulate that new immigrants and Israelis converted by Reform and Conservative Rabbis abroad must be registered by the Interior Ministry as Jews; non-Orthodox representatives and women can on longer be barred from serving if elected to municipal religious councils; and a non-Orthodox burial society was to be granted rights in a cemetery. Also, government allocations to Conservative and Reform institutions were increased to fund courses on Judaism in state *secular* schools. In reaction, religious political parties introduced specific legislation into the knesset opposing religious pluralism, including a law to reverse the High Court of Justice's decision on non-orthodox conversion abroad, and another to reverse a Supreme Court decision that women have a right to pray at the Western Wall (of the Temple Mount in Jerusalem). The atmosphere of religious intolerance was heightened by media denouncements of non-orthodox streams of Judaism and by threats of violence against Supreme Court Chief Justice Aharon Barak for his role in human rights advocacy, particularly on religious issues.

Religious interests and their political manifestation in religious political parties have played a central role in affairs of state within Israel from the time of its founding. Some religious practices and parts of traditional law (*halacha*) are inconsistent with modern secular conceptions of human rights. The debate over the nature of Israel as a Jewish state that is a democracy has been carried on with considerable ferocity in the knesset, in government administration (e.g., over the public school system), and in everyday life. Lack of agreement and strongly polarized opinions have resulted in compromises (two public school systems - one secular and one religious; religious control of matters of personal status). Constitutional/legislative stalemate limits assurance of human rights in some areas of life. Pressure in the form of decisions by the High Court of Justice, the debates surrounding constitutional legislation (basic laws) and specific legislation introduced into the knesset continually test the nature of commitment to human rights in Israeli society. The issues revolve around the fundamental question of whether Israel can continue in the long run to be a state that is both Jewish and democratic. This debate has resulted in slow and halting formal commitment to some aspects of human rights. Reactions to recent legislation, plus polarization over the stress engendered by the Palestine/Israel conflict and the slow peace process have created continuing obstacles to further codification of human rights in areas that relate to religion and society. [2]

Minority Rights

Israel's basic commitment to 'social and political equality for all inhabitants' is codified in the Declaration of Independence and in subsequent human rights legislation. However, the 1950 Law of Return does discriminate in favor of Jews by guaranteeing immediate right of entry to every Jew who arrives and expresses a wish to settle (except those who might pose a danger to public health or security), and the subsequent Nationality Law grants every person admitted under the Law of Return immediate citizenship. While this does not formally discriminate 'against' non-Jewish minorities, who can enter under immigration laws similar to those of other countries, the prominent status of the Law of Return (and challenges to its application over the years from cases posing the question 'who is a Jew?') does set a tone of unequal status for non-Jews as part of the fundamental legal apparatus of the country.

Arab/Palestinian citizens of Israel comprise over 18 percent of the total population. Most of these people (or their immediate families) have been residents and citizens since 1948, but some who formerly lived under Jordanian control became *de facto* residents of Israel proper after extensive areas in the eastern part of Jerusalem were annexed into Israel after the 1967 war. Arab citizens (from 1948) have full voting and citizenship rights; residents of East Jerusalem can claim these rights too, but few choose to do so. Recently, some Palestinian Arab residents of East Jerusalem who had not claimed citizenship have been expelled for reasons of extended residence abroad, which Israeli authorities claim has compromised their rights to residency within Israel.

Despite a basic commitment to equal rights for minorities, Israel was founded after a war, and an atmosphere of ethnic conflict continues to pervade the society. Much Arab land was confiscated for Jewish settlement in the early years of the state. Also, the Arabs of Israel were feared as security risks, and from 1958 until 1966 most lived in areas subject to military control that limited freedom of movement, economic opportunities, and many forms of potential political expression. Military government has long been eliminated within Israel, but the land claims remain an open source of contention symbolized by the major Land Day demonstrations that began in 1976 (the demonstrations themselves are a protected civil right). Also for security reasons, largely supported by mutual agreement, most Arab/Palestinians do not serve in the military. This basic civic duty within the Jewish sector of Israeli society is accompanied by certain public benefits associated with completion of army service (access to housing, education benefits, loan programs, etc.), which Arab citizens do not receive. (Orthodox former *yeshiva* students, who also are exempt from military service do receive the benefits.) There has been discussion of instituting an alternative form of "national service" for Israeli Palestinians, with accompanying benefits, but so far no action has been taken.

Recognized municipalities within Israel are eligible for public funding under various government programs for infrastructure, public works, schools, etc. However, many Arab settlements have not been accorded formal recognition, and thus are not eligible for government support. Others, while recognized, in practice receive lower levels of support than Jewish settlements.

These specific examples of past and continuing inequalities and discrimination against Arab/Palestinian communities are part of a more general recognition that despite a formal and legal commitment to equality, the Arab minority within Israel is subject to discrimination that compromises their human rights, relative to the rest of society. In analyzing the political status of Arab Israelis, Peled claims they live within a 'two-tiered democracy' in which they are a subordinate ethnic group confined to, but also made secure in the possession of, liberal citizenship rights and allowed the political space to struggle for the consolidation of these rights. Israel's Arab citizens are by no means satisfied with the place accorded them in Israel's political system. However, the limited, liberal citizenship status they enjoy (provides) sufficient rights and privileges to both enable and induce them to conduct their struggle within the constitutional framework of the state, rather than against it. This has (allowed) Israel to maintain a stable democratic regime in the context of an acute ethnic conflict (Peled, 1992, p. 440).

Gender - Women's Rights

Institutionalized gender inequalities characterize many aspects of Israeli society, despite the fact that rights to gender equality in Israel are specified or implied in a number of laws and judicial judgements over the history of the state, from the *Declaration of Independence,* the 1951 *Women's Equal Rights Law* and the 1954 *Women's Employment Law* through the 1964 *Equal Pay Law*, the 1988 *Equal Employment Opportunity Law* (Raday 1991a, b) and the 1992/94 *Basic Laws* described above that establish equality as a basic human right with constitution-like weight.

In controversial test cases before the Supreme Court, the rights of women to serve on local Religious Affairs Councils and on the boards that elect local rabbis were established in 1988 (Pope, 1993, p.216). These reinforced the basic rights to vote and be elected to public office, despite religious opposition. However, the area of law where women's human rights are not protected is that dominated by religious interests—personal status law. According to *halacha* a woman cannot divorce without her husband's permission, and rabbinic authorities have refused to amend *halacha* on this point. While religious courts can order the husband to grant permission, this is rarely done and the mechanism for enforcing the judgement is problematic. Husbands can be jailed for contempt of court, but this is rarely done. By recent estimate, there are more than 7000 *agunot* (women refused divorce) in Israel (Pope, 1993 pp. 216-217). In Moslem religious (*sharia*) courts, ACRI has discovered that marriage registrars (state employees) have added clauses to wedding contracts stating that in the event of a financial dispute, Islamic law (which favors men) will apply, rather than the relevant Israeli civil legislation.

Besides the more blatant aspects of inequality based on religion and religious influence on society, recent writers on the status of women in Israeli society (Swirski, Shafir, and Pope) have identified several aspects of Israeli society that engender systematic inequalities facing women. As a result, a broad range of women's interest groups have emerged within Israel, some with specific goals (e.g., sheltering from family violence and sexual abuse, preventing sexist advertising), some advocating unity and common interests between Jewish and Palestinian/Arab women, some supporting traditional women's roles in an egalitarian, or in a religious society, some protecting rights of working women, etc. (Yishai, 1991 pp. 84-86). A wide range of political ideologies and links to political parties is represented among women's organizations (Pope, 1993, p. 209).

Sources of gender inequality begin with the fact that most Israelis come from backgrounds where patriarchy was a strongly rooted social norm, whether in Eastern Europe or the Middle East, in both Jewish and Arab societies. Though these roots may be several generations in the past, the influences remain because of strong family orientation and the continuing impact of religious tradition, even among the currently secular segments of society.

The primacy of family life, with important in-home roles for women is reinforced by a pro-natalist ideology, stronger among the religious but important throughout Jewish and Arab societies, that is related to the continuing national struggles. Also, family obligations to support children during compulsory military service emphasize women's obligation to keep ever-ready home services for soldiers, and the strong security orientation of Israeli society creates an implicit, but strong, male bias.

Extensive discussion of women's roles in the military has resulted in less severe gender division of labor in the Israel Defense Forces, but women are restricted from combat roles. (ACRI recently, and successfully, petitioned the Supreme Court on behalf of a young woman who wished to participate in tests for candidates for the Israeli air force. The air force had refused to allow her to do so, although she is an aeronautical engineer with a pilot's license, on the basis of standing IDF policy not to employ women in 'combat roles'). At the same time, women's peace activism increased greatly after 1988, in reaction to the *intifada* (Palestinian resistance uprising) (Chazan, 1991).

Early legislation affecting women in the workplace provided protection for employed women (maternity leave, right to post-partum leave without pay for up to a year—with job protection, use of sick leave to care for sick children, and a shorter work day for women with school-age children.) Much of this protection was viewed as discriminatory and most women's rights were converted to 'parental rights' over time. A remaining 'sociopolitical controversy centers on the statutory preservation of a mandatory three month maternity leave and on the prohibition of overtime work after five months of pregnancy. There are those who claim that these prohibitions are paternalistic and restrict women's opportunities, while others assert that they are the minimal protection for women's physical and mental health and that they prevent employers from trying to keep women from enjoying the rights which the legal system grants them' (Raday, 1991b, pp.179-180). Restrictions on equality of employment opportunity resulting from job advertisements in newspapers addressed exclusively to men or women was publicly challenged by women's rights groups. Israel's leading daily papers have changed employment ad headings to remove gender restrictions, but observers still note strong sexist stereotypes in vocations and professions.

Finally, despite prominent examples of women who are active in public life, beginning with Golda Meir, women are grossly under-represented in all aspects of elected and high-level public life. Studies have shown that there are relatively few women in the knesset or in local government, despite active campaigning by women's rights organizations to correct the situation (Yishai, 1997; Pope, 1993, pp. 202-203). Organized feminism and women's political activism have been limited in scale and effectiveness (Swirski, 1991). As Pope (1993, p. 221) concludes,

> the failure of the Israeli feminist movement to establish a broad-based network of support attests to the relatively low level of consciousness among Israeli women (and men) of how political issues affect women . . . . The most important task facing the Israeli feminist movement today is the need to convince the general public that it is in the interests of the whole nation to address their concerns . . . . It is vital to proclaim that matters regarded as 'women's issues' are actually political issues with much broader implications. . . the under-representation of women in political institutions undermines the democratic workings of the state because an enormous wealth of female talent remains untapped. . . . It is the society as a whole which suffers, not just women.

In sum, the human rights situation within Israel has received considerable attention. Protective legislation is in place and the judicial record is one of positive court support for basic human rights, consistent with an active democracy in the modern world system, compromised at times by considerations of national security. A wide variety of voluntary organizations, with foundation funding, campaign and provide support for the rights of individuals and special interest groups. The country lacks a full, formal constitution, and some aspects of human rights legislation have been stalled, because of conflicts between religious and secular interests. The religious-secular debate among Jewish Israelis, protection of the rights of ethnic (Arab/Palestinian) minorities in the context of the continuing national struggle, and gender equity are the three major social issues around which the debate on human rights is likely to continue. Of these, growing activism among Israeli Arabs in solidarity with the Palestinian national movement may increasingly link the second issue to the more controversial one of Israeli human rights treatment of people in the occupied territories.

Notes

1.   Special thanks to Pnina Lahav for advice and materials used in preparing this chapter.
2.   While the question of whether Israel can be both a Jewish and a democratic state is unique to the country, on the more general question of the compatibility of religion and state in the Middle East, comparisons can be in order. The rise of Islamic fundamentalism throughout the Moslem and Arab world, beginning with the establishment of a fundamentalist government in Iran in 1979, has challenged many governments (and societies) to decide how to react to 'political Islam.' Can Islamic movements be accepted as 'political parties' the way religious parties are institutionalized in Israel? Can fundamentalist movements accept a position in a Moslem (or pluralist) society where they are a part of a political spectrum, but not the only (perhaps not the dominant) political force? What mixture or co-existence of Islam and democracy is possible?

References

Amnesty International (1997), *Amnesty International Report - 1996*, New York.
Barzilai, Gad (1997), 'Political Institutions and Conflict Resolution: The Israeli Supreme Court and the Peace Process," chap. 5 in Ilan Peleg (ed.) *The Middle East Peace Process: Interdisciplinary Perspectives*, State University of New York Press, Albany.
Chazan, Naomi (1991), 'Israeli Women and Peace Activism,' pp. 152-160 in Swirski and Safir (eds.) *Calling the Equality Bluff: Women in Israel*, Permagon: New York.
Freedom House (1996), *Freedom in the World*, University Press of America, Latham MD.
Gavison, Ruth (1994), *Human Rights in Israel*, Ministry of Defense, Israel (in Hebrew).
Gavison, Ruth and Hagai Shindor (eds.), (1991-92), *Human Rights and Civil Liberties in Israel - a Reader*, Association for Civil Rights in Israel, Jerusalem. (3 vols., Vol. 3 edited by Tali Ben-Gal et al.) (in Hebrew).

Gross, Aeyal M. (1996), *Theories and Discourses on Rights and Democracy: A Comparative Inquiry on the U.S. and Israel*, doctoral thesis, Harvard Law School, Cambridge, Mass.

Hirschl, Ran (1997), 'The "Constitutional Revolution" and the Emergence of a New Economic Order in Israel,' *Israel Studies*, vol.2, no. 1, spring, pp.136-155.

Hofnung, Menachem (1996), *Democracy, Law and National Security in Israel*, Dartmouth, Aldershot, England.

Human Rights Watch (1997), *Human Rights Watch World Report - Events of 1996*, New York.

Lahav, Pnina (1993), 'Rights and Democracy: The Court's Performance.' chap. 7 in Sprinzak, Ehud and Larry Diamond, (eds.), *Israeli Democracy Under Stress*, Lynne Reinner: Boulder, CO.

Lawson, Edward (1996), (with the cooperation of the United Nations Center for Human Rights), *Encyclopedia of Human Rights, 2nd. ed.*, Taylor & Francis, Washington D.C.

Peled, Yoav (1992), 'Ethnic Democracy and the Legal Construction of Citizenship: Arab Citizens of the Jewish State,' *American Political Science Review* Vol. 86, No. 2, pp. 432-443.

Peleg, Ilan (1995), *Human Rights in the West Bank and Gaza*, Syracuse University Press, Syracuse N.Y.

Pope, Juliet (1993), 'The Place of Women in Israeli Society,' chap. 11 in Kyle, Keith and Joel Peters, (eds.), *Whither Israel? The Domestic Challenges*, I.B. Taurus: London.

Raday, Frances (1991a), 'The Concept of Gender Equality in a Jewish State,' pp. 18-28 in Swirski and Safir, *Calling the Equality Bluff: Women in Israel*, Permagon: New York.

Raday, Frances (1991b), 'Women, Work and the Law,' pp. 178-186 in Swirski and Shafir *Calling the Equality Bluff: Women in Israel*, Permagon: New York.

Sharfman, Dafna (1993), *Living Without a Constitution: Civil Rights in Israel*, M.E. Sharpe: Armonk, New York.

Swirski, Barbara (1991), 'Israeli Feminism New and Old,' pp. 285-302, in Swirski and Safir, *Calling the Equality Bluff: Women in Israel*, Permagon: New York.

Swirski, Barbara and Marilyn Safir (eds.), (1991), *Calling the Equality Bluff: Women in Israel*, Permagon: New York.

U.S. Department of State, 'Israel and the Occupied Territories - Report on Human Rights Practices for 1996.' Descriptions of the Israeli governmental and legal system, as well as a historical outline, from various government publications are found at www.state.gov/www/global/human_rights/1996_hrp_report/israel.html www.knesset.gov.il (web site).

www.nif.org (web site of the New Israel Fund).

www.nif.org/acri/index.html (web site of the Association for Civil Rights in Israel).

Yishai, Yael (1991), *Land of Paradoxes: Interest Politics in Israel*, SUNY Press: Albany, N.Y.

Yishai, Yael (1997), *Between the Flag and the Banner: Women in Israeli Politics*, SUNY Press: Albany N.Y.

10 Human Rights in the West Bank and the Gaza Strip: Politics and Law in Transition

ILAN PELEG

Introduction

The conflict between Israeli Jews and Palestinian Arabs is, without a doubt, among the most intense conflicts of our era. It is a struggle which goes back to the late 19th century and only recently serious moves toward its resolution have begun to be taken. Over the last 30 years, the geographical focus of the dispute has been on the West Bank and Gaza, territories conquered by Israel in 1967.

The goal of this essay is to evaluate the status of human rights in these territories (the West Bank and the Gaza Strip). This task, however, cannot be accomplished without first dealing with the political and legal condition of the areas in question. Human rights are, after all, not fixed entities but a function of legal and political status of territories and people.

Moreover, the signing of the Oslo agreements on September 13, 1993, created both a new political situation in the territories, with the establishment of the Palestinian National Authority (thereafter: PA), and a new legal situation, with the transfer of authority in more areas and in more aspects to the hands of the PA. So much so, that after 1993 there are two governmental structures to be evaluated in terms of human rights in the West Bank and Gaza, one Israeli and the other Palestinian.

This chapter would, therefore, deal not only with Israel's human rights record in the quarter century between 1967-92, but will also dwell on human rights under the Oslo Accord, that is, with the period of transition from occupation to the final status of the territories in questions. A view into the future of human rights in the West Bank and Gaza will bring this chapter to a conclusion.

Political and Legal Territories in Limbo

An analysis of the human rights situation in the territories conquered by Israel during the 1967 War cannot be very productive without an essential understanding of the unique status of the West Bank and the Gaza Strip since this fateful war. Of particular interest is the political status of the territories, status which has determined the legal framework under which they have (or should have been) ruled, governed and administered. Politics and law in the territories have always been intimately interwoven, a reality of immediate relevance for the conditions of human rights.

The area known as the West Bank was until June 1967 under the de facto control of the Hashemite Kingdom of Jordan. This territory, originally allocated to the 'Arab State' in the famed United Nations Partition Resolution (General Assembly, #181), was formally annexed by Jordan in 1950, but this annexation was not accepted by the vast majority of the countries in the world, including the Arab states.

East Jerusalem, taken by the Arab Legion during the 1948 war, was an integral part of the West Bank until 1967. Nevertheless, while the Israeli authorities annexed East Jerusalem into the expanded municipal borders of Israel's capital, the fate of the rest of the West Bank remained undetermined, a condition which prevailed into 1998.

In contrast, the West Bank and East Jerusalem, the Gaza Strip, although under Egyptian rule since 1948 (with a brief interlude in 1956), was never annexed by Egypt but merely held under Egyptian administration. It remained under Israeli occupation even after the Sinai Peninsula was returned to Egypt's sovereignty in 1982.

Since 1967 there has been a fierce political disagreement regarding the status of all these territories. One of the most fundamental issues in the debate (and of great importance for human rights) has been whether the territories ought to be regarded as 'occupied.' If the territories are occupied, the 1949 Fourth Geneva Convention Relative to the Protection of Civilian Persons in Time of War (hereafter: Geneva IV) is applicable and the Israeli government--in actual control of the territories for 30 years-- assumes a variety of human rights obligations there.

Two diametrically opposing positions in regard to the status of the territories have emerged after 1967. One stance accepted the territories as legally occupied and saw them politically as areas to be exchanged, all or in part, in return for peace with Israel's Arab neighbors, and possibly the Palestinians. This position characterized the majority in the Labor Party and all factions of the Israeli left. A second position claimed that the territories were, in fact, 'liberated,' taken away from usurpers (Egypt and Jordan) and destined to be, eventually, annexed by Israel (or simply to remain in Israeli hands since a country does not need to annex that which already belongs to her).

By adopting the first position, Labor governments under the leadership of Eshkol, Meir, Rabin and Peres (1967-77 and 1992-96) left the issue of the applicability of Geneva IV vague, although Labor's stance that the territories would eventually be 'exchanged' for peace implied that they were, in fact, occupied. When Likud took over (1977) the official Israeli position became less equivocal. In one of his first Knesset speeches as prime minister, Menachem Begin declared that as far as international law was concerned, Israel's rule over Eretz Israel was not that of an occupying power. Begin and others maintained that the West Bank and the Gaza Strip belong to Israel not only by right of history and tradition, but also because Israel liberated these territories in a war of self-defense (Blum, 1968, 1979; Helms, 1990). To the Likud and its supporters, the application of Geneva IV to the territories was unacceptable on ideological as well as legal grounds.

The views of the Israeli right on the status of the territories proved to be problematic on a number of grounds: (a) the removal of Egypt and Jordan from Gaza and the West Bank, respectively, was done through coercive means, and led, in fact, to the occupation of the territories by the Israeli Defense Force (IDF); moreover, Israel immediately established a military government there, thus treating the territories as 'occupied;' (b) the West Bank and Gaza Strip were both allotted to the would-be Palestinian-Arab state by the U.N. General Assembly on November 29, 1947; thus, Israel's claim to sovereignty on these territories amounted to a direct challenge to the legitimate will of the international community (the very same legitimate will that brought Israel into existence); (c) the claim for national, historical or religious rights in the West Bank and Gaza--rights that, presumably, justify annexation--is not based on any acceptable legal document granting Israel the right to the land in its entirety; in fact, the 1947 General Assembly resolution specifically *partitioning* the land between the warring parties was accepted by Israel's Provisional Government and, thus, committed Israel to the principle of partition; (d) finally, no permanent territorial changes are allowed under the doctrine of contemporary self-defense or modern international law, in general; if there are to be such changes, they must be negotiated as part of a peace settlement (Feinberg, 1977, pp. 60-2).

In recognition of the uniqueness and complexity of the sovereignty question, Gerson suggests that Israel be viewed as a 'trustee-occupant' in the territories, a power whose duty is to temporarily manage the territories in accordance with the rules of international law (specifically those of belligerent occupation), including Geneva IV (Gerson, 1973). Israel's status will continue to be that of a trustee-occupant until a formal cessation of belligerency is obtained through peace negotiations. In essence, this was the position taken by the Israeli government following the 1967 war, but it was completely rejected by the government established after the 1977 elections (Gazit, 1985). Jordan's decision in 1988 to cut off all links to, and withdraw all claims on, the West Bank strengthens Gerson's perspective on the status of the territories. So does the Israeli-Palestinian agreement of September 13, 1993.

This approach to Israel's status in the territories means that Israel is an occupier bound by the laws of belligerent occupation. Most analysts believe that these laws apply to all de facto occupied territories, regardless of their sovereignty status. In fact, Geneva IV is quite specific as to its own applicability. It 'was meant to be people-oriented, not territory-oriented' (Boyd, 1971, p. 260). Cohen notes that Geneva IV emphasized the 'inviolability of the rights of protected persons' rather than territorial issues; above all, it is concerned with the human rights of the civilian population of occupied territories and intentionally ignores the legal status of these territories (Cohen 1985, pp. 53-4). Gerhard von Glahn, an authority on the international law of war, agrees (von Glahn, 1968, p. 693).

It seems that the applicability of Geneva IV to Israel's rule over the West Bank and Gaza Strip can be argued for either directly or indirectly. If Jordan is recognized as the pre-1967 sovereign in the West Bank, then Israel is straightforwardly the occupying power and bound by the provisions of Geneva IV. If the Palestinian Arabs are perceived as the true sovereign in the territories, Israel could be perceived (as proposed by Gerson) as a trustee-occupant, governing the territories temporarily but equally bound by Geneva IV.

Geneva IV also applies, albeit indirectly, if the area is somehow perceived as politically 'vacant,' a territory in limbo, a land over which there is no clear-cut sovereignty. As a person-oriented, humanitarian document, Geneva IV applies to any territory occupied as a result of a military confrontation between signatories to it. Not surprisingly, for more than two decades there has been a virtual unanimity in the international community that Israel is bound by Geneva IV. Even Israel's closest friends have held this opinion (U.N. Human Rights Commission, 1988, p. 56).

Although Geneva IV may give the population in the occupied territories a measure of protection, it guarantees only minimal protection. One can, therefore, argue that additional human rights documents, such as the 1948 Universal Declaration of Human Rights (UDHR) and the two 1966 human rights covenants must also be applied. The UDHR and other documents have 'assumed the status of customary international law'

(Fleishman, 1988, pp. 206-7), and their application is, therefore, not unreasonable.

Israel's Human Rights Record, 1967-92

The Settlement Project

The human rights situation in the West Bank and Gaza ought to be understood within the context of the Israeli settlement policy in the territories and especially its intensification by the right-wing governments after 1977. Many human rights violations can be directly linked to the settlement program; many other violations resulted from the reaction of the Palestinian population to the settlement effort.

Toward the end of Labor rule (mid-1977), its relatively restrained settlement policy began to crumble under the combined pressure of the opposition and the extra-parliamentary activity of radical right-wing groups. Leading the charge was Gush Emunim, a religio-nationalist group founded in February 1974. The organization began establishing settlements without government authorization. Moreover, many of the settlements were purposely established close to and even inside major Arab cities, notably Hebron and Nablus. The implications for the human rights of the local Arab population, although unforseen at the time, proved far-reaching.

Following Likud's first electoral victory (1977), Gush Emunim's settlement program and priorities were adopted, for all intents and purposes, by the Israeli government. This development was ominous in terms of human rights. The Palestinians in the West Bank and Gaza sensed that their very existence as a community was threatened. Their anxiety led to violence and, in turn, to an increasingly oppressive policy.

The most negative aspect of Likud's settlement program, from a human rights perspective, was the massive confiscation of Arab land. The cautious land acquisition policy of Labor was replaced by the considerably more aggressive policy of the Begin government. In 1980 the government began declaring vast areas in the West Bank as 'state lands,' transferring them to the hands of the State and, in turn, to the Jewish settlers (Shehadeh, 1989; Benvenisti, with Abu-Ziad and Rubinstein, 1986). Insofar as the purpose of this policy was to transfer Arab lands to the permanent control of Israeli civilians, it was a clear violation of Geneva IV. Not only was the transfer of settlers into the territories illegal, but the land acquisition project was accompanied by fraud, intimidation of potential sellers, and shady deals. On the eve of the Intifada (December 1987), Israelis controlled between 52-

60 percent of the West Bank (Benvenisti et al, pp. 120-1; Shehadeh, p. 213).

Not only the land acquisition policy, but the land use policy of the Likud government proved highly threatening to the local population. Especially counterproductive were the following policies: (a) the shift from settlement in uninhabited, peripheral areas to the Arab population centers; (b) the restriction on Arab construction outside Palestinian villages and towns; (c) the building of Israeli settlements in order to separate Arab towns and encircle them.

The Israeli settlement effort in the territories and its human rights implications cannot be fully understood without attention to the Jewish settlers (Peleg, 1987, pp. 117-22). The settlers have become an important factor in determining the type and extent of human rights violations in the territories.

During Begin's tenure in office, Gush Emunim became a main instrument not only of settlement but also of coercion. By orders of Chief of Staff Eitan, the settlers were organized into units of the IDF Territorial Defense. All settlements in the territories were defined as border settlements, and their population was heavily armed by the IDF. The settlers were used to control the increasingly restless Palestinian population in Judea and Samaria.

An important phenomenon in the territories was the enthusiasm of some Gush members for using violence. Many cases of vigilantism by Gush settlers were reported. Avraham Achituv, the former director of Israel's General Security Services (Shin Bet, equivalent to the FBI), thought Gush Emunim settlements had become a 'psychological hothouse for the growth of Jewish terror' on the West Bank (Davar, Aug. 19, 1983). He wrote that since the rise of the Likud, the settlers learned that their actions, even if illegal, 'are made kosher because of the political homefront that backs them.' Achituv's words, unusual for the head of the secretive Shin Bet, were later substantiated at length by a committee of jurists appointed by Israel attorney general and headed by his deputy (Karp Report, in Peleg, 1995, pp. 147-53).

Members of Gush Emunim and other West Bank settlers had the greatest impact on human rights when they acted as vigilantes, taking the law into their own hands and committing acts of violence against the inhabitants of the territories. Although on occasion the leaders of the settlers declared that they had no intention of initiating actions to maintain their own security, recognizing that this was the role of the army (FBIS Reports, ME, Feb. 3, 1985), in fact the settlers as individuals, and sometimes as groups, often reacted on their own to Arab attacks or even initiated violence. On numerous occasions settlers arrived at Arab towns, villages, and refugee camps and randomly committed acts of violence and destruction, often attacking not only the Arab residents but also Israeli soldiers trying to restore order. Some Israeli commentators believe that because the settlers realized that Jews were not settling the West Bank in large numbers, extremists among them were trying to encourage an Arab exodus as an alternative (Kretzmer, 1987).

Numerous violent attacks by settlers on Palestinians have been dealt with ineffectively, or not at all, by the army, the police, and the judicial system. In an article published in 1982, Knesset member and law professor Amnon Rubinstein reported that settlers often refused to answer questions put to them by the police regarding incidents in the West Bank, a phenomenon also documented in the Karp Report. Wrote *Ha'aretz* about the situation: 'The police do not dare question or arrest Jewish suspects, fearing a violent confrontation with the settlers' (April 5, 1982).

Beginning in December 1987, with the outbreak of the Intifada, the rate and intensity of acts of settlers' vigilantism increased dramatically, so much so that many in Israel and elsewhere came to believe that 'vigilante action by Jewish settlers could push the country to the brink of civil warfare' (*New York Times*, June 22, 1989). Settlers attacked not only Arabs, but also IDF personnel (including high-ranking officers), political opponents, and members of the international and national media. Some Knesset members argued that the settlers had established 'an armed militia' that carried out, on a daily basis, actions designed to punish, terrorize, and take revenge against the Arab inhabitants (*Israel Shelanu*, Feb. 17, 1989).

Organized violent activity against Arabs by Jewish settlers, especially individuals associated with (and often leaders of) Gush Emunim, was not a new phenomenon. In July 1985, members of a group known as the Jewish Underground in the Territories or the Jewish Terror Group were convicted by an Israeli court for an attempt on the lives of three Arab mayors (in retaliation for a Fatah attack on Hadassah House in Hebron in May 1980, in which six settlers were slain), an attack on the Islamic College in Hebron in which three students were killed in July 1983 (in response to the murder of yeshiva student Aaron Gross), a plot to blow up the Dome of the Rock on Temple Mount in Jerusalem in preparation for rebuilding the Temple, and a plan to attack Arab buses in East Jerusalem with explosives. In response to the arrest, conviction, and imprisonment of the perpetrators, a lobby of more than twenty Knesset members from the religious parties, Tehiya and the Likud, was organized to assist in the early release of the convicted men, all of whom were associated with Gush Emunim (Segal, 1987).

Measures of Enforcement and Punishment

The prolonged Israeli occupation of the territories has generated an increasingly active resistance from the local Palestinian population. This resistance often led to harsh Israeli responses. Although the Israeli authorities decided to forgo the imposition of the death penalty, other severe penalties were extensively adopted. In this section I will deal, however briefly, with some of the most severe enforcement actions. In their totality, these penalties can be regarded as Israel's human rights violations repertoire.

Expulsion

One of the most controversial penalties imposed on many Palestinians since the commencement of the occupation has been deportation from the territories to neighboring countries. Thus, between 1967-85 Israel deported about 2,000 persons, and as late as December 1992 Israel had expelled over 400 Palestinians for alleged links to radical Moslem organizations. Israel adopted the expulsion policy despite the fact that it is specifically banned by Geneva IV, Art. 49 (deZayas, 1975; Hiltermann, 1988). Moreover, the policy proved controversial because Israel often used it to punish political activists, exactly the type of people against whom actual acts of terrorism could not have been proven. Known political moderates were often among the deportees. In justifying the expulsion policy, the Israeli authorities argued that it was not only necessary, but legal. They relied on article 112(1) of the Defense Emergency Regulations (Shamgar, 1971), which the State of Israel inherited from the British upon the termination of their Palestine Mandate in 1948.

A few arguments were made on behalf of expulsions: (a) Article 49 of Geneva IV relates solely to mass deportations and not to the deportations of individuals (High Court of Justice 785/87); (b) as saboteurs and terrorists, and persons who act against state security and public order deserve expulsion; (c) deportation is preferable to lengthy administrative detention; (d) when deportees were taken to Jordan, supporters of the practice maintained that they actually remained within the same sovereignty; (e) finally it was maintained that Israel was not bound by Geneva IV.

The vast majority of the international community has not accepted these claims. As for the breadth of Art. 49, it clearly prohibits *all* deportations (including those of individuals who live under occupation), as recognized, for example, even by Supreme Court justices Bach (High Court of Justice 785/87) and Cohn (High Court of Justice 698/80), as well as by

Israeli legal scholars such as Cohen (1985) and Dinstein (1978, 1979, 1981). The absolute nature of the prohibition on expulsion forcefully invalidates most of the pre-expulsion arguments, and specifically the second, third and fourth arguments above. The question of the binding nature of Geneva IV, discussed above, has direct bearing on the illegality of any deportation.

Administrative Detention

A very large number of Palestinians have been the subject of administrative detention orders since 1967, and especially since the beginning of the Intifada. Thus, *B'Tselem* reported that over 14,000 administrative detention orders had been issued between December 1987 and September 1992 (*B'Tselem*, 1992, p. 7). Most of the detainees spent six months in prison, and many were detained for much longer. The practice of imprisonment through administrative (rather than judicial) means was defended as a means for preventing persons thought to be dangerous from committing acts against state security. In other words, the procedure was depicted as preventive.

An examination of the policy of administrative detention requires a broader perspective than one merely focusing on belligerent occupation. Article 9(1) of the Universal Declaration of Human Rights states that 'no one shall be subjected to arbitrary arrest, detention or exile,' a language retained by the 1966 International Convention on Civil and Political Rights. Article 10 of the UDHR demands due process, specifically 'fair and public hearing by an independent and impartial tribunal.' On the other hand, Article 78(1) of Geneva IV allows the occupying power to detain persons, although only for 'imperative reasons of security.' In other words, political internment is unacceptable.

Although administrative detention is not, as a matter of principle, incompatible with Geneva IV, its extensive use by Israel has come under persistent criticism. Critics argue that: (1) secret evidence against the 'accused' is often used, making a legal defense virtually impossible, especially since detainees are rarely given the reasons for their detention (Amnesty International, 1989, p. 1); (2) appeals of detainees to the High Court of Justice are invariably unsuccessful; (3) many cases target political activists, not 'terrorists' (U.S. Department of State, 1988, pp. 1379-80). Concerning the conditions of administrative detention, many analysts noted that (1) Palestinians are often detained in Israel, rather than in the West Bank or Gaza, a violation of Geneva IV (Amnesty International, ibid., p. 2; Lawyers Committee for Human Rights, 1988, p. 12); (2) international bodies examining the conditions of detention concluded that they were highly unsatisfactory, also in violation of Geneva IV's provisions (Lawyers Committee for Human Rights, 1988, p. 13); (3) particular attention was directed at the detention facility in Ketziot, known for its severe conditions. Even the Israeli High Court of Justice recommended the appointment of a committee to monitor the conditions in this camp (Amnesty International, ibid., p. 8: High Court of Justice 258/88).

Despite the severe conditions of administrative detention, several arguments were offered to defend it:

1. Every state has recourse to administrative detention in times of national emergency (Cohen, 1985, pp. 295-6) and occupiers, specifically, have recognized rights to use administrative detention in order to maintain order in territories under their control (Krauthammer, 1990, pp. 77-8).
2. Israel made use of the procedure in a controlled manner (Cohen, 1985, p. 121), used it against specific individuals and not against population groups (ibid., p. 128), and its record in comparison with other countries (e.g. U.S. During World War II: Dershowitz, 1971) is quite good.
3. Administrative detention ought to be judged against other security measures; it is, according to its defenders, less severe than either deportations or house demolition (Cohen, 1985, p. 128).

Despite these arguments, many international observers believe that administrative detention has been used too often and too extensively in situations where regular judicial proceedings should be employed. These observers emphasized that administrative detention is flawed in terms of due process. Evidence is ordinarily not shared with detainees. Even official Israeli reports found that the human rights of detainees were often violated (e.g. The Landau Report of October 1987).

In general, it is clear that political interests rather than security considerations have driven the policy on administrative detention since 1967. Thus, the outbreak of the Intifada saw the intensification of the policy as a means of reestablishing control over the population and punishing the rebellious Palestinians. All sections of Palestinian society were greatly impacted by the policy.

Although the Israeli system of administrative detention has not been wholly devoid of safeguards against abuse, Amnesty International found that it 'falls short of international human rights standards' (Amnesty International, 1989, p. 34). The Israeli authorities have mistakenly detained many innocent persons as well as persons who were nonviolently exercising their right of free expression.

House Demolition

Although Israeli authorities have used house demolition in the West Bank/Gaza from the very beginning of the Israeli occupation, they intensified its use after 1987, and especially as a result of a package of sanctions approved by the Israeli government in March 1988 (*B'Tselem*, 1989, p. 26). The use of this punishment technique fluctuated from period to period, but there is no doubt that several thousands of houses were demolished (Cohen, 1985, p. 97, p. 170; International Center for Peace in the Middle East, p. 158). In the first year of the Intifada alone Israeli authorities demolished about 150 houses (Al-Haq, 1988, p. 218).

From a legal point-of-view, house demolition has been extremely controversial. Although Israeli authorities argued that the Defense Emergency Regulations (no. 119) authorize the practice, and the High Court of Justice has accepted this position on several occasions (e.g. 698/85, 987/86), Article 53 of Geneva IV clearly *prohibits* the destruction of private property except in cases where it is 'absolutely necessary by military operations.' The Hague Regulations (Article 23g) are even more limiting. The International Committee of the Red Cross, in interpreting Article 53, determined that destruction of property is allowed only if it is 'absolutely necessary, i.e., militarily indispensible for the armed forces' of the occupant (Shehadeh, 1989, p. 155).

A few arguments justifying demolition have been offered through the years: (a) sometimes it is a military necessity to destroy houses from which terrorist operate (Shamgar, 1974, pp. 275-6); (b) the definition of 'military necessity' is left in Article 53 to the discretion of the occupant; (c) house demolition is essential for effectively deterring terrorism (Lorch, 1971, pp. 376-81; Gerson, 1980, pp. 22-5).

By and large, those arguments and others have failed to change the opinion of the international community. In fact, it was argued, most house demolitions have not been 'absolutely necessary' by military considerations; only 'a genuine military emergency' justifies destruction of property (Von Glahn, 1957, pp. 227-8). Procedurally, the practice has been highly problematic: quick execution of an administrative order, depriving the owners of the house of the possibility of appealing, etc. But above all, house demolition was judged to be an extremely severe collective punishment because in practically all cases the alleged offender lives in a family residence. The 'collective character' of house demolition (Cohen, p. 103) clearly violates Article 33 of Geneva IV, which forbids collective punishment or reprisals against the occupied population.

Human Rights under Oslo: The Danger of Transition

In September 1993 Israel and the Palestine Liberation Organization signed a Declaration of Principle, and then a few additional agreements, designed to lead eventually to the withdrawal of Israeli forces from all or most of the West Bank and Gaza and to the establishment of a Palestinian entity there. The election of Benjamin Netanyahu as Israel premier (May 29, 1996), and the actions taken by his government, significantly slowed down the process, but did not stop it completely. In this section I will assess the condition of human rights in the territories under the 'Oslo environment,' an inherently complicated, volatile milieu.

In the long run, the implementation of the Oslo Accords is likely to lead to considerable improvement in the human rights situation in the West Bank and Gaza. Yet, the transition period is extremely dangerous and could produce massive violations of human rights. While the withdrawal of the IDF from major Palestinian cities during 1994 dramatically reduced daily clashes between the Palestinian population and Israel's security forces, the process also generated actions on the part of Jewish extremists like Dr. Baruch Goldstein, Yigal Amir, and Noam Freedman, and on the part of Arab extremist organizations like Hamas and the Islamic Jihad. There is a link between progress toward a final Israeli-Palestinian settlement, on the one hand, and the motivation of the opponents of such a settlement to commit major human rights violations as a mechanism for preventing a peaceful, negotiated settlement. The closer the parties come to a settlement, the more intense the motivation of its enemies to destroy it. The current transition period is, thus, extremely unstable.

The Oslo Accords reflected, *inter alia*, by the Rabin government's recognition (1992-95) that the array of coercive actions against the Palestinian population has miserably failed. The massive violations of human rights, especially after the outbreak of the Intifada, inflamed the population and increased its resistance to the occupation. A broad-based international consensus emerged, viewing Israel as a major violator of human rights. Most Israelis reached the conclusion that Israel must eventually withdraw from most of the Occupied Territories (Barzilai & Peleg, 1994).

From the broadest political perspective, Oslo represents the first, somewhat tentative step toward the resolution of the 100-year old Arab-Jewish conflict. The mutual recognition between Israel and the Palestine Liberation Organization leads necessarily, albeit implicitly, to a two-state solution. In terms of human rights, the Oslo Accord, and particularly Oslo II (1995), obligate Israel and the Palestinian Authority to respect human rights (article 19). There is today a general agreement that, despite the remarkable progress on the political front, neither Israel nor the Palestinian Authority has lived up to their human rights obligations (al-Haq, 1993; *B'Tselem*, December 1996).

The most significant human rights violations by Israel, since Oslo, include the following:

1. *Torture* of Palestinians under interrogation by the General Security Service, sometimes with the explicit authorization of Israel's High Court of Justice (*B'Tselem*, January 1997; December 1996).
2. Long-term and widespread restriction on the *movement* of Palestinians, banning them from moving freely inside the Territories, travelling to Israel, and enjoying free passage between Gaza and the West Bank in direct violation of Oslo (*B'Tselem*, April 1996, pp. 19-33).
3. *Collective punishment* of innocent people, including not only curfews and closures, but the demolition of homes of suspects in attacks on Israelis (resulting in the punishment of their family members).
4. Continued *settlement* of Israelis in the Territories, especially in East Jerusalem and in areas around Jerusalem (*B'Tselem*, March 1997; *B'Tselem*, January 1997) and, at the same time, revoking the rights of many Palestinians to live in East Jerusalem (*B'Tselem*, April 1997).
5. *Detention*: according to IDF statistics, as of December 4, 1996, 284 Palestinians were held in administrative detention, that is: held in prison without trial and for long periods. According to *B'Tselem*, in mid-May 1997, Israel held 249 individuals in administrative detention (*B'Tselem*, July 1997, p. 90).

By and large Israeli security forces in areas which are still under Israeli control--practically the entire West Bank save the major cities--continue to commit 'the same kinds of abuses as in past years' (Human Rights Watch, World Report, 1996, p. 288). It is safe to assume that these human rights violations will continue until the occupation ends (Peleg, 1995, ch. 5). The Palestinian National Authority has also violated, in a systematic way, a series of fundamental rights (*B'Tselem*, 1995):

1. *Torture* of detainees has become widespread, leading in at least 10 cases to the death of prisoners.
2. The right to *a fair trial* has been violated by conducting quick and secret 'legal' proceedings (although some of these in order to prevent extradition to Israel).
3. *Freedom of expression*, guaranteed by many international covenants as well as by the Palestinian Press Law (Art. 2), has not been established;

in fact, many newspapers have been closed, journalists arrested, cameras destroyed, etc.

4. The activity of human rights organizations working in the areas of the Palestinian Authority has been seriously impaired, especially as a result of the detention of human rights activists.

The Future

It is possible, although by no means certain, that eventual Israeli withdrawal from the Territories, will reduce the number and severity of human rights violations by the Palestinian Authority. At the same time, it is highly likely that during the transition from occupation to 'permanent status' (if such a transition eventually occurs), human rights will continue to be massively violated by both Israeli and Palestinian authorities. Israeli violations will be motivated by 'security considerations' as well as by Palestinian resistance to the occupation. Palestinian violations of human rights in the transition period will continue to be determined by two major factors. Internally, violations of human rights within the territory transferred to the Palestinian Authority will be influenced by Arafat's effort to establish a centralized, authoritarian regime. Externally, Arafat will continue to be under strong Israeli pressure to fully control 'his' population, and especially those who oppose the peace process, even if the price is serious violations of human rights (including those of innocent persons).

A more severe human rights problem--inherent in the peace process--is the confrontation between Israeli settlers and the Palestinian inhabitants of the West Bank and Gaza. As the peace process moves forward, this confrontation could become even more severe than it has been over the last three decades. Moreover, the human rights violations associated with Israeli settlement in the Territories could prevent the peace train from ever reaching its destination, a two-state solution. The settlers and their leaders are fully aware of the intimate relations between the violation of Palestinian human rights (e.g., via open and massive attacks on Palestinians) and the possibility of derailing the peace train.

Nowhere in the Territories is the link between peace, settlement, and human rights violations clearer than in Hebron, where the constellation of forces is deadly. Close physical proximity between Jewish settlers and Palestinian inhabitants, an ultranationalist Jewish community and strong Arab fundamentalist presence, religious sites of great importance to both Islam and Judaism, and a bloody history of communal massacres, make

Hebron a recipe for continued violence, human rights violations, and extremist politics.

Despite and maybe because of the movement toward an overall Israeli-Palestinian settlement, further confrontations between the settlers and the Palestinian population seem unavoidable. The settlers would like to stop the impending withdrawal from most of the West Bank. They believe the way of doing so is to commit outrageous acts of violence against the Arab population. What might be called the 'Goldstein Rationale' still dominates among many of the radical settlers. It is doubtful that the Israeli authorities could or would offer the local Palestinian populations protection against further settlers' violence. In the past, violent actions taken by settlers resulted in curfews and closures on the Palestinians.

The election of Benjamin Netanyahu as Israel's Prime Minister in May 1996 could prove, as it already has to some extent, a significant blow to human rights in the transition period, even (and maybe especially) if the government continues to move toward permanent political settlement. On a number of occasions since his election, Netanyahu behaved not only in a non-compromising manner (e.g., in stalling the negotiations over Hebron) but even in an utterly provocative fashion (e.g., in the opening of the Jerusalem tunnel in late 1996 or in establishing a new settlement in Har Homa). Such behavior has led to the most serious violence in the occupied West Bank since the height of the Intifada.

Netanyahu's approach could become a recipe for further human rights violations, confrontations and delays in the arrival at a permanent solution. The traditional demonization of Arafat, which dominated Israeli attitudes for decades, returned under Netanyahu. Such demonization strengthens the ultraright opposition to a settlement with the Palestinians insofar as it reaffirms their own analysis of the Arabs.

On a deeper level, beyond negotiation style, the Netanyahu government has not given good signals in terms of its commitment to an acceptable final settlement; this omission could be fatal in terms of human rights. Since its return to power, the Likud government (a) has reclassified the settlements in the Occupied Territories as priority development areas, (b) has announced its intention of making 3,000 apartments in the Territories, 'frozen' by the previous government, available, and (c) has pushed further the agenda of additional settlement in East Jerusalem. There can be no doubt that an agenda focused on the intensification of settlement must lead to the derailment of the peace process and to more violations of human rights.

References

Al-Haq (1993), *A Human Rights Assessment of the Declaration of Principles on Interim Self-Government for Palestinians, Jerusalem.*

Al-Haq/Law in the Service of Man (1987), *Demolition and Sealing of Houses*, Occasional Paper no. 5, Ramallah.

_____ (1986), *Israel's Deportation Policy*, Occasional Paper no. 2, Ramallah.

_____ (1988), *Punishing a Nation: Human Rights Violations During the Palestinian Uprising*, Ramallah.

Amnesty International (1989), *Israel and the Occupied Territories: Administrative Detention During the Palestinian Intifada*, New York: Amnesty International.

Barzilai, Gad and Ilan Peleg (1994), 'Israel and Future Borders: Assessment of a Dynamic Process,' *Journal of Peace Research* 31(1), February, pp. 59-73.

Benvenisti, Eyal (1990), *Legal Dualism: The Absorption of the Occupied Territories into Israel*, Westview Press: Boulder, Colo.

Benvenisti, Meron (1987), *The West Bank Data Base Project: 1987 Report*, Jerusalem Post: Jerusalem.

_____ (1984), *The West Bank Data Project: A Survey of Israel's Policies*, Washington, D.C.: American Enterprise Institute.

Benvenisti, Meron with Ziad Abu-Ziad and Danny Rubinstein (1986), *The West Bank Handbook: A Political Lexicon*, Jerusalem Post: Jerusalem.

Blum, Yehuda Zvi (1968), 'The Missing Reversioner: Reflections on the Status of Judea and Samaria,' *Israel Law Review* 3, pp. 279-301.

Boyd, Stephen M. (1971), 'The Applicability of International Law in the Occupied Territories,' *Israel Yearbook on Human Rights*, pp. 258-77.

B'Tselem (1997), *Brutality for Its Own Sake: And the Beatings Continue: Beating and Abuse of Palestinians at the Hands of the Border Police and Soldiers in May-August 1997*, Report, August.

_____ (1997), *Prisoners of Peace: Administrative Detention During the Oslo Process*, July.

_____ (1997), *The Quiet Deportation: Revocation of Residency of East Jerusalem Palestinians*, April.

_____ (1997), *Israeli Settlement in the Occupied Territories as a Violation of Human Rights: Legal and Conceptual Aspects*, March.

_____ (1997), *A Policy of Discrimination: Land Expropriation, Planning and Building in East Jerusalem*, January.

_____ (1997), *Legitimizing Torture: The Israeli High Court of Justice Rulings in the Bilbeisi, Hamdan and Mubarak Cases*, January.

_____ (1996), *Without Limits: Human Rights Violations Under Closure*, April.

_____ (1995), *Neither Law nor Justice: Extra-Judicial Punishment, Abduction, Unlawful Arrest, and Torture of Palestinian Residents of the West Bank by the Palestinian Preventive Security Service*, August.

_____ (1992), *Detained Without Trial: Administrative Detention in the Occupied Territories since the Beginning of the Intifada*, Jerusalem.

_____ (1990), *Collective Punishment in the West Bank and the Gaza Strip*, Jerusalem.

_____ (1989), *Demolition and Sealing Houses*, Jerusalem.

Cohen, Esther Rosalind (1985), *Human Rights in the Israeli-Occupied Territories, 1967-1982*, Manchester University Press: Manchester.

de Zayas, Alfred M. (1975), 'International Law and Mass Population Transfers,' *Harvard International Law Journal* 16, pp. 207-58.

Dershowitz, Alan (1971), 'Preventive Detention of Citizens During National Emergency--a Comparison Between Israel and the United States,' *Israel Yearbook of Human Rights* 1, pp. 295-321.

Dinstein, Yoram (1981), 'The Deportation of the Mayors from Judea,' *Tel Aviv University Law Review* 6, no. 1, pp. 158-71.

_____ (1978), 'Deportations from Administered Territories,' *Tel Aviv University Law Review* 13, no. 2, August, pp. 403-16.

_____ (1979), 'Settlements and Expulsion in the Administered Territories,' *Tel Aviv University Law Review* 7, no. 1, September, pp. 188-94.

Drori, Moshe (1978), 'The Legal System in Judea and Samaria: A Review of the Previous Decade with a Glance at the Future,' *Israel Yearbook on Human Rights* 8, pp. 144-77.

'Excerpts from the Landau Commission's Report on Shin Bet Practices,' *Jerusalem Post*, November 1, 1987.

Feinberg, Nathan (1977), 'The West Bank's Legal Status,' *New Outlook* 20, October-November, pp. 60-2.

Fleischman, Lisa M. (1988), Appendix B (Legal), in 'Committee to Protect Journalists and Article 19,' *Journalism Under Occupation*, pp. 199-221.

Gazit, Shlomo (1972), 'Administered Areas Aspects of Israeli Policy,' in *Information Briefing*, Ministry of Foreign Affairs: Jerusalem.

_____ (1985), *Hamakel ve'Hagezer* (The stick and the carrot), Zmora, Bitan: Tel Aviv.

Gerson, Alan (1973), 'Trustee-Occupant: The Legal Status of Israel's Presence in the West Bank,' *Harvard International Law Review* 14, pp. 1-49.

Helms, Jesse, 'Law and the Territories,' *Jerusalem Post*, May 4, 1990.

Hiltermann, Joost R. (1988), *Israel's Deportation Policy in the Occupied West Bank and Gaza Strip*, Al-Haq Occasional Paper no. 2, 2nd ed., Ramallah: Al-Haq/Law in the Service of Man and Gaza Centre for Rights and Law.

Human Rights Watch World Report (1996), Washinton, D.C.

International Center for Peace in the Middle East (1985), *Human Rights in the Occupied Territories 1979-1983*, International Center for Peace in the Middle East: Tel Aviv.

Karp Report (1984), Institute for Palestinian Studies: Washington, D.C.

Krauthammer, Charles, 'Judging Israel,' *Time*, February 26, 1990, pp. 77-8.

Kretzmer, David (1987), 'The Legal Status of Israeli Settlers on the West Bank,' *Israeli Democracy* 1, no. 3, Fall, pp. 16-8.

Kuttner, Thomas S. (1977), 'Israel and the West Bank: Aspects of the Law of Belligerent Occupation,' *Israel Yearbook on Human Rights* 7, pp. 166-221.

Lawyers Committee for Human Rights (1988), *An Examination of the Detention of Human Rights Workers and Lawyers from the West Bank and Gaza and Conditions of Detention at Ketziot*, Committee for Human Rights: New York.

Middle East Watch (1991), *Prison Conditions in Israel and the Occupied Territories*, Middle East Watch: New York.

Palestinian Human Rights Monitoring Group and B'Tselem (1996), *Human Rights in the Occupied Territories Since the Oslo Accords: Status Report*, December.

Peleg, Ilan (1995), *Human Rights in the West Bank and Gaza: Legacy and Politics*, Syracuse University Press: Syracuse.

_____ (1987), *Begin's Foreign Policy, 1973-1983: Israel's Move to the Right*, Greenwood Press: Westport, Conn.

Peleg, Ilan and Ofira Seliktar, eds. (1989), *The Emergence of a Binational Israel: The Second Republic in the Making*, Westview Press: Boulder, Colo.

Playfair, Emma (1989), *Administrative Detention in the Occupied West Bank*, Occasional Paper no. 1, Ramallah: Al-Haq/Law in the Service of Man.

Rubinstein, Ammon (1986), 'The Changing Status of the 'Territories:' From Escrow to a Legal mongrel' (Hebrew), *Tel Aviv University Law Review* 11, no. 3, Oct., pp. 439-56. Also in English in *Tel Aviv University Studies in Law* 8 (1988), pp. 59-79.

Sarid, Yossi and Dedi Zucker (1989), 'A Year of Intifada,' *New Outlook* 8, January, pp. 48-50.

Sela, Michal, 'Half a Million Detentions—All in the Territories,' *Koteret Rashit*, February 25, 1987.

Shamgar, Meir (1971), 'The Observance of International Law in the Administered Territories,' *Israel Yearbook on Human Rights* 1, pp. 262-77. Also published in John Norton Moore, ed., *The Arab Israeli Conflict*, Vol. 2: *Readings*, Princeton University Press: Princeton.

Shehadeh, Raja (1982), *Haderech Hashlishit* (The third way), Adam Publishers: Jerusalem.

_____ (1989), *Occupier's Law: Israel and the West Bank*, Rev. Ed., Institute for Palestine Studies: Washington, D.C.

Sheleff, Leon (1992), 'The Green Line is the Border of Judicial Activism: Queries about Supreme Court Judgments in the Territories,' *Tel Aviv University Law Review* 17, no. 2, November, pp. 757-809.

U.S. Department of State, *Country Reports on Human Rights*, U.S. Department of State: Washington, D.C., annual.

Von Glahn, Gerhard (1986), *Law Among Nations: An Introduction to Public International Law* 5th ed., Macmillan: New York.

_____ (1957), *The Occupation of Enemy Territory*, University of Minnesota Press: Minneapolis.

_____ (1971), 'The Protection of Human Rights in Time of Armed Conflict,' *Israel Yearbook on Human Rights* 1, pp. 208-27.

Weiner, Justus R. (1986), 'The Settlements in Judea and Samaria: A Legal View,' *Midstream*, August-September, pp. 24-6.

11 The Rise and Fall of Democratization in the Maghreb

MOHAMMAD-MAHMOUD MOHAMEDOU

The past decade was a seminal period in North African history. At the end of the 1980s, a transition to democracy was initiated in the countries of the Maghreb region in response to social pressures for social emancipation and political renewal. Wherever and whenever the opportunity beckoned the people put forth these demands. The movement gathered momentum in the early 1990s in the wake of the end of the Cold War and the revolutions in Eastern Europe. Following the 1990-91 Second Gulf War, as change gained urgency in the Arab world, the Maghreb was becoming a democratizing neighborhood. By 1993-94, however, disillusion set in as the promised changes failed to materialize. The experiments had become aborted (Morocco), co-opted (Mauritania and Tunisia), crushed (Algeria) or altogether absent (Libya). Today, as democratization is only paid lip service by the governments, the wave is all but gone.

This chapter pinpoints the nature of the political transformation in the Maghreb within the time-frame 1987-98, identifies the specific issues relevant to each one of the five countries, and assesses the sociopolitical impact and the dividends of these changes on the development of the Maghreb region. While focusing on the internal situation of each one of the five Maghrebi states, the analysis places the current regional political liberalization reconfiguration within the context of the general changes and asks what the process of change reveals or conceals. Underpinning the discussion is the relationship between political stabilization and political turbulence in the context of the demand for more political participation on the part of civil societies. Is the region heading towards protection of human rights, democracy and stability or, toward oppression, autocracy, and unrest? Have the restructuring scenarios paved the way for a forging ahead of the democratic impulse with substantive reforms carrying institutional and procedural implications or have they led to a growth of radicalism?

Thus far democratization in North Africa has been but an attempt to reconsolidate the power of the state. Democratization has weakened the societies and strengthened the regimes. While the state has been conceding to global pressures and retreating from the economic sphere (Strange, 1996), domestically it has resisted calls for sociopolitical change. Neo-authoritarianism has been born in democratic guise. There has been no eradication of political repression or conflict (Carothers, 1997). There has been no period of trust-building between the regimes and their citizens. The electoral processes have not succeeded in infusing a sense of political legitimacy. The emergence of organized opposition movements was possible only because of the gradual development of an increasingly informed and involved public. The setback to the democratization wave has also been compounded by an intensifying struggle between the regime and its political opponents, in particular Islamist militants. Despite the presence of embryonic civil societies, the region has not yet fully developed a democratic tradition. Deeply entrenched élites have stood in the way of liberalization. Consequently, the nexus of state and society is increasingly a troubled one in the Maghreb.

The Changing Maghrebi Picture

As the western part of the Arab world, the North African area was historically known as *jazirat al maghrib* (the western island). With its 71.6 million inhabitants and 6 million square kilometers the self-contained region displays a certain distinctiveness within the Arab world. With the exception of Libya and the Western Sahara sector, all of the Maghreb was colonized by France. French rule lasted 132 years in Algeria (1830-1962), 75 years in Tunisia (1881-1956), 52 years in Morocco (1904-56), and 40 years in Mauritania (1920-60). Algeria was a French province, Mauritania a colony, and Morocco and Tunisia protectorates. In sum, 92 per cent of the Maghrebi population experienced French colonial influence. The Italians remained in Libya for 31 years (1912-43) followed by an eight-year United Nations mandate (1943-51), and Spain controlled the Western Sahara between 1884 and 1976, some 92 years.

The primary result of the colonial imprint has been the triggering of nationalistic feelings. Consequently, human rights and democratic emancipation were first manifested through nationalism. The struggle for the respect for human rights had its origins in the national movements that struggled for independence (Feliu, 1996). The idea was to fight colonialism by using the very same principles that the colonists sought to propagate (Leveau 1989; Karem, 1993). The notion of self-determination as a group right was an intrinsic aspect of the mobilization against the foreigner. However, a real debate on political liberalization only began in the 1970s in Morocco and Tunisia, in the 1980s in Algeria and Mauritania, and it has yet to start in Libya. A second consequence of the colonialist experience has been the introduction of modernizing influences that have undermined the role of traditional institutions. Decolonization was alternatively brutal or soft, but it always marked a break with local traditions. As a result, North African countries have had dysfunctional political systems since gaining independence (Conry, 1997).

Another factor which allows us to analyze the Maghreb as a single unit is the similarity of Maghrebi societies to one another. Despite the existing political variety – a strong monarchy (Morocco), a military junta system (Algeria), authoritarian republican regimes (Mauritania and Tunisia), and a revolutionary socialist state (Libya) – there is an underlying societal and civilizational continuity. In addition to Arab ethnic homogeneity (alongside significant Berber and Black-African minorities) and linguistic continuity, the Maghreb has witnessed a tension between modernity and tradition, secularism and religion. Yet it remained a rather self-contained Islamic civilization in microcosm. The historical experience of the North African region has been deeply Islamic. Some local politicians have pursued Maghrebi political culture simultaneously founded on Islamic precepts and democratic values. Yet the disparity between ideal and real is highlighted by the fact that Islam can be thought and rethought by different groups and towards different ends. Thus, the Maghreb is home to one of the most liberal and westernized Arab societies (Morocco) at the same time that it houses the most radical Islamist factions (the Armed Islamic Group in Algeria).

In the 1970s, the national struggle became one for governance. As local groups were brought in, the inherited system gradually showed its limits – it was not calibrated to the societies at hand. Reshaping of society and indigenizing the polity became the order of the day. Nevertheless, the post-colonial Maghrebi state also inherited repressive colonial measures. Although constitutionally based civil liberties were introduced, democracy was put on hold in the name of state-building imperatives. Statist economic choices shaped the societies in a similar vein.

Since the early 1980s, the region has been in turmoil. Seeking to limit the military's dominant political role, social formations started making forceful demands for their basic rights. A mosaic of groups pressured for social change and called for accountability on the part of the rulers. Refuting symbolic participatory politics that had prevailed in the previous decades, opposition groups started to flourish in the Maghreb. What is distinctive about the situation that came to pass is, on the one hand, the attempt by pressure groups to monopolize the state and, on the other, resistance and protest that could no longer be accommodated within the existing framework (Hermassi, 1993). Nevertheless, governments resisted and suppressed demands and dealt violently with their opponents. The formal introduction of a multiparty system– in Tunisia in 1988, Algeria in 1989, and Mauritania in 1991–brought uncertainty to the polity, but did not undermine the power of the army. To be sure, military authoritarianism remained prevalent. Witness the fact that four out of the five current heads of state originated from army and intelligence sectors. These include: General Liamine Zeroual, General Zine al Abidine Ben Ali, Colonel Maaouiya Ould Sid'Ahmed Taya, and Colonel Moammar Qadhafi. The momentum of change in the late 1980s has been followed by a period of uncertainty.

Chaos in Algeria

The Algerian case dominates the North African picture. The 1991-1998 period has been one of civil war. In the wake of rampant human right abuses and riven by political and ideological cleavages the country is today living through anomie, anarchy, and alienation. Algeria's identity crisis encompasses ethnic, linguistic, and regional cleavages. Taken together, these rifts underscore the deep-seated divisions inhibiting national unity, and the recent years of open conflict have allowed these long-standing differences to fester (Yacoubian, 1997). The 4-5 October 1988 riots sounded the opening salvo of Algeria's transition to democracy. In large part the result of the alienation of urban youth (75 per cent of the 28 million Algerian population is under 30 years of age) whose frustration had been germinating for years in the metropoli. The unrest had been compounded by overpopulation, overurbanization, an enduring economic crisis, a high rate of unemployment, a complex process of internecine power struggles, and popular rejection of the political and economic monolithism of the one-party system. The events allowed for an acceleration of liberalization and highlighted the need to negotiate a new relationship with society. After 1988, mosques, schools, colleges, and universities became politicized. By then, Algeria's society had outgrown the confining economic and political outfit imposed by former President Houari Boumedienne's 1965-1978 Socialist regime (Malley, 1996; Stone, 1997). As the failure of socialist ideology became obvious and as the dissonance between popular mobilization and a faltering and aging one-party system was no longer tenable, opposition emerged from all segments of society. The government recognized that new political mapping and, in an initial attempt to manipulate the democratization movement, the authorities encouraged the creation of civic groups, be they Berberist cultural movements, social associations, or student unions. However, when the political liberalization of 1989 opened legitimate contestatory avenues, that space was overwhelmingly occupied by the Islamist opposition.

In the immediate aftermath of the October 1988 riots (3,743 arrests and 600 dead), several measures were taken in the direction of liberalization. On 10 October, President Chadli Benjedid gave a speech in which he announced that 'profound changes' would soon take place. On 3 November, a referendum for the adoption of a new Constitution was held with a 92.27 per cent vote in favor and an 83.08 per cent participation rate. The Constitution was adopted on 23 February 1989 formally ending the socialist era, installing a multiparty system, and lifting press censorship. An edict on information was adopted on the following 4 April and a law on associations with political character on 7 August. Inasmuch as the 1979-88 period had been characterized by efforts at institutionalizing the monopoly of the ruling Jabhat al Tahrir al Watani or Front de Libération Nationale (FLN), the reforms were not the outcome of any democratic consultation or debate. They had been forced on the regime by the 'street' (Zoubir, 1995).

The first multi-party electoral contest – the 12 June 1990 provincial and municipal balloting – saw al Jabha al Islamiya li al Khalass al Islami or Front Islamique du Salut (FIS) win 853 out of 1,540 communes, securing the control of 32 of the 48 Algerian *wilayas* (provinces). With 54.25 per cent of the vote, the recently-formed Islamist party was a clear winner, triggering concern amongst leaders of the FLN and the army. Demanding a modification of the electoral plan for the upcoming parliamentary elections, as well as President Benjedid's resignation, the FIS launched a general strike on 25 May 1991. Although FIS leaders Madani Abassi and Ali Benhadj[1] had met with Prime Minister Mouloud Hamrouch on 29 May to express their opposition to violence, on the night of 3-4 June the police attacked the Islamist militants gathered in the Martyrs' Square in Algiers. The battle yielded a death toll of 84 and 400 wounded. On 5 June, a state of siege was decreed, and the army entered the capital. The government of Mouloud Hamrouch resigned, and Sid'Ahmed Ghozali was appointed Prime Minister while General Laarbi Belkheir became Minister of Interior. The FIS then moved to open confrontation calling for Benjedid's immediate resignation and demanding legislative elections. Following a second meeting with the Prime Minister on 7 June, the Islamist leaders called off the strike and Ghozali announced that legislative and presidential elections would be held within six months at such time when the mandate of the Assemblée Nationale Populaire (ANP)– which had been elected in 1987 for a five-year term–would expire (Charef,

1994). However, on 15-18 June, 469 FIS activists were arrested. Then, on June 28, Madani Abassi issued a 48-hour ultimatum to the army to evacuate the cities. Two days later, Abassi and Benhadj were detained along with five other leaders of the FIS (Omar Abdelqader, Abdelqader Boukhamkham, Nourredine Chegara, Ali Djeddi, and Kemal Guemmazi). Their detention was followed by 1,293 arrests of militants. On 15 August, the FIS newspapers *Al-Mounquid* (the savior) and *Al-Forkane* (the proof) were ordered to cease publication. The perception that the FIS leaders had been used by the government for deceptive purposes became widespread.

In the first round of parliamentary elections on 26 December 1991, in which 49 out of the existing 58 parties participated, the FIS won 47.26 per cent of the vote, while the FLN and the Jabhat al Quwat al Ishtirakiya or Front des Forces Socialistes (FFS) of Hocine Ait-Ahmed respectively won 23.38 per cent and 7.40 per cent. In this first round, the FIS had succeeded in getting 188 seats out of 340, dwarfing the 25 seats of the FFS and the 16 seats of the FLN. But, 198 seats remained undecided with the Islamist party poised to win 135 more seats. The possibility that the FIS could end up controlling 323 of the 430 seats of the Algerian assembly was a serious one. For all practical purposes, the monopoly of the state-FLN was shattered (Rouadjia, 1994). However, the second round scheduled for 16 January 1992 never took place.

On 31 December, a Comité National pour la Sauvegarde de l'Algérie (CNSA) was set up to oppose the FIS and prevent its victory. It was made up of the Ligue Algérienne des Droits de l'Homme (LADH), the Hizb al Talia al Ishtirakiya or Parti de l'Avant-Garde Socialiste (PAGS), the Berberist and French-oriented Rassemblement pour la Culture et la Démocratie (RCD), and the Union Générale des Travailleurs Algériens (UGTA) who joined forces with the government. On 2 January 1992, an anti-FIS demonstration was attended by 135,000 in Algiers, and the RCD, whose leader Said Saadi had been particularly active in opposing the Islamists, called for a boycott of the second round. Sensing further trouble, on January 8, FIS acting-president Abdeqader Hachani (who had played a decisive role in securing his party's electoral success) asked President Benjedid and the Constitutional Court to guarantee respect for the election's results. The FIS had played by the rules, and now it felt that it was about to be robbed of its victory. However, on 11 January, Benjedid resigned and announced that he had dismissed Parliament on 4 January. The next day, the Constitutional Council declared that the simultaneous dissolution of the National Assembly and the resignation of the President was an unprecedented and unforeseen situation, and that power should therefore be assumed jointly by the army, the Prime Minister, the Constitutional Council, and the judicial authorities. Prime Minister Ghozali then met with the Haut Comité de Sécurité (HCS) to announce the impossibility of pursuing the electoral process, the creation of a Haut Comité d'État (HCE) endowed with executive powers, and the establishment of a Conseil Consultatif National (CCN) to serve as parliament. On 16 January, the army called upon one of the founders of the FLN, Mohammed Boudiaf, to head the HCE. On 22 January, Hachani was arrested; on 3 February, the headquarters of the FIS were stormed by the police, and on 4 March, the authorities announced the dissolution of the Islamist party and arrested 8,900 of its members. This intense period of unrest culminated in the assassination of President Boudiaf on 29 June. These events resulted in an absolute bipolarity between the Islamists and the military.

Notwithstanding the constitutional camouflage, this was a de facto coup. The dissolution of the National Assembly on 4 January was unambiguously unconstitutional since article 120 of the 1989 Constitution stipulated that before acting the President must consult both the President of the Assembly (Abdelaziz Belqacem) and the head of the government (Sid'Ahmed Ghozali). That did not happen. In addition, the decision-making power of the Haut Comité de Sécurité was null since the HCS, a purely consultative body, could only meet at the request of the President. The creation of the HCE by the HCS was also in violation of article 68, which posited the principle of popular sovereignty.

The Algerian government's refusal to abide by the 1991 election results, followed by a silent coup d'État and an anti-Islamist campaign including emergency military trials, torture, and assassinations, led to a civil war between the Algerian army and the three main Islamist groups: the FIS and its military wing, al Haraka al Islamiya al Musalaha or Mouvement Islamique Armé (MIA), and al Jamaa al Islamiya al Musalaha or Groupe Islamique Armé (GIA). Nothing of what the FIS did during the twenty-nine months that it lasted had invited governmental reprisal. From the beginning the FIS leaders pursued a strategy of respectability and a desire for institutional integration, as evinced by their participation in the 1990 and 1991 elections. They followed a non-violent strategy up until the coup.

The following six years saw Algeria plunge into a vicious civil war with a death toll of 90,000 to 100,000. Despite the 16 November 1995 presidential election – boycotted by the FLN, the FFS, the banned FIS, and the short-lived al Haraka li al Dimuqratiya fi al Jazair or the Mouvement pour la Démocratie en Algérie (MDA) of Ahmed Ben Bella – in which General Liamine Zeroual, President since January 1994 of the army-controlled Conseil National de Transition (CNT), was elected by 61.3 per cent of the vote, the crisis has endured and the government has resisted all appeals to open a dialogue. On 13 January 1995, a covenant was signed in Rome by six opposition parties along with the Ligue Algérienne pour la Défense des Droits de l'Homme (LADDH): the FLN, the FFS, the FIS (represented by Rabah Kebir and Anwar Haddam), the MDA, Hizb al Oumal or Parti des Travailleurs (PT) of Louisa Hanoune, and Ennahda (Renaissance) of Abdallah Jaballah. On the basis of the 1989 Constitution, the covenant called for the release of Islamist prisoners, a halt to the fighting, and the creation of a transitional government. The government reacted by calling the meeting a 'non-event' and rejected it globally and in detail.

On 11 May 1996, President Zeroual outlined a constitutional reform proposal that would enforce the separation of religion and politics. He announced that legislative and municipal elections would be held in 1997 and that the constitution would be modified (see Roberts, 1996). Against this background, a National Conference was held on 14-15 September in Algiers with 1,000 delegates representing 28 parties and 37 associations. Aimed at the establishment of a national pact of reconciliation in preparation for the upcoming 1997 legislative and municipal elections, this gathering– boycotted by the FFS, the RCD, and other groups such as the Communist party al Tahadi (Unification)–failed to adopt a binding general platform of principles and reforms to end the civil war. A referendum was held on 28 November for the adoption of a new constitution that bans political parties based on religion, language or regionalism, and strengthens the powers of the president. The new National Assembly has little power. It is under the tutelage of an indirectly-elected Senate of which one-third is appointed by the President from among leading personalities, union leaders, and civil servants. Any law voted by the Assembly must be approved by all members of the Senate. With his third, the President has de facto control of the legislative process.

The parliamentary balloting of 5 June 1997 further altered the balance of power in favor of Liamine Zeroual and resulted in more violence. Amid widespread use of fraud by the authorities, the newly-created government-controlled al Tajamu al Watani li al Dimuqratiya or Rassemblement National pour la Démocratie (RND) won the election capturing 156 of the 380 seats. The government majority was reinforced by the 62 seats of a revamped FLN stripped of its more democratic figures such as its former Secretary-General Abdehamid Mehri. While the FFS (20 seats) and the RCD (19 seats) were big losers, the moderate Islamist parties of Ennahda and the Harakat Mujtama al Salam or Mouvement de la Société pour la Paix (MSP, formerly Hamas) of Mahfoudh Nahnah were allowed to have some representation with 69 and 34 seats respectively. Subsequently, the

FLN and the MSP were each awarded seven portfolios in the 30-member cabinet.

Besides electoral apathy – participation went down by 9 per cent when compared to the presidential election of November 1995, and by 14 per cent when compared to the constitutional referendum of November 1996– the major problem of this parliamentary balloting was that it did not accurately reflect the state of Algerian society and polity. The three parties that obtained the most votes in the last free election (the FIS, the FFS, and the FLN had received a combined 78 per cent during the December 1991 contest) have been ostracized from the political process. The election simply strengthened the government's hold on power without diminishing violence or the existing opposition. The regime's strategy has remained a mixture of co-opting and weakening the opposition parties by engaging them in periodic dialogues (Pierre and Quandt, 1996).

The June 1997 legislative round yielded a competition in which the moderate Islamists of Ennahda and the MSP matched each other; the Berber groups RCD and FFS did the same: The RND towered above the others (using the FLN). The 23 October local balloting further advanced President Zeroual's control over the political process through the RND which obtained 55 per cent of the vote. With 7,242 out of 13,123 municipal seats, and 986 out of 1,880 departmental seats, the RND overshadowed the FLN (2,864 and 373), the MSP (890 and 260), the FFS (645 municipal seats), the RCD (444 municipal seats), and the Ennahda (290 municipal seats). As several thousand protesters took to the street on 31 October to denounce the massive use of fraud by the government, it was obvious that the 1997 elections were but a further confirmation of the devolution of Algeria's transition process.

The regime's strategy of isolating and weakening the FIS took a new turn when, on 8 July 1997, Abdelqader Hachani was freed from the Serkadji prison where he had been held for the past five years without a trial. A week later, Madani Abassi was released after six years of detention. These high-profile liberations were designed to neutralize the leaders of the FIS–to the notable exception of Ali Benhadj who remained jailed under harsh conditions– while putting pressure on the GIA to seek a compromise. On 1 September–six weeks after his release–Abassi was placed under house arrest for calling, in a letter to United Nations Secretary General Kofi Annan, for an end to bloodshed and the opening of dialogue.

Thus, the government's policy as of early 1998 was a balanced effort to appease key sectors of society and to pull the rug out from under the opposition, be they moderate Islamists such as the MSP, RCD pro-Berbers or democrats such as the FFS, while simultaneously seeking to violently eradicate Islamism. The government claimed it had dealt effectively with violence, and that the outbreaks of violence were only 'residual terrorism.' However, the surge of massacres that took place in the six months following the June election was a deadly reminder that President Zeroual had failed in his promise to crush the six-year-old insurgency.

Against this background, the Algerian situation remains essentially dominated by a conflict between a military junta and organized but fractious Islamist groups attempting to overthrow the government and establish an Islamic-oriented state and society. In the wake of six years of civil war, there is little doubt that the Islamists remain the most organized anti-status quo challenger in the country, systematically seeking to gain control of the government. For one analyst at least, an Islamist victory is possible and not necessarily a negative prospect for Algeria (Fuller, 1996). The Islamists and the military government are in effect the real power-brokers. Jockeying for leverage, the other major political parties stand on the side. Indeed, all real power in Algeria revolves around the 125,000-men strong Armée Nationale Populaire (ANP). Whoever controls it, controls the country. The military has held power since the September 1962 coup against the Gouvernement Provisoire de la République Algérienne (GPRA) of Ferhat Abbas, and it has directly controlled the nation's affairs since President Houari Boumedienne coup on Ahmed Ben Bella on 19 June 1965. During the last decade, the armed forces have intervened three times (October 1988, June 1991, and January 1992) to alter the course of the political process.

The threatening consequences to the military of the 1991 election led to a reorganizing of the army's structure. After an initial period (1992-94) of direct confrontation between the army and the Islamists, and in the wake of several desertions and infiltration by Islamists, the government decided to create paramilitary defense groups staffed with citizens. In February 1994, the government freed some 10,000 common law prisoners who were then paid to form anti-Islamist militias called the Groupes de Légitime Défense (GLD) or 'Patriots.' On 4 January 1997, these former convicts were formally entrusted to enforce law and order. The result has been the militarization of Algerian society. The army has also created a 50,000-men special task force to fight the insurgents in urban centers, the Groupes d'Intervention et de Surveillance (GIS) known as 'Ninjas.' Since 1995, therefore, the first line of defense has been made up of militias and paramilitary groups. The army has adopted a defensive strategic approach choosing to concentrate the bulk of its troops around key sites such as oil and gas fields, the ministries, and the élite residential neighborhoods (like the Club des Pins in the periphery of Algiers).

Lower- and middle-class Algerian citizens are the main victims of the crisis. In addition to generalized insecurity and state of siege laws, they have experienced a steady erosion of their economic, political and civil liberties (300,000 families live in shantytowns). According to the Algerian Ministry of Justice, there were in 1995 some 16,000 political prisoners in the country. During the last six years, six hundred schools have been burned down and there has been approximately $2 billion worth of material losses. Some 85 Imams and 70 intellectuals have been killed; 500 journalists have left the country; and at least 2,500 people have disappeared. To this, one must add devastating psychological and sociological effects such as the generalization of fear, the increase in banditry and the growth of feelings of hatred.

The country's agony is illustrated by savagery and rituals of violence (mutilations, throat-slittings, beheadings, disembowelments). In 1997, violence steadily increased in the triangle of cities Algiers-Blida-Laarba with the secondary routes of the Mitidja area (Boufarik, Bougara, Chedli) being the most dangerous zones. In the summer of that year, there were 2,000 dead in seven weeks. On 29 August, three hundred villagers were killed in Rai in the single largest massacre in the history of independent Algeria.

Besides the usurpation of power, there has been since 1992 a consistent pattern of human rights abuses by the authorities prompting revenge killings on the part of the insurgents. In fact, there is an increasing suspicion among Algerians that many of the terrorist acts, up to and including assassinations of police officers, may be the work of élite units of the security forces themselves or their agents provocateurs among the Islamists (Ciment, 1997). To be certain, the violence used by the state is at least equal to that used by its Islamist opponents (Mongin, 1997). Vigilante groups such as the Organisation de la Jeunesse Algérienne Libre (OJAL) and the Organisation de la Sauvegarde de la République Algérienne (OSRA) perpetrate gross human rights violations with impunity. There are at least fifteen detention centers in Algiers, and concentration camps (officially called 'state security camps') have been formed. A June 1991 presidential decree allows the state to deport without trial any citizen on suspicion of guilt for an undetermined period. Arbitrary arrests, summary executions, mass killings, and systematic torture in specialized centers (such as the Superior Police School of Chateauneuf, and the Algiers-based military centers of Ben Aknoun, Bourouba, and Bouzarea), as well as tribunals of exception with no right of appeal and limits to defense rights, are the order of the day in Algeria (see Amnesty International, 1996; Human Rights Watch, 1997; Reporters Sans Frontières, 1997; and Fédération Internationale des Droits de l'Homme, 1997).

Among observers, there is a widespread perception that the majority of the Algerian population is convinced that the government is the principal instigator of the violence of the past six years. As Séverine Labat (1995) aptly remarked, 'violence is a result of the closing of the polity, of the disappearing of mediation elements within the FIS, and of the Islamist movement's inability to fully manage the tensions inherent in its dual nature. Violence is equally anchored in Algerian social practices as it is rooted in the way leaders since 1962 have cultivated the memory of the founding violence of the war of independence. Violence also originates in the way the FLN and then the HCE have all along repressed their opposition thereby confirming the idea that there is no other way to govern or to take power than violence.'

A decade later, Algeria was back to where it was before the October 1988 riots. Following that popular uprising, the army presented itself as the protector of democracy and order, against Islamism. The parties and associations – some consciously, some naively – went along with this claim which was proven wrong by the coup d'État of January 1992 and the civil war that followed. During the past ten years, the Algerian military only acted to maintain its hold on political power. The absence of negotiation and dialogue among all political partners, including the FIS, so as to reestablish a democratic process from which all violence-advocating parties would be excluded, has created a calamitous situation for the country. Endorsed by the *mafia politico-financière* (a formula coined by President Mohammed Boudiaf a few weeks before he was gunned down by one of his bodyguards in Annaba), the security strategy of General Mohammed Lamari and General Tewfiq Mediene known as *tout sécuritaire* still prevails. If not diffused, the crisis has been fragmented. Playing on selective co-optation of moderate Islamist parties, the generals can live with violence as long as the major strategic choices are not affected.

By interrupting the electoral process in January 1992, the army brought an end to a process that could have led to a negotiated settlement of the crisis. Six years later, violence became institutionalized in Algeria, and the government appeared to be stuck in a repression cycle. In such a context, the idea of democratization has all but vanished. The republican and democratic option has not prevailed because the aim of the government was the protection and the perpetuation of the existing power configuration. Before the debate on democracy can be resumed, legitimacy, law, and human rights must be reestablished in Algeria.

Paralysis in Libya

In contradistinction to the struggle in Algeria, Libya exhibits few demands for political change. Even though the self-styled Libyan revolutionary state – initially founded on the emulation of Gamal Abd al Nasser's regime in

Egypt (1952-70)–has come under attack by an increasingly assertive Islamist opposition, Libyans voice few calls for change. This is surprising since Libya faces political uncertainty equal to that of its Maghrebi neighbors. Moreover, since April 1992, the country has been living under a regime of sanctions imposed by the United Nations because of Libya's alleged implication in the December 1988 bombing of Pan Am Flight 101 which exploded over Lockerbie, Scotland.

The military governs the country according to a March 1977 charter giving executive powers to Colonel Moammar Qadhafi, as Guide of the Revolution of the Great Socialist People's Libyan Arab Jamahiriya, and legislative authority to a 1,112-member People's General Congress. Abolished in 1969, the Libyan Constitution was replaced by several revolutionary charters issued in 1973, 1977, 1984, 1989, and 1992. The country's governing principles flow from Qadhafi's 1976 three-volume *Green Book* – an idiosyncratic mélange of Islam and pan-Arabism. The General Congress is elected by Popular Committees set up at the level of municipalities, rural communes, unions, and civic organizations. Political parties are non-existent. Referred to as 'contemporary dictatorships' by Qadhafi, they were banned by a 1972 law. The only authorized party active after the 1969 revolution–al Itihad al Ishtiraki al Arabi (Arab Socialist Union)–was abolished when the jamahiriya (mass republic) was declared. Instead, 1,100 committees serve the purpose of institutionalizing political activity.

Prior to Qadhafi, Libya was ruled by the Sanussi monarchy, and the population was not politically mobilized. The monarchy was replaced by a rigidly controlled military-nationalistic revolutionary system with a pronounced proclivity for populist appeals. Inasmuch as Libya is a relatively affluent country in comparison to its neighbors, there has been no rioting due to poverty and deprivation. The debate about democratic values, human rights, and civil liberties is, by and large, absent. However, the abuses of security services have, since the late 1970s and early 1980s, fueled an increasing resentment towards the regime.

In the absence of parties, some underground political opposition groups developed, such as the Libyan National Movement, the Libyan National Group, the General Organization of Libyan Students, and the Libyan Democratic Front. In the 1980s, the regime repressed all these groups. The Libyan opposition has since remained a weak, amorphous movement causing only sporadic nuisance to Qadhafi. Most importantly, it has lacked a popular base. Besides London-based opponents sponsored by the royal Sanussi house and led by the former Crown Prince Mohammad al Hassan al Ridha al Sanussi, the grand-nephew of King Idris I, the principal opposition to Qadhafi has come from al Jabha al Wataniya li Inkadh Libya

(National Front for the Salvation of Libya, NFSL) formed on 7 October 1981. Initially led by Islamist-oriented and former Ambassador in Qadhafi's government, Mohammad Youssef al Maghariaf, the NFSL organized a failed coup on 8 May 1984, following which 200 people were executed and 6,000 arrested. It has remained active and, in 1992, it launched a 'Platform for the Future' emphasizing rights, institutions, and democracy. On 1 September of that year, al Maghariaf issued a statement establishing a clear connection between Qadhafi's departure and a democratic alternative. The Front announced that it would suspend all laws enacted since 1969, dissolve existing institutions as well as the revolutionary and popular committees.

Other Islamist opposition include al Dawa al Islamiya (Islamist Appeal) and the Jihad (Islamic Struggle). Most of these activists were arrested in 1990. That same year, the regime formed the Popular Guard to monitor activity around mosques. The Islamists have gradually become the most politicized segment of the Libyan population. Moreover, the circle of dissatisfaction with the regime is widening and has extended into the all-important tribal world (Joffé, 1996). Tribalism still plays a significant role in the Libyan political process, as it does in Mauritania. The al Abaydat tribe (part of the nine-member tribal confederation of Saadi) has lent support to the Islamists, and a 1993 failed coup attempt in Beni Walidwas was led by members of the al Warfalla tribe.

To diffuse the discontent, some liberalization measures were taken in the late 1980s. On 2 March 1988, Qadhafi delivered a speech to the General People's Congress criticizing security services. He called for legal reforms to provide safeguards against abuses of authority. Subsequently, he freed 400 political prisoners and lifted travel restrictions. Then, on 12 June, Congress issued a Green Charter on Human Rights. It also introduced some economic liberalization measures, but genuine democratization prospects remained dim.

The institutions of government in their traditional sense were done away with on 2 March 1977 with the proclamation of the Jamahiriya. No presidential elections take place, political parties are still banned, and civil society organizations remain tightly controlled. All power is held by Qadhafi, his security apparatus, and the military (whose leaders are constantly shifted by the Colonel). Associations, unions, and professional groups are tightly controlled by the government, and the media are the property of the state. Qadhafi's interference and veto power predominate at all levels and on all matters.

As a rentier state that derives all of its income from royalties from oil and gas extraction, Libya has been under little pressure to effect sociopolitical change. Qadhafi has ruled with a narrow political base and clientelistic ties with businessmen and tribal leaders. Still, the idiosyncratic communal vision of values and the legitimacy of Qadhafi–which rests on a Koranic morality, a secular dynamic, and a unionist utopia (Djaziri, 1996)–have been seriously affected in the 1990s. His directives are not followed with the same enthusiasm as before. The regime has been seeking a new legitimacy through a better handling of the economy (Vandewalle 1995, 1996), but without popular consultation (Burgat, 1989).

As Moncef Djaziri (1992) asks: How can one speak of a democratization process in a country where the political regime is perceived as totalitarian? Indeed, under the existing coercive system, Libyans have no right to change their government. Citizens are institutionally prevented from contesting the official line. In a 25 August 1975 speech, Qadhafi insisted on the need for party members to refrain from personally interpreting the decisions taken by the popular congresses, and a 1972 law mandates the death penalty for those opposed to the principles of the revolution. In this context, the most important function of the revolutionary committees has been to insulate Qadhafi from the bureaucracy and the rest of society (El-Kikhia, 1997).

In sum, Libya is the only country of the North African region where not even a partial democratization has been formally initiated. Confrontation is muted but an Islamist tumult is present underground, felt primarily in university circles. Apprehensions about Libya's future persist since the country is hardly immune to the Algerian-Tunisian Islamist wave. Clashes between Libyan governmental forces and Islamist guerrillas took place in March and September of 1996. In addition, the country is dominated by one man's political vision and the practice of nepotism–through which Qadhafi's cousins are appointed to sensitive political and military offices– is widespread. All of this does not bode well for Libya's future, since the nurturing of a civic culture has been overly delayed.

Cosmetic Democratization in Mauritania

The Islamic Republic of Mauritania entered the uncharted waters of democratization in 1991. In the spring of that year, al Lajna al Askariya li al Khalass al Watani or Comité Militaire de Salut National (CMSN)–a military council that had ruled the country since the 10 July 1978 overthrow of the post-colonial civilian government of President Mokhtar Ould Daddah–announced that it would be introducing liberalization measures to bring an end to the social unrest that had prevailed between 1980 and 1990. On 15 April, President Maaouiya Ould Sid'Ahmed Taya –a French-trained army colonel who had seized power on 12 December

1984–delivered a speech in which he announced the upcoming adoption of several democratization measures. The new constitutional apparatus included a house of representatives, a senate, a constitutional council, freedom of expression, association, and organization, the right to unionize, as well as a multi-party system.

On 20 July, the new Constitution was adopted formally by 97 per cent of the vote, and a week later, a general amnesty for political crimes was developed. Subsequently, between 19 August 1991 and 15 January 1992, fourteen political parties were formed and legalized. Presidential balloting was then held on 26 January 1992 with Ould Tay receiving 62.65 per cent of the vote and his main challenger, Ahmed Ould Daddah, 32.75 per cent. The two other candidates–former Nouakchott Mayor Mohammed Mahmoud Ould Mah and former President Mustapha Ould Saleck– obtained respectively 1.36 per cent and 2.85 per cent. According to the US Department of State 1996 Human Rights Report, 'The vote in the four-way presidential contest was regarded as fraudulent.' Following publication of the results, clashes took place in Nouakchott and Nouadhibou between the police and supporters of the leading opposition party, Itihad al Quwat al Dimuqratiya or Union des Forces Démocratiques (UFD). Three people died, and a curfew was imposed. On 4 March, a massive opposition demonstration took place in Nouakchott. Five days later, the conservative al Tajamu li al Dimuqratiya wa al Wihda or Rassemblement pour la Démocratie et l'Unité (RDU) decided to boycott the legislative round. Thus, the parliamentary election was massively won by Ould Taya's party, al Hizb al Joumhouri al Dimuqrati al Ijtimai or Parti Républicain Démocrate et Social (PRDS), which obtained 67 of the 79 seats–the remaining seats being filled by independent candidates. By the time, senatorial elections were held on 3-10 April, disinterest in the process had settled in as the PRDS won 35 out of 53 seats and independent candidates took the remaining 18.

Mauritanian democratization was still born. The Mauritanian state had been asked to hand down authority, and it managed to avoid the disengagement (Baduel, 1991). By devising strategies for an organized rather than disorganized state retreat, the regime ended up surviving, even regenerating itself in the process. This was further demonstrated in the course of the 28 January-4 February 1994 municipal elections. In the midst of renewed popular interest (participation was up to 69 per cent from 47 per cent in the 1992 presidential contest), the election was characterized by the emergence of alliances and counter-alliances–the PRDS was supported by the RDU, while the UFD and the Nasserist-oriented al Tahaluf al Shaabi al Taqadumi or Alliance Populaire Progressiste (APP) joined forces in some cities– violence (one person died as a result of clashes), tribal confrontation (particularly between the Laghlal and the Awlad Nasser), as well as massive fraud by both the government and opposition parties. Ultimately, the PRDS won 172 of the 208 communes.

Rather than share power, the authorities went on to govern unilaterally. The ruling PRDS party controlled the political process, winning the April 1996 senatorial elections by a wide margin (97 per cent) and repressing the opposition. When, in January 1995, economic hardships triggered riots, the government sent the army into the streets. The 3-day spontaneous demonstration was violently suppressed, and the leaders of the main opposition parties arrested and detained for two weeks.

Much of the old, authoritarian military regime remained intact, and a tribal-regional-ethnic quota system continued to determine who got what how and when. President Ould Taya's effort at dividing the opposition was successful. Internal rivalries undermined the opposition's action. On 7 July 1992, former Foreign Minister Hamdi Ould Mouknass resigned from the UFD and went on to create his own party, al Itihad li al Dimuqratiya wa al Taqadum or Union pour la Démocratie et le Progrès (UDP). Despite its leader's detention in June 1993 and January-February 1995, the UDP ultimately adhered to the presidential majority on 8 June 1997. Another leading member of the UFD, Messaoud Ould Boulkheir, left that party and formed the Action Civique (AC), a movement that champions the rights of the Haratines (former slaves). In 1997, however, the opposition showed signs of maturity as five parties banded together to create the Front Uni des Partis de l'Opposition (FUPO). Presided over by Mohammeden Ould Babbah, the loose coalition which included the UFD, the AC, the UDP, the APP, and the Baathist party al Taliaa (the Vanguard) called on the government to open a dialogue with the opposition, set up an independent voting commission, and adopt an electoral code.

Although there has been some small-scale Islamist activism in Nouakchott and Nouadhibou it offers no threat to the regime. The Islamist movement has been participating peacefully in the political process – albeit informally, since its sole party, Hizb al Umma al Islami (the Islamic Nation Party), has not been granted recognition by the authorities. In this overwhelmingly Muslim North African country, Islam reigns but does not govern. Tribalism and ethnic conflict remain key determinants of political life. Mauritania's societal structure still resembles in many ways what Ibn Khladoun termed *al umran al badawi* (the Bedouin civilization). Even though Mauritania had witnessed the attrition of tribal politics from 1960 to 1990 (see Marchesin, 1992), tribalism has reemerged strongly since 1991 and has impeded the development of a genuinely independent civil society.

The regime repressed and intimidated opponents. On 19-30 September 1994, ninety-four Islamist militants were arrested. In January of 1995, following 'bread' riots, opposition leaders including Ahmed Ould Daddah and Hamdi Ould Mouknass were detained. The following October, seventy-two Baathists were imprisoned for several weeks. The leaders of AC and the APP, including Messaoud Ould Boulkheir and Mohamed Ould Hafed Ould Ismail, were arrested on 22 January 1997. Following student demonstrations on 10 March, twelve members of the Syndicat Indépendant des Professeurs de l'Enseignement Secondaire (SIPES) were placed under house arrest, and on 18 September, twenty high-ranking Nasserite civil servants were fired for protesting the government's policies.

The Mauritanian democratization process was characterized by the personalized form of government of President Ould Taya and entrenched tribalism. Following the transformations in Eastern Europe, the changes in Algeria and Tunisia, the aftermath of the Second Gulf War, as well as the growing unrest at home, in 1991 the regime in Nouakchott was under regional, international, and domestic pressure to act (Balta, 1992). To face the challenges, Ould Taya originally turned to conservative forces. After securing a rubber-stamp parliament by wooing tribal leaders, he turned to the modernizing élites and used them to ostracize opposition parties. On 13 September 1995, Ould Taya declared in Paris that 'the democratic process in our country is over.' In reality, Mauritania's staccato democratic experiment was at best superficial. Following successive waves of arrests in 1994-97, popular resentment towards the rule of President Ould Taya has gradually multiplied. The regime's treatment of its opposition falls well below the standards expected in a democracy (Wiseman, 1996).

Paradoxically, Mauritania's economic picture has dramatically improved. Economic growth rose from 1.6 per cent in 1992 to 4.9 per cent in 1996, and to a record 7 per cent in 1997. Similarly, international funding and investment has steadily increased. In November 1996, the European Union (EU) announced the granting of a $100 million funding package under the European Development Fund (EDF). On 14 July 1997, the International Monetary Fund (IMF) praised the economic reforms in Mauritania and approved a $59 million loan as part of an enhanced structural adjustment package. Unlike the economy, Mauritania's democratization process is not moving forward.

Uncertain Transition in Morocco

The 1990s ushered in a new era of human rights in Morocco. For many years the question of human rights had been the achilles heel of the Moroccan political system (Tredano, 1996). However, in the 1990s human rights abuses have significantly decreased. On 8 May 1990, King Hassan II announced the creation of a Conseil Consultatif des Droits de l'Homme (CCDH) to investigate violations of citizens' rights. The CCDH had three committees in charge of (i) complaints against the police; (ii) conditions in prisons; and (iii) relations with international human rights organizations. On 12 December of the same year, a National Charter of Human Rights was signed by the three main human rights organizations: the Ligue Marocaine pour la Défense des Droits de l'Homme (LMDDH), the Organisation Marocaine des Droits de l'Homme (OMDH), and the Association Marocaine des Droits de l'Homme (AMDH). On 25 April 1991, parliament adopted new laws proposed by the CCDH regarding detention conditions, and in November of 1993, a Ministry of Human Rights was formed. According to local human rights organizations, there were in 1992 approximately 500 political prisoners in the country. By 1996, according to the same sources, the number was down to 68 (of whom 50 were Islamists). In 1994, the King issued a global pardon and allowed the return of exiled opponents. The destruction of several prisons and the release of prominent political prisoners heralded a new human rights era in Morocco.

There has also been an attempt at creating the conditions for a dialogue between different political expressions by improving the law. On 18 May 1992, the Itihad al Ishtiraki li al Quwat al Shaabiya or Union Socialiste des Forces Populaires (USFP) of Abderrahman El Youssoufi, Hizb al Istiqlal or Parti de l'Istiqlal (PI) of M'Hamed Boucetta, al Hizb al Shaabi al Ishtiraki or Parti Populaire et Socialiste (PPS) of Ali Yata (PPS), al Mounadhama li al Amal al Dimuqrati wa al Shaabi or Organisation pour l'Action Démocratique et Populaire (OADP), and al Itihad al Watani li al Quwat al Shaabiya or Union Nationale des Forces Populaires (UNFP) of Abdallah Ibrahim formed a democratic coalition of opposition parties known as al Koutla al Dimuqratiya (the Democratic Bloc), and published a national charter calling for significant constitutional reform and a more representative government. Originally created on 4 August 1970, by the PI and the UNFP as al Koutla al Wataniya (the National Block), this front was revived in a larger configuration. An electoral amendment was passed on 4 June 1992 by the Chamber of Deputies reducing the minimum voting age from 21 to 20 years and the candidacy age from 25 to 23. A new constitutional text was submitted to referendum the following 4 September. However, the opposition saw these measures as insufficient and decided on a boycott. When the constitution was adopted by 99.98 per cent of the vote with a 97.5 per cent participation rate, to many, the process lost credibility. After irregularities had qualified the 16 October local elections won by the government coalition, the Wifaq (Entente), the opposition parties considered not participating in the following parliamentary round. But in February 1993, the parties of the Koutla agreed to cooperate with the national commission for the supervision of electoral operations, and the King agreed to delay parliamentary elections from April to June.

Direct parliamentary elections were held on 25 June 1993 for 222 seats. In the first round, the PI won 43 seats and the USFP, 48. With 91 seats, the opposition seemed to be on the verge of a first victory since the conservative majority parties of the Wifaq–al Haraka al Shaabiya or Mouvement Populaire (MP), al Tajamu al Watani li al Ahrar or Rassemblement National des Indépendants (RNI), and al Itihad al Doustouri or Union Constitutionelle (UC)–had received respectively only 32, 28 and 27 seats. However, after indirect elections were held on 17 September to select the last third (111 seats) of the representatives, the opposition ended up with only 123 seats, when it needed 167 for a majority. After the opposition parties protested the second-round election, King Hassan II invited them (the USFP, the PI, the PPS, and the OADP) to participate in the government. These parties refused, however arguing that their main condition–the removal of Minister of Interior Driss Basri–had not been done.

The impasse prevailed for the next three years. Then, on 3 March 1996, the King announced the creation of a bicameral Parliament with a House of Representatives and a House of Counsellors. This constitutional reform was adopted through a referendum held the following 13 September amid a massive popular participation (85.95 per cent of the 12.3 million registered voters) and the opposition's active support (see White, 1997). On 11 October, the King delivered a speech before the Parliament in which he confirmed all the changes, and a few days later he met with leaders of the political parties. On 28 February 1997, the parties and the government signed a charter by which the government agreed to punish those responsible for abuses and illegal maneuvers during the elections. The parties, in turn, agreed to recognize 'the sincerity of the elections and the credibility of the institutions.' This pledge was signed by the PI, the USFP, the PPS, the OADP, the UC, the MP, the RNI, al Hizb al Watani al Dimuqrati or Parti National Démocratique (PND), al Haraka al Wataniya al Shaabiya or Mouvement National et Populaire (MNP), and al Haraka al Dimuqratiya wa al Ijtimaiya or Mouvement Démocratique et Social (MDS).

Communal elections were subsequently held on 13 June 1997. With 34 per cent of the vote, the Koutla emerged as the largest bloc. Still, the expected landslide victory of the opposition did not occur. More importantly, the elections were marked by the proliferation of independent candidates and by several instances of violence (4 dead and 15 wounded), fraud, corruption, vote-buying, and intimidation. Similarly, the long-awaited 14 November 1997 parliamentary balloting – in which 3,319 candidates from 16 political parties took part – did not alter fundamentally the political status quo. Since no one party controls more than 20 percent of the parliament, the process will in all likelihood favor the monarchy.

Between 1960 and 1972, in the wake of state of siege laws and continued unrest, the power of Moroccan parties had been undermined. Over the next twenty years, it was gradually co-opted as the King was able to reshuffle the players and increase the number of his partners who found themselves locked in a contest of influence rather than representation. In the meantime, the *makhzen* (royal house) remained the key element and the polity fragile. The result of this evolution is that the difference between the union of opposition parties, the Koutla, and the coalition of governmental parties, the Wifaq, has less significance today than the difference between the rich and the poor. There are increasing divisions within Moroccan society. Moroccan youths, for instance, have sought democracy primarily as a way to achieve more emancipation (Bennani-Chraibi, 1995). Bred by economic, social, and cultural frustrations, the opposition between the *shaabi* (man of the street) and the *makhzen* has been fueling calls for more social justice.

The Moroccan social crisis is energized by an economic recession and Islamist organizations that lead the social protests. Although the latter have not yet garnered enough power to revolutionize Morocco, their presence is increasingly being felt by the authorities (Munson, 1993). The Islamists' influence is particularly perceptible in high school and university circles in Marrakech, Casablanca, Oujda, Fes, Meknes, Rabat, and Tangiers. The 3 February 1991, 500,000-strong demonstration in support of Iraq was dominated by 20,000 Islamists. Besides traditional figures such as Abdalbari Ibn al Siddiq (the son of Islamic scholar al Fqih al Zamzami), seventy-year old Sheikh Abdessalam Yassin has remained, since his confinement to house arrest in the mid-1970s, the leading personality of the growing Islamist militantism. Yassin has primarily emphasized the issues of socialization, moral education, and spiritual preparation. His movement has taken the form of a network of religious associations such as the al Adl wa al Ihsan (Justice and Welfare), an organization created in 1979 and banned in 1989, but still active and aiming at becoming a political party within the existing constitutional framework. Other religious associations politically active include al Tawhid wa al Islah (Unity and Reform), al Tajdid wa al Islah (Renovation and Reform), Rabitat al Mostaqbal al Islami (Coalition of Islamic Future), and al Shabaab al Islami (Islamic Youth).

Like political parties and civil society organizations, Islamist groups are never openly critical of the King (Cubertafond, 1997). Their appeal is often more ideological and economic than political. Expressing an Islamism of compromise, their discourse revolves primarily around questions of social injustice, excessive Westernization, and moral deprivation. The centralization by the monarchy of religious legitimacy – the King is *amir al mumineen* (commander of the faithful) – confines the *ulama* (religious scholars) to a management role of religion. But the existence of numerous moderate Islamist groups evinces an increasing infiltration of society. Some have gained a foothold in the political system. In the June 1997 local election, for instance, 100 members of al Tajdid wa al Islah were elected as independents. Similarly, in the parliamentary balloting held in November of the same year, Islamists from al Haraka al Shaabiya al Destouriya al Dimuqratiya or Mouvement Populaire Constitutionel et Démocrate presented 148 candidates and won 6 seats.

Still, with the Algerian situation next door, the monarchy is on guard. The liberal and leftist segments of Moroccan civil society are equally opposed to the rise of a successful Islamist movement. Most members of the civil society approve of the containment of Islamists and criticize their activism within academic circles. However, the Islamist movement reflects discontent with the existing socioeconomic conditions (Entelis, 1989). A fertile site for the frustrations of the poor classes and the proliferation of petty corruption, the urban periphery is where Islamism has its origin. Distributional inequalities in Morocco are the key to a potential radicalization of the Islamists.

Certainly, the Moroccan political system is in the throes of change. By and large, Moroccans harbor little doubt as regards the dominant role of the monarch in the conception and orchestration of local politics (Eickelman, 1994). The monarchy transcends any and all political actors. Its ability to renew its social basis by changing allies (who constantly attempt to curry favor with it) is one of the keys to its survival. Still, with a minimal program the Koutla has worked as a positive force. It has played a balancing role, so that, even though constitutional conservatism is still the prevailing norm, a *demakhzenization* of Moroccan politics seems to be under way.

Amid uncertainties about the resolution of its democratic transition, a persisting economic crisis, mounting social tension, and the evolution of the Alawi dynasty which has ruled Morocco since 1664, will Crown Prince Mohammed Ben Hassan, poised to become King Mohamed VI, have the strength and political acumen of his father, or will he be replaced by his younger brother, Moulay Rachid? Morocco is at the crossroads. Since the recent consultations left much to be desired, the issue of political *alternance* (rotation of power) has remained a nagging question. How can political pluralism coexist with the principle of consultation and monarchical prerogatives? What kind of political modus operandi will emerge from a new, more democratic arrangement? As it seeks an alternative to the existing management of the country's affairs, the opposition, it seems, is no longer ready for half-hearted compromises. Specifically, the nature of the new constitutional rearrangement with a clear specification of the role of the monarchy and the rights of the government, as well as the place and status of political parties, is being hotly debated.

The Successful Tunisian Police State

Although it has had one of the earliest modern-day human rights traditions in the Islamic world going back to the 1857 Pacte Fondamental, Tunisia is the part of the Maghreb where human rights conditions and democratization have regressed the most since 1987. To the dismay of many Tunisians and the 4 million tourists who visit the country each year, authoritarianism has remained the norm.

On 2 October 1987, General Zine Abidine Ben Ali was appointed Prime Minister replacing Rachid Sfar. Five weeks later, Ben Ali conducted a 'medical' coup d'État on 84-year-old President Habib Bourguiba ending his 31 years of rule. On 27 February 1988, Bourguiba's party, al Hizb al Ishtiraki al Destouri or Parti Socialiste Destourien (PSD) became al Tajamu li al Destour wa al Dimuqratia or Rassemblement pour la Constitution et la Démocratie (RCD) with Ben Ali at its helm. Initially, the new president liberated thousands of political prisoners, including Sheikh Rached Ghannouchi, the leader of the Harakat al Itijah al Islami or Mouvement de la Tendance Islamique (MTI, renamed Hizb al Nahda in January 1989), who had been imprisoned for life by President Bourguiba. The Constitution was amended, and a new law on parties passed in April 1988. The 1975 press code was restructured by an organic law on 2 August. Ben Ali also abolished the presidency-for-life law. Amnesty International was allowed to open a section in Tunis in April of 1988, and the Association Tunisienne des Femmes Démocratiques (ATFD) was legalized.

A certain dose of Islam was reintroduced in governmental institutions as a Secretary of State for Religious Affairs was appointed – a clear departure from Bourguiba's professed secularism. On 5 April, Ben Ali met with the leaders of the two main unions, Habib Achour of the Union Génèrale des Travailleurs Tunisiens (UGTT), and Abdelaziz Bouraoui of the Union Nationale des Travailleurs Tunisiens (UNTT) to discuss new agreements and convince the two competing syndicates to sign a pact of collaboration. Clearly, a new partnership was being sought. Several thousand prisoners were set free, including members of the MTI, and militants from al Hizb al Tahrir al Islami or Parti de la Libération Islamique

(PLI). In total, 2,487 amnesties were granted in 1987. Between March and November 1988, another 4,106 prisoners were released. Ben Ali also abolished state security courts and allowed some eighty self-exiled political figures to return to Tunisia. New parties, such as al Hizb al Ijtimai li al Taqadum or Parti Social du Progrès (PSP) and al Itihad al Dimuqrati al Itihadi or Union Démocratique Unioniste (UDU), were legalized in 1988. Clearly, the country was witnessing a process of dilution of the excessively centralized presidential power inherited from Bourguiba (Bras, 1996). The pursuit of consensus culminated in a National Pact signed in September of 1988 between several political forces. The Pact aimed at a historical compromise between different views, emphasized the actors' commitment to democracy, human rights, and state institutions. It also provided for the reconstruction of the UGTT. On 5 November–two days before the promulgation of the Pact–Ben Ali met with Ghannouchi and invited the MTI to join the agreement on the conditions that the party renounce violence and accept the principle of democratic competition.

However, the reforms did not bring democracy to the country (Gasiorowski, 1992). The hopes for reconciliation and civil peace weakened as the momentum toward liberalization slowed with the April 1989 presidential and parliamentary balloting in which independents and eight parties participated: the RCD, the UDU, the PSP, the leftist Hizb al Itihad al Shaabi or Parti de l'Unité Populaire (PUP) of Mohamed Benhadj Amor, the centrists of Harakat al Dimuqratiyoun al Ijtimaiyoun or Mouvement des Démocrates Sociaux (MDS) of Ahmed Mestiri, al Tajamu al Ishtiraki al Taqadumi or Rassemblement Socialiste Progressiste (RSP) of Mohamed Nejib Chabbi, al Hizb al Tounoussi al Shouyoui or Parti Tunisien Communiste (PTC) of Mohamed Harmel. Two-thirds of the independents were Islamists of the Nahda. The RCD received 80 per cent of the vote followed by independents/Islamists (14.5 per cent) and the MDS (3.76 per cent). In some urban centers such as Tunis, the Islamist list received 25 per cent of the vote. With 141 seats out of the 144 in the Assembly, the RCD had almost absolute control. As the sole presidential candidate, President Ben Ali won with 99.27 per cent of the vote.

The 1989 legislative elections delivered a blow to all who had hoped for significant change (Waltz, 1995). Opponents to the Tunisian regime, such as former Prime Minister Mohammed Mzali, Ahmed Manai, Nasserite Arab Socialist Forum led by Faysal Kaabi, and the Democracy Now society of Youness Ben Othman became disenchanted. On 13 May 1989, Ghannouchi left the country in self-imposed exile. His departure marked the end of cooperation between the Nahda and the authorities. On 22 May 1991, several hundred Nahda members were arrested and tried in August of 1992. Overall, some 8,000 arrests were made between 1990 and 1992 dramatically reversing the advances of 1987-89. By late 1991, the political climate in Tunisia had come to resemble the latter days of the Bourguiba era (Gasiorowski, 1992).

In March of 1993, the electoral code was modified. The following year all 144 seats of the assembly were captured by the RCD in the parliamentary contest. In the presidential election of 20 March 1994, Ben Ali was the sole candidate. Two other individuals who had intended to participate in the contest were imprisoned for four months. The Tunisian President was reelected by 99.92 per cent of the vote (only 1,753 Tunisians refused to vote for Ben Ali)–the highest score ever in the Arab world. Then, during the municipal elections of May 1995, the ruling RCD party won all but 6 of the 4,090 seats contested. When the new president of the MDS, Mohamed Moada, wrote an open letter to Ben Ali criticizing the results of the election and denouncing the government's 'hegemonic' rule, he was arrested and sentenced to 11 years in prison. He was conditionally released in December 1996.

Starting with the legislative elections of April 1989, repression policies have reached most Islamists, human rights activists, and liberal opposition groups such as the MDS, the PUP, and al Tajdid (Renewal) party. On 21 October 1997, President Ben Ali declared in Paris that his government had 'no political prisoners'– even though there was evidence of at least 2,000 such detainees. A clear contradiction has emerged in Tunisia between an authoritarian and repressive regime's self-congratulatory discourse on respect for human rights and a reality characterized by the growing decline of fundamental liberties (Baudoin and Dhonte, 1997; Ibrahimi, 1997). The current picture is one of widespread use of torture, intimidations, repression, arrests, passport privations, telephone and fax surveillance, and mail interception. Satellite television antennas are sold only with authorization, and internet access is limited, supervised, and subject to governmental clearance. Police are omnipresent on campuses and their number has quadrupled since 1987. The Ligue Tunisienne des Droits de l'Homme (LTDH) was shut down between 1992 and 1994 (it was allowed to reopen later with a new co-opted board).

President Ben Ali's government has also consistently demonstrated a pattern of intolerance of public criticism, stifling freedoms of press, speech, and association. Government critics have been severely sanctioned. Academic papers to be delivered at conferences have to be vetted by the Ministry of Education. There is regular censorship of international newspapers such as *Le Monde* and *Al Hayat*. On 6 June 1997, the World Association of Newspapers suspended the Tunisian Newspaper Association for failing to protest governmental interference (the editors of six independent newspapers had met with Ben Ali in September 1996 to argue against *talimat* or directives sent by government members). Not surprisingly, the prevalence of self-censorship in the Tunisian press has led to the proliferation of underground publications.

As in Mauritania, the disparity between economic and political reforms is significant. With a 4.5 per cent growth rate, Tunisia's economy is rapidly modernizing. Several state-owned enterprises have been privatized, with the government providing subventions (see Harik, 1992). On 17 July 1995, Tunisia signed the first Euro-Mediterranean accord with the European Union (EU). Coming on the heels of this free-trade agreement with the EU was the setting-up of a Conseil National Supérieur des Exportations (CNE). These and other measures have reinforced the role of the state in the economy. By meeting the demands of the new compradore middle class, the state has created a buffer zone between itself and the populace. Thus, the maintenance of political hegemony has been accompanied by economic liberalization (Hermassi, 1993).

Tunisia has gradually and consistently moved toward increased authoritarianism since 1987. The store of experience accumulated by President Ben Ali during his earlier years in intelligence and police work has been used to control the nine million Tunisians and to 'neutralize the polity' (Camau, 1997). Much like his Mauritanian and Libyan counterparts, the Tunisian President has gradually excluded all his challengers from political participation. Whereas former President Bourguiba had had several high-profile prime ministers (Bahi Ladgham, Hedi Nouira, Mohamed Mzali, and Rachid Sfar), Ben Ali has had none. Ben Ali has derived his power from control of the security forces and the specter of an Islamist state (Waltz, 1995). He has also weakened the Islamists, not by boosting his religious legitimacy (as King Hassan II or Qadhafi have done), but by unmitigated repression, and by promoting a modern (read secular) and economically-successful Tunisia.

Collapsed Liberalizations and the Return of the State

This overview shows that the North African ship of political liberalization may be sinking. In spite of some minor advances, the democratization picture in the Maghreb remains unambiguously dim. Whether it is because of suppression (Algeria), immobility (Libya), manipulation (Mauritania), frustration (Morocco), or repression (Tunisia), democracy's precarious situation in the Maghreb of the late 1990s is obvious. Maghrebi governments, in particular those battling Islamism, are not ready to accept a true form of political pluralism—which they perceive as fundamentally endangering their monopoly—nor are they willing to allow a greater role to civil society organs in policy-making. So far, democratization has been but a convenient way for the North African regimes to hang on to their monopoly of power while claiming some minimum legitimacy. As Samuel Huntington (1997) has said: democratic development occurs only when political leaders believe they have an interest in promoting it or a duty to achieve it.

In the Maghreb, however, the governments have systematically rigged elections. Whereas democracy is the stuff of uncertainty, the regimes want to be absolutely confident about any and all electoral outcomes. The objective is the neutralization of the political process. This was forcefully demonstrated in the four elections (presidential, referendum, parliamentary, and municipal) in Algeria between November 1995 and November 1997. What has come into existence is a hybrid mixture of elements of economic liberalization, renewed authoritarianism and failed democratization. The perpetuation of authoritarian rule and the alienation of the electorate is also the result of the inability of the political systems to produce credible opposition parties (Zartman, 1994). Too often, the opposition has been the mirror image of the governments, and secular groups have proven to be undemocratic forces. Certainly that is the case of the self-appointed Algerian democrats such as the RCD, who welcomed the cancellation of the 1991 elections.

One central theme runs through this essay. It is that of a retreating society and an expanding state. The initial pressures from within the population for democratic change have been met by the consolidation of state power. First, between 1987 and 1992, the liberalization process was captured by society. Then, beginning in 1992, the process was gradually recaptured by a reconstructed state. Authoritarianism today in the Arab world is indeed different from the authoritarianism of the past (Ghadbian, 1997). No longer concerned with pursuing genuine legitimacy it is propelled by a logic of exclusion combined with iron-fisted security measures. All governments in the Arab Maghreb do the following: (i) they retain executive supremacy, (ii) they exercise tight media controls, (iii) they provide no guarantee of basic rights, (iv) they face a dearth of genuine political opposition, (v) they engage in suspect elections, (vi) they do not adhere to the principle of equality before the law, and (vii) they create continued constraints on voluntary associations (Sivan, 1997).

The emergence of a more assertive state is also symbolized by the adoption of policies of economic liberalization. As *infitah* dynamics unfolded throughout North Africa, recentralization of power has paradoxically become linked in part to greater reliance on the international capital needed for local development (Hermassi, 1994). Moreover, the state also adopts a 'scare strategy' by which it links the potential success of its opponents (Islamists and democrats alike) to situations of unrest. The idea is to rally a populace alarmed by the doomsday scenario of a revolutionary takeover. Finally, the state has also reappropriated the discourse on transformation, so that change is no longer embodied by the opposition. This tactic has been used with great success by Mauritanian President Ould Taya whose 1992 electoral motto was *al taghayour fi al istiqrar* (change within stability), and with moderate and temporary success by Algerian President Liamine Zeroual in 1995. The other half of the equation–security through stability–is best embodied in Ben Ali's 1994 campaign leitmotiv, *al baladou al amin* (the safe country).

What this narrative captures then is the abridgment of a democratization process. A degree of generalization was unavoidable. In effect, one cannot equate Morocco–where, in recent years, there has been less muscularity in dealing with opponents–and Mauritania–where freedom of speech is relatively well protected–to the horror unfolding in Algeria or, for that matter, the atmosphere of repression prevalent in Tunisia, let alone the political void in Libya. Still, there is an element of continuity in the complex tapestry of Maghrebi politics. The interruption of the democratic experiment is illustrated by a general picture wherein the regimes stuff ballot boxes, orchestrate pro-government votes in military barracks, illegally bar observers from polling sites, and restrict freedom of the press.

Having stated these limitations, we must acknowledge that the region is not doomed to authoritarianism. The 1987-92 movement toward democracy has irrevocably altered Maghrebi societies. There are too many North Africans–intellectuals, independent journalists, women groups, and moderate Islamists–who are keen on asserting their democratic rights. Democratization remains their goal. Nevertheless, the political game in its formal and informal aspects is still largely controlled by the regimes. One analyst pithily argued that it is inappropriate to announce either the triumph or the exhaustion of the democratic impulse in Africa. Rather, he noted, we must recognize that the region has embarked on forking, circuitous, and contested paths (Bratton, 1997). That being as it may, the Maghreb can ill afford the current state of political disintegration. There is an urgent need for redemocratization in the Maghreb.

Note

1.   There exists confusion as regards both men's names. Ali Benhadj's last name is oftentimes erroneously transcribed as 'Belhadj.' Similarly, Madani Abassi's last name is systematically reported as his first name. This is due to the vestiges of a colonial practice through which French authorities registered and referred to Algerians under their family name first, e.g. Didouche Mourad for Mourad Didouche.

References

Addi, Lahouari (1995), *L'Algérie et la Démocratie - Pouvoir et Crise du Politique dans l'Algérie Contemporaine*, La Découverte: Paris.

Amnesty International (1996), *Algeria - Fear and Silence: A Hidden Human Rights Crisis*. London.

Ayubi, Nazih H (1995), *Over-Stating the Arab State - Politics and Society in the Middle East*, I.B. Tauris: London.

Baduel, Pierre Robert (1991), 'Mauritanie: De la Répression à l'Esquisse d'une Transition Démocratique ou des Capacités d'Adaptation d'un Régime Autoritaire', *Annuaire de l'Afrique du Nord* 30, pp. 887-927.

Balta, Paul (1992), 'La Mauritanie à l'Heure du Multipartisme', *Confluences Méditerranée* 3, pp. 130-36.

Baudoin, Patrick and Xavier Dhonte (1997), 'Les Droits de l'Homme Bafoués en Tunisie', *Le Monde*, 21 October 1997, p. 17.

Bennani-Chraibi, Mounia (1995), 'Sujets en Quête de Citoyenneté: Le Maroc au Miroir des Législatives de Juin 1993', *Les Cahiers de l'Orient* 148, pp. 17-27.

Bonnefous, Marc (1997), 'Deuxième Guerre d'Algérie: Deuxième Phase', *Défense Nationale* 53, 4, pp. 115-21.

Bras, Jean-Phillipe (1996), 'Tunisie: Ben Ali et sa Classe Moyenne', *Pôles* 1, 1, pp. 174-95.

Bratton, Michael (1997), 'Deciphering Africa's Divergent Transitions', *Political Science Quarterly* 112, 1, pp. 67-93.

Brumberg, Daniel (1995), 'Authoritarian Legacies and Reform Strategies in the Arab World', in Brynen, Rex, Bahgat Korany, and Paul Noble (eds.), *Political Liberalization and Democratization in the Arab World, Volume 1 - Theoretical Perspectives*, Lynne Rienner Publishers: Boulder, pp. 229-59.

Burgat, François (1989), 'Les Aléas de la Transition Démocratique en Libye', *Annuaire de l'Afrique du Nord* 28, pp. 309-18.

Camau, Michel (1997), 'Tunisie: D'Une République à l'Autre – Refondation Politique et Aléas de la Transition Libérale', *Monde Arabe Maghreb Machrek* 157, pp. 3-16.

Carothers, Thomas (1997), 'Democracy Without Illusions', *Foreign Affairs*, 76, 1, pp. 85-99.

Charef, Abed (1994), *Algérie - Le Grand Dérapage*, Éditions de l'Aube: Paris.

Ciment, James (1997), *Algeria - The Fundamentalist Challenge*, Facts on File, Inc.: New York.

Conry, Barbara (1997), 'North Africa on the Brink', *Mediterranean Quarterly* (Winter), pp. 115-30.

Cubertafond, Bernard (1997), *Le Système Politique Marocain*, L'Harmattan: Paris.

Daoud, Zakya and Brahim Ouchelh (1997), 'Vers une Transition Tranquille? Le Maroc Prêt pour l'Alternance', *Le Monde Diplomatique* 519, p. 8.

Djaziri, Moncef (1992), 'Libye: Pouvoir Gestionnaire, Pouvoir Révolutionnaire', *Confluences Méditerranée* 3, pp. 145-57.

_____ (1996), *État et Société en Libye - Islam, Politique et Modernité*, L'Harmattan: Paris.

Eickelman, Dale F. (1994), 'Re-Imagining Religion and Politics: Moroccan Politics in the 1990s', In Ruedy, John (ed.), *Islamism and Secularism in North Africa*, Macmillan: London, pp. 253-73.

El-Kikhia, Mansour O. (1997), *Libya's Qaddafi - The Politics of Contradiction*, University Press of Florida: Gainesville.

Entelis, John P. (1989), *Culture and Counterculture in Moroccan Politics*, Westview Press: Boulder.

_____ (1994), 'Islam, Democracy, and the State: The Reemergence of Authoritarian Politics in Algeria', in Ruedy, John (ed.), *Islamism and Secularism in North Africa*, Macmillan: London, pp. 219-51.

_____ (1997), *Islam, Democracy and the State in North Africa*, Indiana University Press: Bloomington.

Fédération Internationale des Droits de l'Homme (1997), *La Levée du Voile: L'Algérie de L'Extrajudiciaire et de La Manipulation*. Paris.

Feliu, Laura (1996), 'Human Rights in Morocco: Politics Beyond Ethics', In Gillespie, Richard (ed.), *Mediterranean Politics, Volume 2*, Pinter: London, 1996, pp. 179-97.

Fuller, Graham E. (1996), *Algeria, The Next Fundamentalist State?* Rand: Santa Monica.

Gasiorowski, Mark J. (1992), 'The Failure of Reform in Tunisia', *Journal of Democracy 3*, 4, pp. 85-97.

Ghadbian, Najib (1997), *Democratization and the Islamist Challenge in the Arab World*, Westview Press: Boulder.

Harik, Ilya (1992), 'Privatization and Development in Tunisia', in Harik, Ilya and Denis J. Sullivan (eds.), *Privatization and Liberalization in the Middle East*, Indiana University Press: Indianapolis, pp. 210-32.

Hermassi, Abdelbaki (1993), 'State, Legitimacy, and Democratization in the Maghreb', In Goldberg, Ellis, Resat Kasaba, and Joel Migdal (eds.), *Rules and Rights in the Middle East - Democracy, Law, and Society*, Seattle: Univ. of Washington Press.

_____ (1994), 'Socioeconomic Change and Political Implications: The Maghreb,' in Salamé, Ghassan (ed.), *Democracy Without Democrats? The Renewal of Politics in the Muslim World*, I.B. Tauris: London, pp. 227-42.

Hidouci, Ghazi (1995), *Algérie - La Libération Inachevée*, La Découverte: Paris.

Human Rights Watch/Middle East (1997), *Algeria: Elections in the Shadow of Violence and Repression*, Washington.

_____ (1998), *Algeria: Neither Among the Living nor the Dead: State-Sponsored 'Disappearances' in Algeria*. Washington.

Huntington, Samuel P. (1997), 'After Twenty Years: The Future of the Third Wave', *Journal of Democracy 8*, 4, pp. 3-12.

Ibrahimi, Hamed (pseudonym) (1997), 'Les Libertés Envolées de la Tunisie', *Le Monde Diplomatique 515*, pp. 4-5.

Joffé, George (1994), 'Elections and Reform in Morocco' in Gillespie, Richard (ed.), *Mediterranean Politics, Volume 1*, Pinter: London, pp. 212-26.

_____ (1996), 'Unrest in Libya', *Mediterranean Politics 1*, 2, pp. 261-67.

Kapil, Arun (1990), 'L'Évolution du Régime Autoritaire en Algérie: le 5 Octobre et le Réformes Politiques de 1988-1989', *Annuaire de l'Afrique du Nord 29*, pp. 499-534.

Karem, Mohamed (1993), 'La Question des Droits de l'Homme au Maghreb', in Martin, Gema Munoz (ed.), *Democracia y Derechos Humanos en el Mundo Arabe*, Agencia Espanola de Cooperacion: Madrid, pp. 125-47.

Labat, Séverine (1995), *Les Islamistes Algériens - Entre les Urnes et le Maquis*, Éditions du Seuil: Paris.

Leveau, Rémy (1989), 'Éléments de Réfléxion sur l'État au Maghreb', *Annuaire de l'Afrique du Nord 28*, pp. 269-80.

Malley, Robert (1996), *The Call from Algeria - Third Worldism, Revolution, and the Turn to Islam*, University of California Press: Berkeley.

Marchesin, Phillipe (1992), *Tribus, Ethnies et Pouvoir en Mauritanie*, Karthala: Paris.

Merzouki, Moncef (1996), La Deuxième Indépendance Arabe – Pour un État Arabe Démocratique *Moderne*, Maison des Trésors Littéraires: Beyrouth.

Mongin, Olivier (1997), 'Le Sale Avenir de la Guerre Civile en Algérie', *Esprit*, pp. 16-26.

Munson, Henry (1993), 'The Political Role of Islam in Morocco (1970-1990)', in Joffé, George (ed.), *North Africa: Nation, State and Region*, Routledge: London, pp. 187-202.

Ould-Mey, Mohameden (1996), *Global Restructuring and Peripheral States - The Carrot and the Stick in Mauritania*, Littlefield, Adams Books: Lanham, MD.

Pazzanita, Anthony G. (1996), 'The Origins and Evolution of Mauritania's Second Republic', *The Journal of Modern African Studies* 34, 4, pp. 575-96.

_____ (1997), 'State and Society in Mauritania in the 1990s', *The Journal of North African Studies*, 2, 1, pp. 16-39.

Pierre, Andrew J. and William B. Quandt (1996), *The Algerian Crisis: Policy Options for the West*, Carnegie Endowment for International Peace: Washington, DC.

Przeworski, Adam (1997), 'Democratization Revisited,' *Items* 51, 1, pp. 6-11.

Reporters Sans Frontières (1997), *Algeria – Civil War Behind Closed Doors*, Paris.

Roberts, Hugh (1996), 'The Zeroual Memorandum: The Algerian State and the Problem of Liberal Reform', *The Journal of Algerian Studies* 1, 1, pp. 1-19.

Rouadjia, Ahmed (1994), *Grandeur et Décadence de l'État Algérien*, Karthala: Paris.

Sadiki, Larbi (1997), 'The Impasse of Liberalising Arab Authoritarianism: The Cases of Algeria and Egypt', in White, Paul J. and William S. Logan (eds.), *Remaking the Middle East*, Berg: Oxford, pp. 59-85.

Sivan, Emmanuel (1997), 'Constraints and Opportunities in the Arab World', *Journal of Democracy* 8, 2, pp. 101-13.

Spencer, Claire (1993), *The Maghreb in the 1990s*, Adelphi Paper No. 274, *International Institute of Strategic Studies: London*.

Stone, Martin (1997), *The Agony of Algeria*, Columbia University Press: New York.

Strange, Susan (1996), *The Retreat of the State: The Diffusion of Power in the World Economy*, Cambridge University Press: New York.

Tlemçani, Mohamed Benlahcen (1993), 'Les Leçons des Élections Législatives au Maroc', *Les Cahiers de l'Orient* 31, pp. 129-136.

Tredano, Abdelmoughit Benmessaoud (1996), *Démocratie, Culture Politique et Alternance au Maroc*, Les Éditions Maghrébines: Casablanca.

Vandewalle, Dirk (1995), *Qadhafi's Libya, 1969-1994*, St. Martin's Press: New York.

_____ (1996), 'Qadhafi's Failed Economic Reforms: Markets, Institutions, and Development in a Rentier State', in Vandewalle, Dirk (ed.), *North Africa - Development and Reform in a Changing Global Economy*, St. Martin's Press: New York, pp. 203-225.

Waltz, Susan E. (1995), *Human Rights and Reform - Changing the Face of North African Politics*, University of California Press: Berkeley.

White, Gregory (1997), 'The Advent of Electoral Democracy in Morocco? The Referendum of 1996', *The Middle East Journal* 51, 3, pp. 388-404.

Wiseman, John A. (1996), *The New Struggle for Democracy in Africa*, Avebury Press: London.

Yacoubian, Mona (1997), *Algeria's Struggle for Democracy*, Council on Foreign Relations: New York.

_____ (1997), 'The Rise of Illiberal Democracy,' *Foreign Policy* 76, 6, pp. 22-42.

Zartman, I. William (1994), 'The Challenge of Democratic Alternatives in the Maghrib', in Ruedy, John (ed.), *Islamism and Secularism in North Africa*, Macmillan: London, pp. 201-218.

Zoubir, Yahia H. (1995), 'Stalled Democratization of an Authoritarian Regime: The Case of Algeria', *Democratization* 2, 2, pp. 109-39.

Acknowledgments

Research for this chapter was conducted in 1997 while the author was a Visiting Scholar at the Center for Middle Eastern Affairs at Harvard University. The author wishes to thank Samuel Huntington and Susan Miller for their kind assistance, and acknowledge his indebtedness to Keith Krause and Benjamin Rivlin for their comments on an earlier draft.